Sinister histories

Manchester University Press

Sinister histories

Gothic novels and representations of the past, from Horace Walpole to Mary Wollstonecraft

Jonathan Dent

Manchester University Press

Published by Manchester University Press
Altrincham Street, Manchester M1 7JA, UK
www.manchesteruniversitypress.co.uk

British Library Cataloguing-in-Publication Data is available

ISBN 978 0 7190 9597 9 *hardback*
ISBN 978 1 5261 4351 8 *paperback*

First published by Manchester University Press in hardback 2016

This edition first published 2019

Typeset by Out of House Publishing

For my family

Concordia et industria

Contents

Acknowledgements

I would like to thank several people who have provided support during the writing of this book. First and foremost, I am very grateful to Nick Freeman and Carol Bolton for their generous sharing of knowledge and encouragement over many years. My book has benefited enormously from their constructive and supportive criticism. I would like to thank Caroline Franklin and Julian Wolfreys for their comments, conversations and thoughts. My gratitude is also due to Manchester University Press for their patience and support. The insights of the three anonymous readers have strengthened this book considerably. Sections of this study have been presented at conferences and university seminars over the years and have benefited from the perceptive comments and questions of those who attended events hosted by the Universities of Loughborough, Sheffield, Oxford, and Cambridge. My thinking on the Gothic, and the relationship between literature and history, has been shaped by my teaching. Special thanks are, therefore, due to the undergraduate students that I have taught at Loughborough University and De Montfort University. Gratitude is also due to my friends for their backing and unwavering ability to make me smile. Above all, my heartfelt thanks go to my parents and my sister for believing, supporting and listening to me throughout the course of this project. It is to these three people that I dedicate this book.

Abbreviations

The following editions are used throughout this book:

CW   William Godwin. *Caleb Williams*. Edited by Pamela Clemit. Oxford: Oxford University Press, 2009.

H   Paul M. Rapin de Thoyras. *History of England*. Translated by Nicholas Tindal. 15 vols. Dublin: A. Rhames, R. Gunne and G. Ewing, 1726–32.

HE   David Hume. *The History of England*. 6 vols. Indianapolis: Liberty Fund, 1983.

M   Mary Wollstonecraft. *Maria, or The Wrongs of Woman*. Edited by Anne K. Mellor. New York: Norton, 1994.

O   Horace Walpole. *The Castle of Otranto*. Edited by Michael Gamer. London: Penguin, 2001.

OEB   Clara Reeve. *The Old English Baron*. Edited by James Trainer and James Watt. Oxford: Oxford University Press, 2003.

R   Sophia Lee. *The Recess; or A Tale of Other Times*. Edited by April Alliston. Kentucky: The University Press of Kentucky, 2000.

RF   Ann Radcliffe. *The Romance of Forest*. Edited by Chloe Chard. Oxford: Oxford University Press, 1999.

Introduction: history and the Gothic in the eighteenth century

I believe this is the historical Age.
David Hume to William Strahan (August 1770)

The first ages of Scottish History are dark and fabulous. Nations, as well as men, arrive at maturity by degrees, and the events which happened during their infancy or early youth, cannot be recollected, and deserve not to be remembered.
William Robertson, *The History of Scotland* (1759)

But when I am sure that in all ages there can be but little dependence on history, I cannot swallow the legends of the darkest period in our annals. In one word, Sir, I have often said that History *in general is a Romance that is believed, and that Romance is a History that is not believed*; and that I do not see much other difference between them.
Horace Walpole to Dr Henry (15 March 1783)

It is a dark and stormy night. Alone inside a room in a ruined abbey located in a gloomy forest, an orphan discovers a secret door that is hidden behind a tapestry. She opens it and, after descending a few steps, finds herself in an ancient chamber. The only sound she can hear is the wind that whistles through the apartment. As she explores her surroundings, the moonlight which shines through a shattered casement is obscured by a cloud and she is temporarily left in total darkness. Trembling, she trips over something on the floor. The moonlight returns and she learns that the object she stumbled over is an old dagger spotted with what appears to be rust. Surveying the room, she discovers mouldering furniture, dust, cobwebs and an old, decaying manuscript. Struggling to read the fragments that are still legible, she learns to her horror that the script was written by someone who was murdered in the abbey many years ago. This chilling sequence of events features, of course, in Ann Radcliffe's *The Romance of the Forest* (1791) and, typical of eighteenth-century English Gothic novels, a repressed and macabre history lurks at the heart of the narrative. In all of the Gothic novels discussed in this book, dark stories and sinister pasts return to haunt the present. Whether it is fragmented scripts, discarded documents, fractured histories, ancient artefacts, decaying architecture, confused ancestry, generational conflict, a preoccupation with origins or the presence of history through supernatural occurrences, the Gothic is obsessed with the nature of the past and our relationship with it. As David Hume's epigraph to this chapter indicates, interest in the systematic analysis and study of the past exploded in the eighteenth century, and the Gothic capitalised on the century's attraction to history.

The Gothic is everywhere fascinated by the past. In recent years, Gothic criticism has witnessed a resurgence of historicised readings of texts and, while this renewed critical focus recognises the importance of historical context, little attention has been paid to how such texts actually construct and represent the past.[1] Why is this genre seemingly fixated with sinister histories? For what reasons is it so concerned with historical authenticity, and what techniques do Gothic writers employ to excavate and dramatise it? How do Gothic pasts differ from each other? To what extent do they portray contemporary anxieties and what are the implications of such pasts for our relationship with history? In his seminal *The Literature of Terror* (first published 1980), David Punter comments that the Gothic represents 'a particular attitude towards the recapture of history' (1996, 1: 4) and that it 'seems to have been a mode of history, a way of perceiving an obscure past and interpreting it' (1: 52). He also comments that the Gothic provides a 'genuine substitute' for history and functions as a means of understanding 'those barbaric areas where knowledge had not quite penetrated' (1: 98). However, characteristic of many critical responses to the Gothic over the decades, Punter conducts predominantly psychoanalytic and Marxist readings of Gothic texts and does not develop these ideas, or their wider implications for the genre.

Considering the relationship between the Gothic and dominant eighteenth-century modes of historical writing, this book employs a historical, contextual and philosophical approach to significantly develop these notions. Indeed, there are currently no studies which focus exclusively on Gothic pasts and few which consider the relationship between early Gothic fiction and eighteenth-century historical writing.[2] Contending that the Gothic can be read as a complex reaction to Enlightenment methods of historical representation, *Sinister Histories* uncovers until-now neglected relationships between Gothic texts and prominent works of eighteenth-century history. Bringing an interdisciplinary approach to the study of the Gothic, this monograph addresses a long neglected aspect of Gothic fiction by discussing the ways in which both well-known histories (such as Hume's *The History of England*, 1754–62) and lesser known historical works (such as Paul M. Rapin de Thoyras's *History of England*, 1721–31) influenced and shaped the genre. Arguing that the French Revolution destabilised Enlightenment notions of historical understanding, it goes on to examine the implications of the events taking place in France for history and Gothic pasts. Tracing the development of the Gothic in chronological order, *Sinister Histories* encompasses both well- and lesser-known novels. As well as discussing authors such as Horace Walpole and Ann Radcliffe, this project breaks from familiar critical histories of the genre by devoting chapters to Clara Reeve and Sophia Lee, important women writers whose works are often ignored or marginalised in discussions of the genre's genesis. By charting the Gothic's complex reaction to Enlightenment conceptions of the past and contemporary anxieties, *Sinister Histories* challenges and broadens our current picture of the genre's historical, political, social, and aesthetic agenda. The Gothic emerges and develops at a time when historical writing was undergoing major changes. In order to fully understand the genre's attitude towards history, it is requisite to situate the Gothic within the wider changes taking place in eighteenth-century historical writing. In terms of the evolution and popularity of history in the eighteenth century, the Gothic emerges at a very telling moment. Although many types of histories were published at this time, including historical biographies, ecclesiastical histories and studies of particular reigns or events, histories of England were by far the most common. Given their popularity and their implications for Gothic fiction, my discussion will concentrate primarily on general histories of England.[3] The following section is not designed to provide a comprehensive account of the development of historical writing prior to the emergence of Gothic fiction; rather, it focuses on the changes in historical works that have significant implications for the Gothic pasts discussed in this book.

Enlightenment: histories of England and the changing nature of eighteenth-century historiography

Throughout the eighteenth century, history was considered one of the noblest forms of literature and its value and literary status were unquestioned. In the first half of the century, attitudes towards history were largely derived from those of continental Renaissance humanism. Classical historians such as Livy, Cicero, Herodotus, Thucydides, Xenophon, Polybius, Sallust, and Tacitus were held in high esteem and it was the aim of English historians to imitate their rhetorical eloquence. The main function of history in this period was not so much to (re)discover the past, but to use it as a vehicle for moral and social improvement in the present. As Laird Okie points out, history was designed to encourage readers to emulate past heroes, arouse affection for their ancestors and country, provide diversion, reveal how God manifests himself in the affairs of humanity, supply shining examples of virtuous conduct, and afford instruction for professional men (1991, 8). For example, in his *Letters on the Study and Use of History* (written in the 1730s but not published until 1752), Henry Bolingbroke transmitted the message of Tacitus and Seneca by emphasising the didacticism of historiography and arguing that history is 'philosophy teaching by examples' (1752, 48). History in this period depended more on the way it was told rather than on accurate scholarship. There was generally less hands-on research with primary texts, little concern with the role of the self in historical writing and few reservations about judging the past by the standards of the present. Late Renaissance history frequently consisted of annals, compilations and chronologies, and scholars often did not distinguish between the primary sources and the finished work of historical writing. As Rosemary Sweet notes, the 'Ciceronian dictum that history only dealt with those things worthy of recollection – what would now be considered as high politics – was still largely unchallenged in the early eighteenth century' (2004, 3). During the first quarter of the eighteenth century, the Battle of the Books had largely been lost by the ancients and, even though its effects continued to be felt, the models used to write history became increasingly Modern or neoclassicist. Furthermore, as Okie points out, the 'Augustan age coincided with the early Enlightenment' (1991, 2), and, in contrast to their predecessors, historians influenced by Enlightenment doctrines became more concerned with methodology, source-criticism and narrative structure.

The Enlightenment was, to use David Williams's words, a 'unique product of various national Enlightenments' (1999, 1). However, even though the Enlightenment was a diverse rather than unitary movement, its adherents were joined together by a commitment to 'modernize' (Porter 2000, xxii). Its advocates prized reason and scientific method, were committed to demystification, debunking tradition and 'clear[ing] away the darkness of ignorance, intolerance and prejudice, … [in order to] move towards a just and better life' (Day 1966, 64). Such Enlightenment characteristics became an integral part of eighteenth-century historical writing, particularly by the mid-century. The age of Enlightenment (or philosophical) history was dawning. As the century progressed, there was a growing frustration with the state of English historical writing and the fact that a history of England worthy of comparison with the ancient historians had not been written.[4] Historians (and philosophers) who were influenced by Enlightenment doctrines addressed this problem. Even though the historiography of the ancients remained important, such histories represented a significant departure from previous historical works.[5] Despite its variety and numerous guises, Enlightenment historical writing has a number of distinguishing characteristics. Whereas traditional humanist history was written, in part, to reveal the workings of divine providence, Enlightenment historiography rejects the providentialist view of history, which saw the narrative of the past as the unfolding of a divine plan. Rather than simply recording great deeds, such historical writing develops a 'more reflective understanding of the operation of society and its political forms, and the relationship between commerce, economy and political order' (Sweet 2004, 4). Works of history influenced by the Enlightenment are not written around the actions of a single protagonist and are not concerned with the politics of a single country. Indeed, such histories have a cosmopolitan outlook and are interested in the general laws of historical development common to all societies.[6] A particularly notable characteristic of histories which embrace Enlightenment doctrines is a commitment to notions of progress and the 'teleology of civility' (Pittock 2007, 262). As William Robertson's epigraph to this chapter reveals, philosophical historians treasured the present moment above all else and were quick to repress or mock the barbarism of previous ages. The follies of the past are condemned while the emergence of reason and learning out of medieval savagery and superstition are celebrated. In accordance with Enlightenment doctrines, liberty of conscience and religious toleration are lauded, while superstition, ignorance and frivolous theology are denounced (Hicks 1996, 179). In the spirit of the Enlightenment, Protestantism is presented as progressive and enlightened, whereas Roman Catholicism is denounced as oppressive and backward. Throughout *Sinister Histories*, historical works that exhibit such characteristics will be referred to as Enlightenment histories. In the eighteenth century, Edward Gibbon's *The Decline and Fall of the Roman Empire* (1776–81) and the historical works of numerous Scottish intellectuals such as Robertson, Adam Ferguson and Adam Smith exhibited such attitudes.[7] In terms of histories of England, however, such characteristics are evident in Hume's *The History of England* and, to a certain extent, Rapin's national history.

As Okie notes, Rapin's *History of England* 'commingled traditionalist elements of the compilation-chronicle mode with a more modern Enlightened approach' (1991, 61). Rapin, a French Protestant who lived in England and the Netherlands, began writing his *Histoire d'Angleterre* in 1707 and continued writing until 1724 when he was interrupted by illness. He died a year later and his completed work was published in The Hague in 1727. The work was made familiar to English readers by Nicholas Tindal's extremely popular translation of Rapin's work.[8] Entitled the *History of England*, it was published in octavo volumes between 1721 and 1731. As Okie points out, Rapin provided new possibilities for history by undermining the traditional chronicle-compilation form of historical writing and effectively 'set the standard for British historical scholarship in the age of [Robert] Walpole' (1991, 47). Introducing many of the characteristics associated with Enlightenment historiography, Rapin's *History of England* consults a wider range of sources than its predecessors, interprets facts rather than lists them, treats sources critically and sceptically, and employs an increasingly secular tone.

As Chapter 2 shows, the secularisation of the historical cause has a number of implications for Gothic fiction. Paving the way for Enlightenment historiography, Rapin shuns military history and significantly broadens the scope of historical enquiry by discussing social and economic factors. For Rapin, the main prerequisites for writing history are common sense, rationality and honesty. As Hicks points out, Rapin had little intention of imitating the classical historians; he complained to readers about the vagueness of classical protocols for writing history and rejected the necessity of conforming to ancient ideals (1996, 149). Whilst Rapin does acknowledge classical historians such as Tacitus, he largely decided to pursue his own agenda (*H* 1: xvi).[9] However, as Chapter 2 discusses, arguing that English liberty could be traced back to the Saxon constitution and citing the late origins of the House of Commons, it was widely acknowledged that, despite its claim to rise above party politics, Rapin's history had a clear Whig bias.

If Rapin represents something of a transitional figure in the history of eighteenth-century historical writing, Hume heralds the era of Enlightenment, or philosophical, history. His *The History of England* was published between 1754 and 1762; the first volume covered the period 1603–49 and was followed by further volumes covering the sixteenth century and two covering the period from Julius Caesar to Henry VII. Hume was initially known as a philosopher, but his multi-volume history met with great acclaim and established his reputation much more firmly than his philosophical works had done. Hume rejected the Whig bias of Rapin's history and attempted to write a more objective history of England that transcended party politics. Characteristically of works influenced by Enlightenment thinking in this period, Hume strives for political detachment and neutrality. His history is interested in the socio-economic factors that drive the historical process and is committed to studying societies in a comparative and cosmopolitan manner. He is quick to mock the follies of previous ages and repress violent incidents, employing a confident and judicious tone to do so. Governed by reason, Hume's work of Enlightenment history is written on a grand scale and sees history as the result of a relationship between cause and effect. Moreover, as Chapter 1 reveals, *The History of England* can be viewed as an extension of Hume's philosophical work and a study of the science of man underpins his historical project. Although Hume is indebted to the 'manner of the Ancients' (Hume 1932, 1: 170) and shared their view that history should have a didactic purpose, his historical work is profoundly 'modern' and represents something of a revolution in eighteenth-century historical thought.[10] As Sweet notes, 'famously associated with Voltaire and his *Essai sur les moeurs*, but also characterised by the histories of David Hume or William Robertson', works of history underpinned by Enlightenment theories influenced 'to a greater or lesser extent the majority of narrative histories of Britain which were published in the second half of the century' (2004, 3–4).

Rapin's proto-Enlightenment and Hume's Enlightenment histories of England are particularly notable for their commitment to explanatory narrative. As Okie points out, by the middle of the eighteenth century, England had 'witnessed a major transformation in historical writing from the traditional humanist chronicle of the Renaissance to an essentially modern style of historical narrative' (1991, vii). Works of history influenced by the Enlightenment are notable for their improved readability. Rapin's history is certainly an example of a narrative history, but Hume criticised his 'despicable' style and endeavoured to write a more elegant history of England (Hume 1932, 1: 179). Indeed, even though Hume's history is written in a philosophical spirit and probes the causes and motives that underpin events, he is still committed to writing a narrative history that is accessible and one that has a commendable literary style. Rationalism and sober judgement may be the most prominent characteristics of *The History of England*, but Hume recognised that historical writing must also entertain: the 'first Quality of an Historian is to be true & impartial; the next to be interesting', he writes (1932, 1: 210). It was this emphasis on narrative, style and literary accessibility that helped to widen the readership and appeal of history in the eighteenth century, and which made such histories so popular. Rapin's history enjoyed enormous success; Tindal's edition was so prevalent that it became one of the most popular scholarly works of the eighteenth century. It was not until the publication of Hume's *The History of England* in the 1750s that Rapin's work of history fell out of fashion. In keeping with the wider aim of the Enlightenment, these histories were designed to make the past accessible to as many readers as possible. In contrast to the historiography of the ancients, history was no longer written and designed exclusively for politicians and the elite; it was increasingly written for a polite middle-class audience. Hume was particularly successful in aiming history at a new female audience. 'There is nothing which I would recommend more earnestly to my female readers than the study of history', he writes, 'as an occupation, of all others, the best suited both to their sex and education, much more instructive than their ordinary books of amusement, and more entertaining than those serious compositions, which are usually to be found in their closets' (Hume 1854, 508). Hume's *The History of England* took history to unprecedented levels of popularity. With seven complete editions during his lifetime and 175 in the century after his death, Hume's multi-volume work became the definitive version of England's past until the publication of Thomas Macaulay's *History of England* (1849–61) in the mid-nineteenth century (Wootton 1993, 285). Other works of Enlightenment history also enjoyed great success. Robertson achieved fame with his *History of Scotland*, and Gibbon's *Decline and Fall* would become one of the most successful histories of all time.[11] History was not a distinct discipline in the eighteenth century and, in terms of the literary marketplace, historical works were in competition with the novel and striving for a central role in contemporary culture.

Literature, history and the rise of the Gothic novel

The historian and the novelist obviously occupy different positions. In the eighteenth century, there was an assumption that literature was about things that had not happened, whereas history was concerned with things that had. Literature was about imagination and invention whereas history was about telling the truth. As Hume's intentions in *The History of England* attest, historians were supposed to write about 'facts' and, using increasingly scientific methods governed by reason and designed to probe the past with a new degree of objectivity, distinguish fiction from myth. However, as Walpole's epigraph to this chapter suggests – that there is not 'much difference' between history and romance (1937–83, 15: 173) – the relationship between the two is far more complicated than this simple opposition suggests. With Enlightenment works of history employing the narrative form, boundaries between history and literature were especially difficult to distinguish by the middle of the eighteenth century. As scholars such as Everett Zimmerman and Robert Mayer have shown by examining the works of canonical eighteenth-century authors, there is a complex interrelationship between literature and history in this period.[12] Historians were utilising literary and narrative techniques from the novel to make their histories more appealing to general readers, while novelists frequently debated historical subjects and were involved in historical pursuits.[13] Eighteenth-century writers predominantly associated with fiction often engaged in historical writing. For example, Oliver Goldsmith published his *History of England* in 1771, while Tobias Smollett's *History of England* (1757–58) sold very well.[14] A number of other popular writers, such as Jonathan Swift and Henry Fielding, experimented with historical writing in this period.[15] Antiquarian works flourished in the eighteenth century. Studying history with particular attention to ancient objects, archives and manuscripts, antiquarians focused more on the empirical evidence of the past than on historical narrative, context, or process. Publishing and corresponding in elaborate networks, antiquaries such as Richard Gough and William Stukeley were instrumental in reconstructing England's past and laying solid foundations for history as a whole.[16] Controversy surrounding the authenticity of James Macpherson's 'Ossian' poems (1761 onwards) and Thomas Chatterton's 'Rowley' works (which date from around 1764) blurred the boundary between history and fiction and truth and falsity, even further.

Moreover, many eighteenth-century novels are preoccupied with the nature of historical writing and knowledge. For example, the works of Fielding, Laurence Sterne, Charlotte Lennox and Smollett continually grapple with early notions of historical consciousness and understanding.[17] As Chapter 3 discusses, Samuel Richardson's immensely popular epistolary fiction raises interesting questions about time and the distance between the perceiving and narrating self. However, even though the nature of history is debated in such novels, very few choose historical settings for their narratives. As Anne H. Stevens points out, in the 1740s and 1750s, Fielding, Richardson and their imitators dominated the literary marketplace and the 'historical settings of seventeenth-century romance were temporarily set aside in favour of modern day, middle-class English settings' (2010, 35). 'This period of the suspension of romance', continues Stevens, 'coincides with the period of the "rise of the novel", where the novel is identified with contemporary settings and a rejection of romance features' (35). However, with historical works enjoying great popularity in the literary marketplace by mid-century, writers of fiction became increasingly drawn to historical settings. Although his authorship of the work is contested, Thomas Leland's *Longsword, Earl of Salisbury* (1762) is a notable example of a novel that elects for a medieval, rather than contemporary, setting. Leland was primarily known as a historian and antiquarian rather than a fictional writer, and his work is an attempt to blend the prestige of history with the novel. However, as Stevens notes (2010, 31), beyond a favourable review and a popular stage adaptation, *Longsword* did not enjoy widespread success. Indeed, it would be another antiquarian and historian who would successfully fuse the eighteenth-century novel with the past.

Capitalising on the popularity of modern histories underpinned by Enlightenment philosophy, and exploiting the fluid relationship between history and literature, Horace Walpole pioneered the Gothic genre with the publication of *The Castle of Otranto* on Christmas Eve 1764. As Chapter 1 discusses, the first edition of *Otranto* was presented as a discovered manuscript. By employing such a device, Walpole's novel raises awkward questions about narrative history and the nature of historical knowledge. In the second edition of *Otranto*, the words 'A GOTHIC STORY' are printed on the title page (*O* 3). Before the publication of this work, Walpole was better known as an antiquarian, historian and son of the British Prime Minister, Sir Robert Walpole. His home at Strawberry Hill became famous for its Gothic Revival style of architecture and vast collection of antiquities. Given his interest in antiquity and history, it should come as no surprise that the past is a source of fascination in *Otranto*. Set in a foreign location and an obscure historical period, Walpole developed a number of themes and tropes that would make the Gothic such a recognisable genre. These include an obsession with history and historical artefacts, the device of the discovered manuscript, a haunted suit of armour, paranormal occurrences, Catholic superstition, an evil villain, dysfunctional families, female oppression, a mouldering castle, macabre pasts, ancestral portraits, irrational behaviour, fantastic coincidences, and scenes of sustained terror and suspense.

Walpole's thoughts in the preface to the second edition of *Otranto* provide a particularly significant insight into the Gothic and its preoccupations. He describes the novel as 'a new species of romance' (*O* 13) and as 'an attempt to blend the two kinds of romance, the ancient and the modern' (O 9). He adds that 'in the former all was imagination and improbability: in the latter, nature is always intended to be, and sometimes has been, copied with success' (O 9). Arguing that the modern novel has 'dammed up' the 'great resources of fancy' by adhering too strictly to 'common life' and that 'old romances' do not depict accurate psychological states, he sets out to reinvent the romance in *Otranto* by finding a way to 'reconcile the two kinds' (O 9). He achieves this by combining the fantastic and macabre aspects of romance with the modern novel's ability to depict realistic psychological states and responses to events (O 9–10). A key preoccupation of most romances, of course, is a focus on events that happened in the distant past. This is certainly the case with Walpole's 'updated' romance; he speaks of *Otranto* as an attempt to identify with the 'actions, sentiments' and 'conversations' of 'ancient days' (O 9). To a readership accustomed to narratives set in the present, *Otranto* marks the return of the past to the literary domain. Indeed, the vague, unspecific medieval historical setting of Walpole's novel is particularly significant. Akin to the sinister past that returns in Walpole's narrative, *Otranto* drags the 'civilised' eighteenth century back to the medieval and un-Enlightened past.

Enlightened pasts versus Gothic pasts

Walpole's *Otranto* transported its readers to a barbaric period ruled by primitive customs, ignorance and superstition: the material that Enlightenment historians tended to overlook. It is a long-standing contention that the Gothic is not simply a rejection of the Enlightenment, but a complex reaction to it.[18] As I mentioned previously, the Enlightenment may have been a diverse and multi-national movement, but it united a number of common characteristics. Its adherents shared Immanuel Kant's motto for the Enlightenment, 'dare to know', and aimed to transform 'the invisible into the visible, the ineffable into the discursive, and the unknown into the known' (Bronner 2004, 19). At the same time that the Enlightenment was challenging religious conceptions of the world and fundamentally changing perceptions of the past, present and future, the Gothic emerged. Embracing irrationality, mysticism and superstition and yet obsessed with legitimacy and the status quo, Gothic pasts have a complex relationship with

Enlightenment doctrines. As Fred Botting notes, the Gothic 'is a site of struggle between enlightened forces of progress and more conservative impulses to retain continuity' (1996, 23). The Gothic texts under discussion in this book continually stage such conflicts. Carol Margaret Davison echoes Botting's words when she contends that the Gothic is a 'battleground bearing traces – among other things – of a momentous confrontation between Enlightenment and pre-Enlightenment belief-systems, ideas and values' (2009, 40).

Sinister Histories shows that there is also a complex interaction between the Gothic and Enlightenment conceptions of history in this period. The Gothic can be read as a reaction to the eighteenth-century's 'new-found confidence in the ability of man to understand the past, improve his present and establish a blueprint for his future' (Williams 1999, 7). In a similar vein to Enlightenment historiography, some of the narratives discussed in this book express anti-Catholic sentiments and stage a movement from a primitive past to a more civilised present. Stevens goes so far as to suggest that the Gothic expresses 'characteristic Enlightenment skepticism about the truth of historical accounts' (2010, 33).[19] However, at the same time that the Gothic seems to accord with the characteristics of such histories, it responds to the Enlightenment's attempt to demythologise the past by delighting in superstition, the supernatural, irrationality, and the inexplicable; aspects of the past that such historians deplore. Indeed, Gothic pasts evince 'multiple and sometimes contradictory stand-points vis-à-vis the Enlightenment' (Davison 2009, 45). As James Carson argues, 'the Gothic novel is at once complicit with and critical of the Enlightenment conceived of as a contradictory ideological formation and intellectual enterprise' (1996, 265). The Gothic's reaction to Enlightenment doctrines becomes more varied and complex as the genre develops. Walpole's *Otranto* may exhibit anti-Catholicism, but, as the next chapter shows, it is predominantly a reaction to the 'cold common sense' that dominates explorations of the past in the eighteenth century (Walpole 1767). Chapter 2 shows how the next Gothic novel to be published after *Otranto* – Clara Reeve's *The Old English Baron* (1778) – embraces images of darkness and light, stages a movement from a barbaric past to a more progressive future, and yet, at the same time, can be read as a response to the secularisation of history. Sophia Lee's *The Recess* (1783–85) rejects nearly every aspect of Enlightenment historiography (see Chapter 3) while Radcliffe's

The Romance of the Forest (1791) demonstrates perhaps the most complex reaction to Enlightenment doctrines. As Chapter 4 shows, Radcliffe's fictional past may embrace reason and ultimately dispel superstition, but it continually draws attention to aspects of the past that Enlightenment historiography ignores. The final chapter of this book reveals that Godwin and Wollstonecraft were very familiar with works of philosophical history and that they viewed (Gothic) romance as an alternative mode of historiography. Although there is a complex interplay between Enlightenment strategies of historical representation and the Gothic, the links between historians and Gothic writers uncovered in *Sinister Histories* reveal that the genre is frequently hostile towards such representations of the past. While acknowledging instances where the Gothic accords with Enlightenment historical doctrines, this book is particularly interested in where the Gothic exploits its blind spots and deviates from such conceptions of the past. The Gothic is a heterogeneous genre in the eighteenth century, but the following characteristics apply – to greater and lesser extents – to all of the Gothic narratives discussed in this monograph.

As I mentioned earlier, the popular historical works of Rapin and Hume (as well as Robertson and Gibbon) forward an Enlightenment agenda by focusing on the development of civil society and, in the latter's case, by forwarding a science of man. The inevitable result of this representational strategy is that aspects of the past that do not conform with reason or the spirit of science are marginalised. *Sinister Histories* contends that the Gothic reacts to Enlightenment history's 'propensity to exclusion' by focusing on aspects of the past that defy reason and that 'resist the effort to force the complexities of the past into a neat synthesis' (Ankersmit 2001, 3). In keeping with the Gothic's contradictory relationship with Enlightenment doctrines, even novels which do eventually provide neat explanations for the past and feature harmonious endings (namely, *The Old English Baron* and *The Romance of the Forest*) still point to aspects of history that challenge rational comprehension. The Gothic is not concerned with accurately reconstructing historical periods. Even though Reeve's and Lee's Gothic novels are set in specific historical periods and involve a number of events from recorded history, their novels are not designed to challenge historians' accounts of these proceedings.[20] As this monograph demonstrates, at the same time that the Gothic is intricately connected with the history of the eighteenth century, it exploits the blurred relationship between literature and history in order to question the extent to which we can know and understand the past. In all of the novels discussed in *Sinister Histories*, the Gothic haunts Enlightenment historiography; it exploits its insecurities, plagues its vulnerabilities, and imaginatively provides fictional presences for its many absences and omissions. In the works discussed in this monograph, the Gothic frequently undermines the confidence exuded by Enlightenment historians. Hayden White's thoughts on the relationship between literature and history are useful here. Exploring sinister aspects of the past that remain outside the premise of Enlightenment historiography and drawing attention to our frustrated access to the past through fragmented manuscripts and decaying buildings, the Gothic qualifies Enlightenment explanatory power by reminding readers that history is a 'discourse' rather than 'an absolute ground of being, an objective process, or an empirically observable structure of relationships' (White 1987, 103). Preying on notions of authenticity and exploiting the tenuous relationship between history and fiction in the eighteenth century, the Gothic serves as a timely reminder that history is the study of the past, not the past itself, and exposes the 'irreducible and inexpungeable element of interpretation' that is part of all historical narratives (White 1985, 51). At a time when the eighteenth century felt confident about its ability to master the past, the Gothic – a genre shot through with pro- and anti- Enlightenment impulses – emerged as a chilling reminder that our relationship with the past is often anything but comfortable and straightforward.

Reminiscent of Davison's earlier quotation, even in works that exhibit historical attitudes associated with the Enlightenment, the Gothic continually harks back to pre-Enlightened conceptions of the past. The Age of Reason is haunted by the spectre of the Gothic. One of the reasons the Gothic endured throughout the eighteenth century (and well beyond) is because it continually questions what it is to be human and preys on primeval anxieties and fears. Gothic works raise disturbing questions about our relationship with history, the persistence of the past in the present and the role of divine agency in human life. The suspense-driven novels discussed in this book show that there is something inherently 'Gothic' about our relationship with history: despite its seeming tangibility in the present, the past is always inherently inaccessible and beyond physical reach. Even in Reeve's and Radcliffe's novels where tidy resolutions are provided, the Gothic frequently preys on our alien connection with the past. Whereas Enlightenment historiography gives the impression that progress and rationality ultimately drive the historical process, the Gothic shows how violence and irrationality frequently dictate the ruthless sweep of history. The authoritative prose and neat narrative structures employed by Enlightenment historians frequently mask our essentially remote connection with history. Drawing attention to the haunting nature of history and aspects of it that transcend Enlightenment historiography, the Gothic explores our most fundamental relationship with the past.

Gothic heterogeneity: historical displacement and the past as subterfuge

The attitudes towards history outlined above may be characteristic of a number of the Gothic responses towards history discussed in *Sinister Histories*, but it is important to recognise the complexity and heterogeneity of Gothic pasts. While all of the novels discussed in this book react to Enlightenment conceptions of history, they do so in very diverse ways and take issue with different aspects of them. Furthermore, Gothic pasts themselves are sites of intense conflict with authors frequently reacting to each others' works. Throughout this study, I will emphasise the genre's instability, hybridity and contending ideologies. As Davison points out, at the same time that the Gothic is a 'tradition with a generic identity and significance with which … its foremost contributors consciously dialogued', there is also a 'tremendous diversity' in its manifestations (2009, 13).[21] The Gothic may be a recognisable genre, but it is not a homogeneous one that develops unproblematically. Walpole may have fashioned many of the tropes that became the hallmark of Gothic fiction and that were utilised by subsequent authors such as Reeve, Lee, Radcliffe, William Godwin, and Mary Wollstonecraft, but they would undergo significant revisions and be deployed for diverse ends. As this monograph points out, within the Gothic genre itself, there are numerous different strains, including Loyalist Gothic and Female Gothic. Still recognisable as works of Gothic fiction, such sub-categories express different attitudes towards history, have conflicting views on the genre's themes and tropes and fiercely contest the meaning of the 'Gothic' as a political term (see Chapters 2 and 4). The Gothic writers discussed in this book set their narratives in very different locations and historical periods and, as well as engaging in debates surrounding history and the Enlightenment, express fears about a range of pressing social, political and historical debates. The Gothic is often much closer to home than general accounts of the genre suggest and, despite the seeming historical, and in some cases, geographical, remoteness of such narratives, they frequently respond to and comment on a number of eighteenth-century events. Gothic pasts may be linked with historical writing, but they are also intertwined with eighteenth-century history and culture. As the following chapters reveal, the Gothic undergoes a number of significant changes in the course of its development.

I have selected 1764, the publication date of the first Gothic novel, as the starting point for *Sinister Histories*. However, it is important to note that developments in eighteenth-century verse, romance and criticism helped to shape the Gothic novel. The 'Graveyard Poets' enjoyed great popularity in the first half of the century and contributed to the development of Gothic fiction by drawing on themes such as death, mortality, religion, melancholy and the supernatural. Thomas Parnell's 'Night-Piece on Death' (1722), Edward Young's *Night Thoughts* (1742–45), Robert Blair's *The Grave* (1743), James Hervey's *Meditations among the Tombs* (1745–47), Thomas Warton's *The Pleasures of Melancholy* (1747), and Thomas Gray's *Elegy Written in a Country Churchyard* (1751) proved particularly influential and are frequently cited as important Gothic precursors. As I discuss in more detail in Chapter 4, Edmund Burke's *A Philosophical Enquiry into the Origin of Our Ideas of the Sublime and the Beautiful* (1757) influenced the Gothic by examining terror, awe, incomprehension, and the irrational. Romances and revivals of 'Celtic', 'Saxon' or 'bardic' poetry by antiquarians were also popular and helped to shape the genre's attitudes towards the past. Thomas Percy's *Reliques of Ancient English Poetry* (1765), the work of 'Ossian', James Beattie's *The Minstrel* (1770–74), Chatterton's 'Rowley' poems, John Carter's *Specimens of Ancient Sculpture and Painting* (1780–94), and Joseph Riston's collections of ancient poetry reveal a fascination with history and contribute to eighteenth-century attempts to reappropriate the past. Novels of sentiment written by authors such as Henry Mackenzie and Richardson focused on the emotions of characters, recorded their feelings in minute detail and revealed their reactions to situations involving despair and anguish. As Chapter 3 discusses, this emphasis on psychology and passion had a large impact on the Gothic novel.

Another work which contributed to the cultural debates that led to the rise of the Gothic and the Gothic novel was Richard Hurd's *Letters on Chivalry and Romance* (1762). Criticising Augustanism and the realistic modern novel, he analyses the literature of the past, calling for the recovery of a native English tradition and urging a reconsideration of romance. Discussing Spenser's *Faerie Queene*, the verse epics of Tasso and Ariosto, and some of Shakespeare's plays, he heralds the imaginative freedom of such works and argues that 'Gothic' (meaning, in this instance, medieval, or outside the classical domain) romances are a welcome alternative to the rigid neo-classical principles that dominate the first half of the eighteenth century. As my earlier discussion of the preface to the second edition of *Otranto* indicates, Walpole, similarly to Hurd, recognised the imaginative potential of romance and fused it with some of the features associated with the modern novel in order to write the first Gothic novel. The revival of romance and ancient forms of poetry proved vital to the rise of the Gothic novel.

However, this monograph is interested in works that are part of, rather an influence on, the Gothic tradition and focuses exclusively on the development of the Gothic novel in the eighteenth century. As the various reflections on historical understanding that feature in the novels of Fielding and Smollett suggest, the novel, with its emphasis on narrative, structure, interpretation, and testimony, is useful for critiquing historiography and draws attention to the literary nature of history. This is even more so with the Gothic novel. Set in the past and replete with framing devices, fragmentation, conflicting testimonies, complex plots, coincidences, and situations that frequently defy reason, the novels discussed in this monograph have profound philosophical implications for Enlightenment, narrative history and destabilise the traditional relationship between fact and fiction, history and romance. One might wonder why, in a book addressing the Gothic novel, I choose to focus on so few and at such length. There are three main reasons for this. First, all of the Gothic novels discussed in this book have strong links to works of history influenced by Enlightenment doctrines and engage with Enlightenment conceptions of the past. *Sinister Histories* carefully excavates hitherto neglected links between Gothic texts and works of eighteenth-century historiography. As the following chapters reveal, Walpole had read Hume's *The History of England*, Reeve was influenced by Rapin's *History of England* as a child and Lee's novel, *The Recess*, engages explicitly with Hume's (and, indeed, Robertson's) history. Radcliffe was a Dissenting Unitarian and, as Chapter 4 reveals, her works are intertwined with Enlightenment notions of history and communicate with the historical debates that were triggered by the French Revolution (a series of events which were heavily influenced by Enlightenment doctrines). Godwin and Wollstonecraft also responded to recent events in France and changing conceptions of late eighteenth-century history (and were familiar with works of Enlightenment historiography). Second, whether it is Ellinor's difficulty recalling past events in *The Recess*, or the decaying manuscript that is splintered throughout *The Romance of the Forest*, the novels discussed in this monograph problematise the nature of historical knowledge in both *form* and *content*. As well as challenging historical authenticity by masquerading as edited or translated works, Gothic novels frequently discuss (often explicitly) the complex issues that arise when it comes to writing the past. Third, I have elected to devote the same time and space to each novel under discussion. This ensures that each work has equal status and serves one of the main aims of this book: to show that authors who are often sidelined in histories of the Gothic novel (Reeve and Lee) are just as important and worthy of critical analysis as canonical writers (Walpole, Radcliffe, Godwin, and Wollstonecraft).

Tracing the genesis of the Gothic in chronological order, *Sinister Histories* begins with an examination of the Gothic's engagement with Enlightenment history by examining the complex and often antagonistic relationship between Walpole's *Otranto* and Hume's *The History of England*. As Walpole's correspondence reveals, he had read numerous volumes of Hume's history before writing *Otranto* and did not think very highly of its content or the methods used to write it. Reassessing the significance of the Gothic in the eighteenth century, this chapter discusses the extent to which Walpole's novel can be viewed as a bold response to, and critique of, Hume's historiography. Focusing on the Gothic trope of the discovered manuscript, violence, textuality, language, and the wider interrelationship between literature and history in the eighteenth century, answers to a number of key questions are sought. For example, why is *Otranto* seemingly fixated with a bygone age? Why is it so concerned with historical authenticity? What techniques does Walpole use to write the past and how do these compare with Hume's methods? Taking into account a wealth of historical evidence, this chapter proposes that Walpole's novel can be read as an imaginative revolt against Hume's multi-volume work of history and that it marks the beginning of the genre's contentious relationship with Enlightenment historiography and the philosophy that underpins it.

Building on the notion that the Gothic is shaped by (and can be read as a reaction to) Enlightenment historiography and shifting conceptions of the past in the eighteenth century, Chapter 2 proposes that *The Old English Baron* can be understood as a response to a popular (and frequently neglected) work of proto-Enlightenment English history that Reeve was very familiar with: this was Tindal's translation of Rapin's *History of England*. Focusing on this previously ignored relationship, the chapter considers the religious and political implications of Rapin's *History of England* for the Gothic past presented in Reeve's novel. Furthermore, in this chapter, I reveal the ways in which the past constructed in *The Old English Baron* can be read as a rewriting of *Otranto* and draw attention to the historical specificity that Reeve introduces to the genre at this time. As Chapter 1 notes, even though Walpole was the son of the Prime Minister and a Whig MP, it is difficult to read his politics into the foreign and Catholic past constructed in *Otranto*: a novel that is written largely in defiance of politics, philosophy, history, and mainstream eighteenth-century literature. The Gothic works which follow *Otranto* have clearer political standpoints and can be linked more accurately with their authors' religio-political orientations and, as a result, the scope of this monograph broadens from this point onwards. Focusing on Reeve's Old Whig political beliefs and the English setting of her novel, I assess the extent to which *The Old English Baron* conveys Whig historico-political nightmares and focus on how her Gothic past betrays contemporary anxieties. Concurring with James Watt's view that Reeve's novel is a work of Loyalist Gothic fiction, this chapter shows how *The Old English Baron* subverts the Walpolean Gothic and responds to the Enlightenment drive to secularise the historical cause.

Influenced by Reeve's use of history in *The Old English Baron*, the Gothic continued to be concerned with the events of recorded history. Lee's *The Recess* is based around Queen Elizabeth's persecution of Mary, Queen of Scots, and the isolation of her two daughters by a secret marriage. The novel bears close resemblance to parts of Hume's *The History of England* and Robertson's *The History of Scotland* and it is likely that it was influenced by these two popular historical works. *The Recess* marks a significant contrast with previous Gothic narratives in that it is narrated predominantly in the first person by the novel's protagonists, Matilda and Ellinor. Emphasising the diversity of the Gothic genre in the eighteenth century, this chapter argues that Lee hijacks certain themes from Walpole and Reeve to write a prototypical Female Gothic novel. Continuing to read the Gothic as a reaction to eighteenth-century historical writing, this chapter contends that Lee focuses on female protagonists and employs Gothic plotlines to critique the male codes of historical representation that govern Hume's Enlightenment historiography. Developing arguments from the previous chapter, I show how, in the hands of female writers, Gothic pasts often express contemporary fears and anxieties, and comment on gender politics in the eighteenth century. Drawing on Gary Kelly's notion that the Gothic enabled women to access the male-dominated realms of history and politics (2002, 1: xxix), I contend that Lee's historically based novel utilises Gothic tropes such as concealed writings and a focus on the law to present a nightmare vision of women's historical and social plight in the eighteenth century. Examining the complex structure of *The Recess*, I conclude by examining the extent to which Lee 'Gothicises' the eighteenth-century epistolary form, and what the novel says about the nature of the past.

The Enlightenment, the French Revolution and the Gothic

Although the nature of the past was debated throughout the eighteenth century, it became a subject of even more intense debate in the 1790s. The speed, scale and intensity of the French Revolution was unprecedented in human history. In just a few short years, the monarchy that had ruled France for centuries was overturned and a new social order based on Enlightenment principles of citizenship was established. Looking on from English shores, there was general amazement at the scale and dizzying pace of events taking place in France. At the same time that events in France were influenced by Enlightenment philosophy, Enlightenment historical theories struggled to explain such developments. Historical discussion moved from multi-volume tomes to political pamphlets. Engaging with events in France and forwarding their own social and political views, writers such as Edmund Burke and Mary Wollstonecraft present conflicting views of history and debate the role of the past in the present. As I discuss in Chapter 4, feelings, romance and contested notions of the political term 'Gothic' become important aspects of historical thought at this time.

Re-evaluating the implications of the French Revolution for Gothic fiction, Chapter 4 examines representations of the past in a novel that is often neglected in Gothic studies: Radcliffe's *The Romance of the Forest*. It was written in the immediate aftermath of the French Revolution, but set in seventeenth-century Roman Catholic France. I discuss the ways in which the novel bears traces of the present and examine the significance of the decaying abbey and fragmented manuscript that feature in the novel. Citing the enormity of the events taking place in France and the challenge they presented to established Enlightenment historical theories and methods, I argue that *The Romance of the Forest* responds to such shifting notions of history by revealing a heightened sense of historical consciousness that is engendered by the French Revolution. Influenced by *The Recess* and utilising the Female Gothic's focus on the heroine, I show how Radcliffe's novel engages with the politics of the past and, more specifically, with the contested 'Gothic' views of history presented in Edmund Burke's *Reflections on the Revolution in France* (1790) and Mary Wollstonecraft's *A Vindication of the Rights of Men* (1790). Drawing attention to Radcliffe as a Rational Dissenter, her links to Burke and the renewed significance of the sublime in the Romantic period, this chapter considers the extent to which the past in *The Romance of the Forest* is shaped by the chaotic events of the early 1790s.

The final chapter of this book begins with a discussion of the insatiable thirst for Gothic novels in England as the French Revolution consumed itself in the Terror and reveals how the historical and geographical settings of Gothic narratives change fundamentally during this period. Amidst the diverse Gothic responses to the crisis in England triggered by the French Revolution, a very different setting for Gothic novels was emerging: the present. The date range of *Sinister Histories* (1764–1798) differs from many other works of Gothic scholarship, and this is due to one of its central contentions: that the French Revolution changed the nature of history and Gothic pasts forever. With the government implementing draconian legislation designed to restrict the spread of radicalism, this chapter argues that late eighteenth-century England had become a frightening place. As a result, some Gothic novels exploited this climate of fear and were situated closer to the present. One such novel to do so was William Godwin's *The Adventures of Caleb Williams* (1794). This chapter examines how Godwin brings the Gothic to bear on the eighteenth century and, by considering the novel as a manifestation of his radical views outlined in *Political Justice* (which was Godwin's rebuttal of Burke's *Reflections*), explores the novel as a response to English anxieties about the French Revolution at home and abroad. Moreover, I examine representations of the past in the novel, particularly in relation to Godwin's essay, 'Of History and Romance' (1797), in which he criticises works of Enlightenment history written by Hume and Robertson. This chapter also discusses the psychological introspection of *Caleb Williams*, the presence of history in the human psyche and the (unwanted) ideological legacy of the past. Mary Wollstonecraft, whom Godwin married and who shared his political radicalism, published *Maria, or The Wrongs of Woman* in 1798. This chapter goes on to explore how, in a similar vein to Godwin, Wollstonecraft refuses to use a fictional past as a subterfuge to comment on the present and uses the Gothic to examine women's plight in eighteenth-century England. Discussing *Maria* in relation to *A Vindication of the Rights of Woman*, I examine how the novel brings the Female Gothic and its political agenda into sharper focus. This chapter discusses Wollstonecraft's exploration of the female psyche, and how Maria's thoughts and actions are governed by anachronistic and patriarchal social customs. I also consider the impact of Godwin's and Wollstonecraft's novels on subsequent Gothic works. *Sinister Histories* concludes by demonstrating that, even though some Gothic works no longer relied on historical displacement, Gothic attitudes towards the past continued to be influenced by the genre's earlier contentious relationship with Enlightenment historiography.

Notes

1 While psychoanalytic criticism has traditionally dominated Gothic studies and remains a prevalent aspect of contemporary criticism, there has been an increasing focus on historical readings over the last decade or

so. Notable examples of this approach include Maggie Kilgour's *The Rise of the Gothic Novel* (1995), David H. Richter's *The Progress of Romance: Literary Historiography and the Gothic Novel* (1996) and Robert Mighall's *A Geography of Victorian Gothic Fiction* (1999). In recent years, Andrew Smith's *Gothic Literature* (2007) and Carol Margaret Davison's *Gothic Literature 1764–1824* (2009) conduct a number of historically based readings.

2 In *British Historical Fiction before Scott* (2010), Anne H. Stevens briefly considers the relationship between Gothic and historical pasts (2010, 48–50) and discusses Walpole's *Otranto*, Reeve's *The Old English Baron* and Lee's *The Recess*. However, as the title of her study suggests, Stevens is more interested in how the Gothic helped to shape the historical novel and is not primarily interested in the Gothic's complex relationship with eighteenth-century historiography. In his introduction to *Varieties of Female Gothic* (2002), Gary Kelly also briefly considers the influence of aspects of Enlightenment historiography on the Gothic (1: xxiii–xxix).

3 For a discussion of the broader and more diverse changes taking place to historical writing in this period, see Thomas Preston Peardon's *The Transition in English Historical Writing 1760–1830* (1933), Mark Salber Phillips's *Society and Sentiment: Genres of Historical Writing in Britain, 1740–1820* (2000) and Joseph M. Levine's *The Battle of the Books: History and Literature in the Augustan Age* (1991).

4 As Philip Hicks points out (1996, 1), intellectuals as diverse as Bacon, Milton, Clarendon, Dryden, Addison, Bolingbroke, Voltaire, and Montesquieu all voiced their displeasure at the fact that England did not have a narrative history written in a grand, majestic manner and containing political deeds, military activity and character sketches for which the classical historians were famous. The aim was not to write a history of the classical period, but to produce a modern history of England that accorded with the conventions of the classical historians. The publication of the Earl of Clarendon's *History of the Rebellion* (1702–4) – a work of historiography modelled after Thucydides – went some way to achieving this and was well received. However, Clarendon had only achieved acclaim with one period of English history, the Civil War of the 1640s, and English critics still longed for a good (neoclassical) account of England's entire past. In a strange twist of fate, it would be two outsiders influenced by Enlightenment doctrines – Rapin and Hume – who would successfully address the perceived 'weakness' of English historical writing.

5 For a thorough discussion of the persistence and assimilation of classical ideas in modern historical works, see Hicks's *Neoclassical History and English Culture: From Clarendon to Hume* (1996). See Note 10 for the influence of ancient historians on Hume.

6 For more information on the cosmopolitanism of histories influenced by the Enlightenment, see Karen O'Brien's *Narratives of Enlightenment: Cosmopolitan History from Voltaire to Gibbon* (2005).

7 Besides Hume's history, the historical works of a number of other Scottish intellectuals trace human development 'through certain common stages of progress from barbarism to refinement' and dismiss much of the past as mere savagery and superstition (Cannon 1988, 201). In his *Lectures on Jurisprudence* (1752–64) – the ideas of which were fundamental to the later *Wealth of Nations* (1776) – Adam Smith develops a four-stage theory of history whereby all societies pass through the following universal historical stages: the hunting stage, the age of shepherds, the age of agriculture, and the commercial stage. Smith's historical ideas proved very influential. Developing Smith's work, Dugald Stewart came up with the idea of theoretical, or conjectural, history in order to address the problem of how we can 'conjecture historical change for which no evidence exists by examining the same stage in development for a society where the evidence does exist' (Pittock 2007, 263). Based on the widespread Enlightenment notion that human nature is essentially the same everywhere at all times, Robertson utilised conjectural history in his analysis of Native Americans in his *History of America* (1777). Smith's historical ideas also influenced John Millar, Lord Kames and Adam Ferguson, who shared Smith's view that social progress is often accompanied by a backward step. For further discussion of Scottish intellectual history, see Murray G. H. Pittock's 'Historiography' (2007) and Alexander Broadie's *The Scottish Enlightenment: An Anthology* (1997).

8 Tindal's translation of Rapin's history surpassed all previous general histories and English readers expressed begrudging praise for the Frenchman's achievement. 'It is somewhat surprising', wrote one English critic, 'that the only account of the English affairs which deserves the name of a history should be writ by a foreigner' (Duncombe 1728, 1).

9 Hicks argues that Rapin 'denied the necessity of following received opinion regarding the writing of history. He did list Caesar, Livy and Tacitus as having the sort of taste historians required … but Rapin decided to press on according to his own lights' (1996, 149).

10 As Hicks notes, even though Hume observed 'ancient protocols for historical writing', *The History of England* was modern and 'revolutionary in its treatment of many religious and constitutional issues' (1996, 170). Influenced by the ancients, Hume's work of history functions as a teacher of moral and political lessons, but many of his 'particular lessons were those commonly associated with the program of the Enlightenment' (179).

11 Robertson's *History of Scotland* is particularly significant in the sense that it was written for the general public. As Peardon notes, he presented his

history (and his many other Enlightenment-influenced historical works) in 'a straightforward narrative without too much encumbrance of academic digression, technical discussion or quotations from documents, and added a concluding section of "proofs and illustrations" devoted to such matters' (1933, 23). Works of history influenced by the ethos of the Enlightenment became increasingly accessible and readable. The most stylistically accomplished historical work published in the eighteenth century was Gibbon's *Decline and Fall.* Sharing the characteristics of numerous works of history influenced by the Enlightenment in this period – a denunciation of religious tyranny, an examination of the causes that underpin events and a persuasive narrative tone – it was an immediate bestseller. Although Gibbon's history was immensely successful, its influence on Gothic fiction is difficult to assess for two main reasons: first, Volume 1 was published twelve years after Walpole pioneered the Gothic genre and, second, there is a lack of historical links between Gibbon's history and the Gothic authors discussed in this book. For a consideration of some of the ways in which Gibbon's *Decline and Fall* may have influenced the Gothic, see Robin Sowerby's 'The Goths in History and Pre-Gothic Gothic' (2000).

12 Discussing the works of authors such as Jonathan Swift, William Godwin, Samuel Richardson, and Henry Fielding, Everett Zimmerman's *The Boundaries of Fiction: History and the Eighteenth-Century British Novel* (1996) argues that novels in this period are concerned with the epistemological problems of historical writing. His study focuses on the ways in which the novel critiques the manner in which historiography makes claims about the past and pays particular attention to the tendency of novelists to entitle their works as histories and to present them as pseudo-documentary 'evidence' presented by pseudo-editors. In *History and the Early English Novel: Matters of Fact from Bacon to Defoe* (1997), Robert Mayer explores the complexity of the relationship between history and fiction and argues that the English novel originates from historical writing.

13 Aware of the success of the novel, histories written in this period were influenced by literary techniques used by novelists and the sentimental movement. In *Society and Sentiment* (2000), Mark Salber Phillips argues that sentiment became integral to historiography and shows how, throughout the century, history broadened its appeal beyond politics and frequently paralleled developments in the contemporary novel. In *Narratives of Enlightenment* (2005), O'Brien also notes the literary aspects of Hume's and Robertson's histories and shows how their historical works sometimes make use of a sentimental historical style. While sentiment most certainly does influence parts of Hume's and Robertson's works, their histories are still largely governed by reason, measured prose and a deliberate detachment and emotional distance from the historical events being described.

14 As Okie notes, Goldsmith's and Smollett's works were 'popularizations of English history' which proved to be 'enormously successful and remunerative ventures' (1991, 9). However, Goldsmith's and Smollett's historical works do not present original contributions to historiography and, therefore, neither are discussed in this monograph. Smollett's instalments of his *History of England* sold 10–20,000 copies a week, but, as Peardon points out, it was 'merely a rapid compilation written as a commercial venture to rival Hume' and was 'long used as a supplement' to the latter's *The History of England* (1933, 77). Goldsmith's *History of England, from the earliest times to the death of George II* proved very popular, but he admits to 'abridging the works of others' (1771, 1: i) in the preface and the Elizabethan section of his work is taken almost directly from Hume. He also published *A History of England in a Series of Letters from a Nobleman to his Son* anonymously in 1764.

15 Okie points out that it is 'striking how many of the literary titans of the age dabbled in history, although their endeavors were frequently never completed or published' (1991, 8). Such writers include Daniel Defoe, Jonathan Swift, Henry Fielding, Samuel Johnson, and Edmund Burke. Swift wrote abstracts for a general history of England while Fielding – a friend of the historian James Ralph – was an 'avid reader of English history and imbued his fiction with profound historical insight' (Okie 1991, 8–9).

16 As Rosemary Sweet observes, the relationship between the antiquary and the historian was 'always more complicated than a simple opposition between narrative and description'. History may have been regarded in much higher esteem than mere antiquities in the eighteenth century, but, nevertheless, the 'historian used the evidence of the antiquary, and the antiquary depended upon the historical narrative of the historian to provide the framework according to which the artefacts of the past could be interpreted'. They were, Sweet adds, 'natural partners, a fact to which their frequent titular pairing is sufficient testimony' (2004, 1–2).

17 Eighteenth-century novels frequently take issue with narrative histories. For example, in the opening pages of *The Adventures of Ferdinand Count Fathom* (published in 1753), Smollett questions the accuracy of historical writing and questions notions of 'historical truth' (1990, 45). Indeed, featuring extreme situations and a graveyard scene including a phantom, *Ferdinand Count Fathom* is seen as an important precursor to the Gothic. For a brief overview of the early origins of Gothic fiction (including a discussion of Graveyard Poetry, sentimentalism and the sublime), see Punter's *Literature of Terror* (1: 20–53).

18 It is beyond the scope of this introduction to discuss the Gothic's relationship with the Enlightenment in detail. For a good overview of this

subject, see Davison's *Gothic Literature* (2009, 22–54). My brief consideration of the Enlightenment and the Gothic here synthesises a number of opinions and views outlined in Davison's account (40).

19 Stevens's observation is a valid one. However, as Chapter 1 shows, Hume's scepticism about our ability to know the past in *The History of England* is often obscured by his authoritative, persuasive narrative tone and strong conviction that the mysteries of the past can be solved by a strict adherence to reason.

20 Reeve's and Lee's novels do not aim to challenge historical accounts, but, by implication, they suggest that romances can provide valuable historical information and insight. This is particularly the case with Lee's *The Recess* (see Chapter 3).

21 In *Contesting the Gothic: Fiction, Genre and Cultural Conflict, 1764–1832* (1999), James Watt argues that the Gothic was 'far less a tradition with a generic identity and significance than a domain which was open to contest from the first, constituted or structured by the often antagonistic relations between different writers and works' (6). While Watt identifies the diversity of eighteenth-century Gothic – an important aspect of such fiction which this book develops – I concur with Davison's counter-claim that, despite its diversity, the Gothic is still a recognisable genre and one that its practitioners deliberately engaged with and debated. As this monograph makes clear, there may be very different variations within the Gothic genre itself, such as the Loyalist Gothic and the Female Gothic, but they are, nevertheless, still identifiable as works belonging to the hybridal literary tradition of the Gothic.

1

Contested pasts: David Hume, Horace Walpole and the emergence of Gothic fiction

Old castles, old pictures, old histories, and the babble of old people,
make one live back into centuries that cannot disappoint one.
Horace Walpole to George Montagu (5 January 1766)

In reality, what more agreeable entertainment to the mind, than to
be transported into the remotest ages of the world, and to observe
human society, in its infancy, making the first faint essays towards
the arts and sciences.
David Hume, 'Of the Study of History' (1741)

Featuring supernatural occurrences, family disputes, ancestral
ambiguity, female persecution, superstitious beliefs, a castle with
subterranean passages, scenes of suspense and terror, and a macabre history that returns to disrupt the present, Walpole's *The Castle
of Otranto* introduced a number of tropes that would feature
prominently in future Gothic works. As Walpole's epigraph to this
chapter indicates, he was enthralled by the past and our relationship with it. His status as a wealthy aristocrat enabled him to pursue his interest in the past and his home at Strawberry Hill came
to resemble a Gothic castle.[1] Walpole was fascinated with medieval history and he was a keen historian and antiquarian.[2] His
Strawberry Hill mansion was filled with paintings and ancient artefacts, and he published a number of works with serious historical
intent.[3] However, as I will show in this chapter, Walpole's engagement with the past in *Otranto* is more frivolous. He does not set
out to challenge the historical accuracy of Enlightenment works of
history such as Hume's *The History of England*. Rather, *Otranto*

cultivates an imaginative identification with the past, raises difficult questions about the nature of historical knowledge and exploits the blind spots of Enlightenment historiography to evoke suspense, fear and terror.

As I discussed in the Introduction, Hume's *The History of England* exhibits many of the qualities associated with Enlightenment historiography and proved immensely successful throughout the eighteenth century. In very diverse ways, both Hume and Walpole were interested in re-configuring history for the demands of an increasingly historical age. The former employed rational narrative frameworks designed to produce a more objective account of England's history while the latter let his imagination run riot and plundered the past for its creative potential. History and literature were closely intertwined in the eighteenth century but, with the emergence of *Otranto* two years after the publication of Hume's final volume of *The History of England*, the relationship between the two became even more convoluted. As I discuss in more detail later, Walpole's letters reveal that he had a contentious relationship with Hume and that he was not fond of *The History of England*. Proposing that *Otranto* can be read as a rebellion against Hume's historical philosophy, this chapter poses a number of questions. For example, to what extent can the novel be read as a reaction to the Enlightenment historical attitudes manifest in Hume's *The History of England*? What is the significance of random occurrences in Walpole's novel and what does *Otranto* say about our relationship with the past? Before answering these questions, it is necessary to thoroughly examine *The History of England* and the philosophy that underpins it.

Containing the past: Hume and historical frameworks

Hume was a philosopher before he was a historian and, whether it is historiography or philosophy, all of his work is historical in the sense that it endeavours to trace effects to perceptible causes. From *A Treatise of Human Nature* (1739–40) to *An Enquiry Concerning Human Understanding* (1748) to *The History of England* (1754–62), Hume examines origins in an attempt to gain understanding and endeavours to banish ignorance by assigning causes to previously inexplicable phenomena. Moreover, his philosophical works outline a variety of narrative strategies that he believes are not only essential for writers in general, but particularly for historians. Throughout his philosophical conjectures, Hume speaks of history as a 'narrative composition' (1826, 27). Less interested in the function of history than some of his contemporaries, he focuses on how the past comes to be written and is concerned with history as a specifically 'literary problem' (Braudy 1970, 32).[4] Hume argues that, like all literary compositions, history must have 'a design': without one, a work would resemble 'more the ravings of a madman' than 'the sober efforts of genius and learning' (1826, 26). History must be contained by a narrative framework or an infrastructure that emphasises coherence and continuity. The 'events or actions' that a historian relates must be 'connected together by some bond or tie' which 'may bring them under one plan or view' (26). In the writing of history, Hume argues, this 'connexion among several events', the one that 'unites them into one body', is invariably the 'relation of cause and effect' (30). The 'more unbroken' the 'chain' of reasoning or causation the historian presents, the 'more perfect is his production' (27).

For Hume then, the chief purpose of historiography is to unearth lines of causation. Even seemingly 'different and unconnected' past events must be comprehended within a 'design' and traced from their origins to their 'most remote consequences' because, 'amidst all their diversity', they still share a 'species of unity' (27). This leads to another important aspect of Hume's philosophy, and one that has fundamental implications for his historiography. Despite its evident scepticism, his philosophy is largely concerned with universalisability.[5] In *An Enquiry Concerning Human Understanding*, Hume declares that 'there is a great uniformity among the actions of men, in all nations and ages' and that 'human nature remains still the same in its principles and operations' (97). Since human nature is 'uniform', he posits, human action necessarily follows certain patterns. To use Terence Penelhum's words (1993, 169), Hume's philosophy implies that there is 'a natural or usual course of behaviour'. Even when there are 'seeming irregularities' (in character or event), 'internal motives' may still 'operate in a uniform manner' (Hume 1826, 103). By 'showing men in all varieties of circumstances and situations' (98) within a coherent, causal, narrative framework, history should illuminate 'secret springs and principles' (27) and ultimately reveal 'the constant and universal principles of human nature' (98).

Such ideas pervade *The History of England*; a work that essentially represents an extension of Hume's philosophical speculations. Written after the majority of his works of philosophy, Hume's philosophical ideas not only inform and shape his multi-volume work of historiography, but are thoroughly tested, evaluated and altered. In contrast to his earlier works, Hume not only conjectures about matters of historical composition, but *implements* his philosophical ideas in *The History of England*. One does not have to read far into Hume's history to discover his continuing concern with organisational frameworks and patterns of human behaviour:

> Most sciences, in proportion as they encrease and improve, invent methods by which they facilitate their reasonings; and employing general theorems, are enabled to comprehend in a few propositions a great number of inferences and conclusions. History ... is obliged to adopt such arts of abridgment, to retain the more material events, and to drop all the minute circumstances, which are only interesting during the time, or to the persons engaged in the transactions.
>
> (*HE* 2: 3–4)

One such framework or 'art of abridgment' implemented in *The History of England* is character analysis. By implying that there is a relationship between personality and a broad range of public events, the analysis of 'eminent personages' (*HE* 5: 327) provides a form of causal explanation, at least in the Stuart volumes. For instance, 'wild' in his 'conduct' and 'unrestrained either by prudence or principle' (*HE* 6: 240), the Duke of Buckingham's character is closely linked to his involvement in certain historical events. Without even considering alternative causes (such as social, political or contingent), Hume argues that it is Buckingham's impulsiveness, his lack of 'secrecy and constancy', that destroys 'his character in public life' (*HE* 6: 240). As Leo Braudy highlights (1970, 46), Buckingham's fiery nature is also somewhat overemphasised in his rivalry with Richelieu and for the cause of the brief England–France segment of the Thirty Years War.

In a similar fashion to Buckingham, Lord Ashley (also known as the Earl of Shaftesbury) is another figure who provides the 'bond or tie' that brings disparate events 'under one plan' (Hume 1826, 26). One of 'the most remarkable characters of the age', Lord Ashley is portrayed as 'the chief spring of all the succeeding movements' (*HE* 6: 240). Possessing 'furious passions', a 'sound judgement of business' and an aptitude for subtle contrivance, Lord Ashley's nature is closely allied with the 'pernicious counsels' and insidious schemes of the infamous Cabal (*HE* 6: 240–89). Indeed, in the Stuart volumes, character analysis provides a framework or design for containing the past and revealing the correlation between human nature and human action. Hume epitomises his own historiographical strategy when he declares that the 'movements of great states are often directed by as slender springs as those of individuals' (*HE* 6: 46). However, *The History of England* is essentially a mélange of historiographical methods and, as is common with works written over a number of years, Hume's techniques, aims and attitudes alter significantly; not only across the six volumes, but within individual volumes. Hume's representation of Oliver Cromwell exemplifies the experimental nature of *The History of England* and signifies a discontent with character as a mode of historiographical organisation.

Where Buckingham and Lord Ashley are represented as rather one-dimensional figures whose stormy natures are directly responsible for the outcome of certain historical events, Oliver Cromwell is presented as a dynamic man with both public and private identities. Conducting himself with great 'regularity' and 'austerity of manners' in court, he has a propensity for 'unguarded play and buffoonery' amongst his 'friends' (*HE* 6: 90–1). We learn that he has a 'vein of frolic and pleasantry', often amusing himself by 'putting burning coals into the boots and hose of the officers' that 'attended him' (*HE* 6: 90). Hume argues that such qualities make Cromwell a 'singular personage' and a rather 'inconsistent' character (*HE* 6: 90). Human nature as uniform and the cause of historical events is profoundly problematised. Hume's desire to see mankind 'the same, in all times and places' lessens (1826, 98). Cromwell's conflicting selves lead Hume to contemplate the validity of character as a form of organisation in historical writing: he notes that Cromwell is capable of provoking both the most 'extravagant panegyric' and 'most virulent invective' (*HE* 6: 107) amongst historians. In his own historical account, Hume does not attempt to resolve the paradoxical qualities of Cromwell's character. He merely represents the disparate qualities of his character and leaves it for the reader to decide. As Braudy notes (1970, 56), the irregularities of Cromwell's character cast Hume's philosophical notions concerning the universalisability of human nature and behaviour into doubt.

The portrayal of Charles II casts further doubt on Hume's earlier philosophical conjectures. 'If we survey the character of Charles II in the different lights, which it will admit of', writes Hume, 'it will appear various, and give rise to different and even opposite sentiments' (*HE* 6: 446). In contrast to the treatment of Cromwell's character, Hume sees a need to contain Charles's character in order to ensure a coherent narrative. 'With a detail of his private life', writes Hume, 'we must set bounds to our panegyric on Charles' (*HE* 6: 447). By volume 5, Hume has almost entirely lost his faith in the relationship between human nature (cause) and human action (effect). Despite Charles I's propensity for 'hasty and precipitate resolutions' (*HE* 5: 542), Hume does not see his personality as the reason for a series of 'hostilities with Spain' (*HE* 5: 354). Rather, Hume argues that antagonism between England and Spain 'proceeded from the advice' and 'importunity of the parliament' who deserted Charles 'immediately after they had embarked him in those warlike measures' (*HE* 5: 354). Indeed, human personality as a means of tracing lines of causation and unifying the vagaries of circumstance that is the past is radically undermined. Hume comes to believe that 'character is not the only or even a major cause in history' (Braudy 1970, 58).

In the Tudor and medieval volumes, Hume turns his back on the character-oriented conception of history almost entirely; history may be expressed through human nature, but it is not ultimately determined by it. Character becomes merely 'one of the many causal streams in the flow of history' (Braudy 1970, 64). The focus is now on the law. As Hume argues in his essay, 'That Politics may be Reduced to a Science', so 'great is the force of laws' that 'consequences almost as general and certain may sometimes be deduced from them' (1825, 13). Consequently, as Braudy points out (1970, 67), the Tudor and medieval volumes accentuate the formation and implementation of the law and attempt to place humankind within the infrastructure of law and time. For instance, Hume's representation of Henry VII's reign is permeated by the 'many good laws' that he 'enacted for the government of his subjects': from a ruling against 'carrying off any woman by force' to laws 'against the exportation of money, plate, or bullion' (*HE* 3: 74–7). At this stage of *The History of England*, Hume suggests that 'the "real" theme of history is the working of law' in each period (Braudy 1970, 68). Discussing feudalism in volume 1, Hume declares that 'feudal law is the chief foundation, both of political government and of jurisprudence, established by the Normans in England' (*HE*

1: 455). Feudal law is so important, argues Hume, that we must 'form a just idea' of it in order to explain the state not only of England, but 'of all other kingdoms of Europe, which, during those ages, were governed by similar institutions' (*HE* 1: 455). The law in effect becomes Hume's latest infrastructure to connect diverse events and to 'comprehend in a few propositions a great number of inferences and conclusions' (*HE* 2: 3–4). In effect, what we have throughout *The History of England* is a quest for a narrative framework to contain and write the past. Elements that fit such infrastructures are kept, whilst elements that do not are omitted. Traditional forms of historiography (such as character analysis) are tried, tested, retained, modified or discarded whilst new forms (such as examinations of laws and the impact on lives) are developed and piloted. From a belief in a static historical reality, Hume eventually perceives the past as a kinetic 'collection of facts which are multiplying without end' (*HE* 2: 3–4).

As Braudy aptly summarises (1970, 59), in Hume's historiography the 'idea of a past filled with notable events and exemplary individuals gives way to a past defined by movement, process, and the tangled accumulation of causes'. Despite searching for an infrastructure to interpret and contain history, Hume still manages to convey a sense of the multiplicity of the past. He freely admits to the shortcomings of the historical record, bemoaning the fact that 'the history of remote ages' should always be 'so much involved in obscurity, uncertainty, and contradiction' (*HE* 1: 3). Moreover, historiography is a speculative art for Hume; his history is ultimately governed by likelihood and probability. He freely admits the limited narratological power of historiography and does not shy away from historical uncertainty. Since 'unavoidable ignorance' often renders one's attempts 'fruitless', Hume argues that it is the job of the historian to supply 'by conjecture what is wanting in knowledge' (Hume 1826, 27). Consequently, Hume's art in *The History of England* is one of rationalism, probability and persuasion:

> It was *probably* the example of the French barons, which first emboldened the English to require greater independence from their sovereign: it is also *probable*, that the boroughs and corporations of England were established in imitation of those of France. It may, therefore, *be proposed as no unlikely conjecture*, that both the chief privileges of the peers in England and the liberty of the commons were originally the growth of that foreign country.
>
> (*HE* 1: 470–1, my emphasis)

As Fiona McIntosh-Varjabédian comments on Enlightenment historiography in general (2006, 110), 'exactitude' is less important than the 'pertinence of the argument' in Hume's history. By employing a measured, authoritative voice and illuminating the multiple interpretations that can be gleaned from the past, Hume attempts to build an intimate relationship with the reader; he encourages them to follow his rational deductions and, thus, to participate in the historical process. His copious footnotes and appendices allow the reader to assess the validity of his verdicts for themselves. However, as McIntosh-Varjabédian points out (2006, 113–14), despite recognising the numerous possibilities of the past, it is ultimately Hume, the historian, that sets the field of probability and privileges select readings above other, equally plausible, explanations. As a narrative strategy which presupposes elements of continuity, probability itself provides a framework that sets a limit to the number of possible readings of the past; in effect, it is another method of containing the past. It is also important to highlight that, as *The History of England* progresses, Hume becomes even more concerned with matters of narrative coherence. As David Wootton notes (1993, 295), Hume perceives digressions (for example, observations on the arts and sciences) as a threat to structure and, consequently, moves them to appendices and footnotes. Furthermore, his rational, authoritarian voice undercuts the multiple impressions of the past that his experimental work of historiography occasionally attempts to convey.

The rise of the Gothic: Walpole's historiographical discontent

Published two years after the publication of the final volume of *The History of England*, Walpole's *Otranto* marks the birth of Gothic fiction. In the context of the eighteenth century and, more specifically, Hume's work of Enlightenment history, the Gothic essentially emerges amidst a storm of historiographical debate and experimentation. In many respects Hume, a writer of history, and Walpole, a writer of fiction, share similar characteristics: both writers are fascinated by the past, interested in developing new methods of writing about it, reject totalising, systematic accounts of history, and draw attention to the role of the self in historical writing. Walpole's interaction with history in *Otranto* is essentially as experimental as Hume's engagement with the past in *The History of England*. For example, Walpole's representation of Manfred (the protagonist of *Otranto*) is, in many ways, comparable to Hume's treatment of Cromwell and Charles I. Capable of 'the most fatal excesses' (*O* 94) and 'exquisite villainy' (*O* 34–5), Manfred simultaneously possesses a propensity for sympathy: he is not, writes Walpole, 'one of those savage tyrants who wanton in cruelty unprovoked' (*O* 30). Indeed, it may be argued that Walpole's treatment of Manfred's character endorses Hume's eventual view in *The History of England*: that character is not necessarily uniform, does not (solely) dictate the course of certain historical events and fails to provide an adequate framework or design for writing the past. Experiments with narrative and how best to write about humans in time and history characterise both Hume's and Walpole's works. Hume is acutely aware of former histories and is keen to break new ground in eighteenth-century historiography: remarks such as 'most historians have thought' (*HE* 5: 510) and 'contrary to the tenor of all the historians' (*HE* 1: 165) are not uncommon in *The History of England*. Walpole uses fiction to paint 'pictures of ancient manners' and to bring the past 'nearer to the imagination' of the reader (1791, 84–5). To use the words of the latter, both Hume and Walpole essentially endeavour to give history a 'new dress' (1768, xi): to break with established modes of historiography and generate new ways of writing the past in a bid to make history attractive to a wider readership. However, this is perhaps where any mutual affinities between the two writers end, Walpole's correspondence underlining this fact.[6]

Walpole's letters reveal not only that he had read well beyond the first few volumes of *The History of England* before writing *Otranto*, but that he was thoroughly disenchanted with Hume's work.[7] Writing to the Reverend Henry Zouch on 15 March 1759, Walpole expresses his discontent with Hume's historiography: although he has 'not advanced far' in his reading of the '*History of the House of Tudor*', he is displeased with what he considers is an 'inaccurate', 'careless' and 'hasty' historical account (1937–83, 16: 28). In a letter addressed to Sir David Dalrymple on 30 November 1761, Walpole berates Hume's history, arguing that 'details' are 'so much avoided by him' and the 'whole rather skimmed than elucidated' (15: 75).[8] Writing to George Montagu on 8 December 1761, Walpole comments, 'I am now in Mr. Hume's England, and would fain read no more' (9: 407).

Negative allusions to Hume and his historiography pervade Walpole's correspondence. He accuses *The History of England* of being 'so falsified in many points, so partial in as many, so very unequal in its parts' (10: 176) and criticises Hume for the 'flimsy, ignorant, blundering manner' in which he treats the 'reigns preceding Henry VII': it is 'a proof', writes Walpole, of 'how little he had examined the history of our constitution' (42: 78). As Rosemary Sweet notes (2004, 6), Walpole heavily criticised Hume for failing to support his statements with references in the first volume of *The History of England*. There were also a number of other disputes and controversies between Walpole and Hume.[9] Indeed, Walpole's enduring frustration with Hume's history (and, to a certain extent, eighteenth-century historiography in general) is epitomised in his preface to *Historic Doubts on the Life and Reign of King Richard the Third*: 'If we take a survey of our own history, and examine it with any attention, what an unsatisfactory picture does it present to us! How dry, how superficial, how void of information!' (1768, ix).

The Gothic provides Walpole with a means of offsetting the inadequacies of *The History of England* and the philosophy that forms an integral part of it. Walpole admits as much in his correspondence with Madame Du Deffand: writing to her on 13 March 1767, he declares that he wrote *Otranto* 'in defiance of rules, of critics, and of philosophers' (Walpole 1767). In terms of the early Gothic, actual historical accuracy (and even coherence) is not important: *Otranto* does not attempt to rationally and realistically chronicle a given historical period. It is more concerned with the ways in which the past comes to be narrativised and structured. The Gothic provides Walpole with a way of fashioning an entertaining, suspense-driven narrative and a means of critiquing Hume's historiography through fiction. The very frame of *Otranto* complicates concepts of historical transmission, organisation and knowledge. In the preface to the first edition, Walpole declares that the 'following work was found in the library of an ancient Catholic family in the north of England' (*O* 5). Printed 'at Naples, in the black letter, in the year 1529', the original date of its composition 'does not appear' (*O* 5). *Otranto*'s very material existence thus undermines the all-encompassing, wide-ranging historiography of Hume and, moreover, rejects the Enlightenment metanarrative of history. As Fiona Robertson points out (1994, 86), Walpole's Gothic novel provides a 'fetishization of the processes of narrative'. Hume is preoccupied with the structure and pertinence of his own argument: the Gothic is fascinated with 'the origin and transmission' of the very 'historical and pseudo-historical materials' that are used to construct such arguments (86). The date of the events recounted in the narrative is not even clear: if 'the story was written near the time when it is supposed to have happened', writes Walpole, it 'must have been between 1095, the æra of the first crusade, and 1243, the date of the last, or not long afterwards' (*O* 5). In contrast to Hume's history, the Gothic is fixated by aspects of the past that resist narrative synthesis.

Uncertainty, ambiguity and disorganisation characterise the past in *Otranto*. Before embarking on a more detailed discussion of the undecidable nature of the past in Walpole's Gothic novel, it is necessary to readdress my earlier discussion regarding the duplicitous representation of Manfred's character. *Otranto* may, similarly to *The History of England*, reveal the inadequacy of character as a method of analysing and ordering the past, but there is a fundamental difference between the two works: the latter still condones frameworks for writing the past whereas the former rejects not only character (as embodied by Manfred) but *any* pre-determined narrative infrastructure employed to write and contain the past. Whether it is character, a revision of character, or the law, the Gothic reveals the futility of employing any abiding framework to interpret and unify the past; it is simply too remote and polymorphous for any infrastructure of understanding. Walpole utilises the Gothic to suggest that the imposition of any conceptual framework to understand and write the past will only inculcate distortion and reductionism. Hume alludes to the multifaceted nature of the past; the Gothic revels in the past's incompleteness, incoherence and fragmentation. In *The History of England*, Hume confidently guides the reader through a defined field of historical probability, assuring them with his measured tones that the reading he privileges is the rational or natural one. In stark contrast to this, the Gothic heralds a loss of faith in humankind's capability 'to (unproblematically) know a past reality', and, therefore, to be able to represent it in a narrative (Hutcheon 1995, 86). What we have in the preface to the first edition of *Otranto* is a growing awareness that, despite Hume's frameworks and measured verdicts, it is impossible to know the past with any degree of certainty.

Otranto and the textual nature of the past

Where Hume's history endorses coherent narrative designs and measured, rational deductions, Walpole's Gothic novel revels in abstruseness and incoherence. Before discussing this in greater detail, it is important to note that, along with frameworks of interpretation, measured, rational deduction characterises *The History of England*. As Peter Jones highlights (1993, 255–80), Hume's history is essentially an exercise in sobriety with 'flat and official verdicts' evident on almost every page of every volume. Hume's philosophy regarding narrative language pervades *The History of England*. As he argues in his essay 'Of Simplicity and Refinement in Writing', 'simplicity' of style should be given preference to excess 'refinement', especially when it comes to the treatment of 'men, and actions, and passions' (1825, 191–2). Furthermore, writers should at all times avoid employing 'uncommon expressions, strong flashes of wit, pointed similes, and epigrammatic turns' (189). Such techniques are, he contends, a 'disfigurement' rather than an 'embellishment of discourse' (189). To quote Hume's words in *The Natural History of Religion*, historical writing should provide a 'clear testimony' (Hume 1976, 26). By employing coherent narrative structures, avoiding figurative language and maintaining a measured voice throughout, he earnestly believes that he can make the past (and the process of its recovery) more transparent. Indeed, *The History of England* is underpinned by Hume's belief that with clear, simplified language and coherent narrative structures, historical writing can, to a large extent, act as an 'enlarged mirror' (*HE* 5: 545) and reflect the past as it was actually lived. The Gothic has a quite contrary view.

The first edition of Walpole's novel is styled as a manuscript and, in effect, presents the reader with an actual fragment from the past. In his critical deliberations concerning Walpole, Sir Walter Scott highlights that (1829, 228), on publication, the authenticity of Walpole's Gothic novel was not doubted: many readers actually believed it was an obscure manuscript from the past. Writing to Walpole on 30 December 1764, Thomas Gray writes, 'we take it for a translation; and should believe it to be a true story if it were not for St Nicholas' (1825, 266). To further complicate matters of historical knowability and authenticity, Walpole assumes the 'personage of a translator' (*O* 9). Originally composed in the 'purest Italian' (*O* 5) by Onuphrio Muralto, William Marshall (Walpole's adopted personage) claims that he has had to translate the manuscript before presenting it to readers. Under the guise of Marshall, Walpole even highlights the difficulties involved in translation. 'Our language', he argues, 'falls far short of the charms of the Italian, both for variety and harmony' (*O* 7). Italian is 'peculiarly excellent for simple narrative', whereas it is 'difficult in English to relate without falling too low or rising too high' (*O* 7). It is so difficult to avoid distortion and to stay true to the original manuscript in the act of translation that Walpole even suggests that he will 're-print the original Italian' (*O* 7) if his work is a success. Walpole's 'translator' is a stark reminder that, despite Hume's longing for a certain amount of objectivity in historical writing, all historians can be compared to translators in the sense that they can only ever generate linguistic *representations* (or approximations) of the past. By revealing that historical knowledge is as much *engineered* by language and narrative structures as it is *discovered* in archives, *Otranto* significantly undermines Hume's historiography. From its very inception, the Gothic draws attention to history not *as* the past, but as a *substitute* for the past.

Traditionally perceived as a distancing device, or a means of protecting the author from the potentially socially incendiary nature of his or her work, the convention of the discovered manuscript has added significance: it symbolises the Gothic's obsession with, and problematisation of, historical knowledge. Styled as a translated manuscript, *Otranto* essentially presents the reader with a paradox: it purports to reveal the reality of the past, but our textualised access to it in the present. The Gothic illuminates the fact that our access to the past is largely conditioned by textuality: in many cases, we can only (re)construct the past from the textual traces that have survived. Moreover, the device of the discovered manuscript (and the difficulties involved in its translation) undermines Hume's rational historiographical interpretations by showing that 'historical representations are necessarily distortions of a past whose real character can never be objectively transmitted' (Holmes 1997, 54). Walpole's contrived manuscript illuminates the contrived nature of all historical representations. Through the medium of fiction, *Otranto* radically 'destabilizes received notions of both history and fiction' (Hutcheon 1995, 88).

The Gothic effectively problematises everything that Hume's history (and much eighteenth-century historiography influenced by Enlightenment doctrines) takes for granted; from the use of language, to narrative structures, to primary sources to historical authentication. The very fashioning of *Otranto* as a forgotten manuscript represents what might be seen as a satiric attack on Hume's historiography: *The History of England* contains virtually no primary sources. Hume enters into 'no Detail of minute, uninteresting Facts' (Hume 1932, 1: 193), simply omitting eye-witness accounts, traditions, superstitious beliefs, legends, and fables. In a letter addressed to Walpole on 2 August 1758, Hume argues that were a reader to be presented with only primary sources, he or she 'wou'd attain but a very confus'd idea' of the 'period' spoken of (1: 285). The sheer volume of material and the difficulty of comprehending it would, Hume informs Walpole, be asking too much of the reader. History should, at all times, be related by a skilled historian who has had adequate training in writing the past. Moreover, Hume believes that a work of history should be 'as complete as possible within itself' and 'should never refer, for any thing material, to other books' (*HE* 1: 455). The device of the discovered script enables Walpole to reveal the irony of Hume's decision to insert 'no original Papers' (1932, 1: 193) in *The History of England*: by its very nature, history is both textual and intertextual. Hume's decision not to present the reader with original material, but to offer his reading of such material against a matrix of possible readings, is ridiculed by Walpole's novel. Furthermore, it is not only the lack of primary sources in *The History of England* that troubles Walpole: he is equally concerned with Hume's attitude towards certain historical resources and beliefs.

Writing the past, writing the present

In the preface to the first edition of *Otranto*, Walpole remarks that 'belief in every kind of prodigy was so established' in the 'dark ages' of which he writes that 'an author would not be faithful to the *manners* of the times who should omit all mention of them' (*O* 6). He is 'not bound to believe them himself', writes Walpole, but he 'must represent his actors as believing them' (*O* 6). These comments suggest that Walpole is not only aggrieved by the lack of primary sources in *The History of England*, but by the deliberate and sustained attack of the most dearly-held values and beliefs of former ages; whether these are religious, superstitious or otherwise. Indeed, it is important to note that the past Walpole constructs in *Otranto* is Catholic. In the first preface, the novel purports to be written by Onuphrio Muralto, a Catholic priest from the church of St Nicholas. The reader is also encouraged to infer that William Marshall (the gentleman who claims to have found the discovered manuscript) and the Catholic family from the North of England (where the script is supposedly found) are 'one and the same' (Miles 2002, 92). *Otranto* marks the beginning of the Gothic's complex relationship with Catholicism by associating Catholic Europe with 'superstition, arbitrary power and passionate extremes' (Botting 1996, 64).[10] Walpole's Gothic novel depicts Catholicism as a superstitious faith and, in this sense, encapsulates the Gothic's complex relationship with Enlightenment historiography: throughout *The History of England* (and many works of Enlightenment history for that matter), Hume also associates the Catholic faith with irrational beliefs. However, in contrast to Walpole, Hume often disregards such beliefs as 'superstition' (*HE* 5: 223). Indeed, rather than simply mocking or repressing the perceived follies of Catholicism or any superstitious beliefs, Walpole gives expression to them and exploits their narrative potential. The Gothic continues to exploit aspects of the past that fall outside the scope of Enlightenment history. Moreover, Walpole focuses on Catholicism and superstitious beliefs not only to prey on the rationality of his largely Protestant readers, but to draw attention to the wider suppression of primitive beliefs in Hume's Enlightenment work of historiography.

Raising an issue that will dominate future Gothic fiction, Walpole highlights that, despite aspirations for objectivity, historians such as Hume fail to divorce themselves from their own present and are, moreover, perpetually unable to obviate the effects of their own subjectivity.[11] Walpole (under the guise of Marshall) highlights this tendency when he writes that, despite the fact that 'more impartial readers' may not be so 'struck with the beauties' of the narrative as he was, it is nonetheless 'natural' for him to be 'prejudiced in favour of his adopted work' (*O* 6). Furthermore, Walpole proposes that the religious views of Onuphrio Muralto (the writer of the original manuscript) may have shaped the events recounted and the moral on which the action is founded: that the '*sins of fathers are visited on their children to the third and fourth generation*' (*O* 6). This moral is weak, argues Walpole, not only because the punishment comes so long after the crime, thus minimising the 'dread' felt by the perpetrator, but because the original author, influenced by his profession, suggests such retribution may be 'diverted by devotion to saint Nicholas' (*O* 7). 'Here', writes Walpole, the 'interest of the monk plainly gets the better of the judgment of the author' (*O* 7). Indeed, the Gothic continually highlights that writing the past is an inherently narcissistic enterprise and that a certain amount of bias is an integral part of all historical writing. In relation to *The History of England*, the question is, however, the extent to which bias informs historiography and the consequences this has for the integrity of written accounts of the past.

Interestingly, Hume set out to write an impartial history of England: one that would be free from Whig and Tory biases and banish ignorance regarding the foundation of some of England's most important institutions. By exposing the myths of political parties, Hume endeavoured to realistically and accurately trace how England arrived at its particular present. Before sending the first volume of *The History of England* off to press in early 1754, Hume (in direct contrast to *Otranto*'s translator) believes in the impartiality of his work. In a letter to Matthew Sharpe dated 25 February 1754, he openly declares, 'I am of no party, and have no bias' (Hume 1932, 1: 185). However, despite his aim to write a history free of bias, Hume's work bears all the hallmarks of subjectivity: from his professed dislike of intertextuality and primary sources, to his sentimental treatment of Charles I (*HE* 5: 220–1), to his religious scorn. Indeed, Hume's personal correspondence betrays the fact that (then) contemporary political references and attitudes shape *The History of England*; even when the periods under discussion are in the very distant past and completely removed from the contemporary sphere of political action. 'My views of *things* are more conformable to Whig principles; my representations of *persons* to Tory prejudices', he writes (1932, 1: 237). In his personal correspondence, rather than in the historiography itself, Hume becomes very conscious of the role of the self in historical writing. In a letter to Sir Gilbert Elliot, dated 21 February 1770, he speaks of his endeavours to 'soften or expunge' the 'many villanous seditious Whig Strokes' which have 'crept into' and characterise previous editions of *The History of England* (2: 216). Despite initial protestations of impartiality and a sustained effort to remain unbiased in the work itself, Hume's multi-volume history is as much a manifestation of personal, eighteenth-century and Enlightenment values as it is a history of England.

In tune with Enlightenment historical attitudes, *The History of England* is especially notable for its derision of religion and superstition. Writing of the Irish insurrection and massacre of 1641, Hume condemns established religion, expostulating that amidst all its 'enormities', the 'sacred name of Religion resounded on every side; not to stop the hands' of the murderers, but to 'enforce their blows, and to steel their hearts against every movement of human or social sympathy' (*HE* 5: 343). Such barbed comments are not uncommon in *The History of England* and resulted in Hume being labelled an atheist when it was first published. Often viewing any type of established religion as a form of superstition, his views on this latter topic are even more hostile. 'Weakness, fear, melancholy, together with ignorance, are', Hume argues in his essay 'Of Superstition and Enthusiasm', the 'true sources of superstition' (1825, 67). Superstition, or 'the child of ignorance' as Hume calls it in *The History of England* (*HE* 1: 215), is derided throughout his work, but especially in the volumes covering medieval times or the 'dark ages': the approximate setting of the events of *Otranto*. Hume's history conveys a strong sense of cultural superiority and intimates that the age in which he is writing is one free from the vagaries of superstition. Indeed, *The History of England* gives the impression that its author is writing from a cultural vantage point by frequently ridiculing, undermining or completely censoring the most dearly held beliefs of former ages and the individuals that believed in them. For example, Hume's abhorrence of the Britons, their regimes and their beliefs is all too apparent: 'Thus, the bands of government, which were naturally loose among that rude and turbulent people, were happily corroborated by the terrors of their superstition' (*HE* 1: 5–6). References to pre-Enlightened beliefs and peoples are invariably followed by derogatory terms such as 'stupidity' (*HE* 2: 519), 'barbarism' and 'ignorance' (*HE* 3: 427). As I mentioned earlier, Catholicism is frequently depicted as a faith with primitive beliefs and dismissed as ignorance and superstition. Seldom outlining what exactly the superstitious beliefs of previous ages were, Hume simply condemns them and uses them as a means of distancing an Enlightened present from an archaic past. In fact, Hume is so averse to primitive beliefs that he proposes that history, by exhibiting the 'horrid and deformed' aspects of former eras, can even act as an 'antidote against superstition' (*HE* 2: 519).

Walpole's assertion that 'partiality man cannot intirely divest himself of' (1768, xii) epitomises his sentiments regarding Hume's history and is a notion that greatly influences *Otranto*: a work that can be read as a bold response to the bias and negation of superstition evident in *The History of England*. In contrast to Hume's history, Walpole's Gothic novel *is* faithful to the manners of the times because it details elements of superstition and represents the individuals who believe in them. Walpole chooses to represent rather than repress beliefs associated with Catholicism and, by doing so, preys on the superstitious beliefs that continue to haunt the Protestant faith and the imaginations of his readers. On hearing peculiar noises, Matilda (Manfred's daughter) asks Bianca (her maid), if anyone is staying in the chamber directly below them. 'Nobody has dared to lie there', she answers, since 'the great astrologer' that tutored Conrad (Matilda's recently deceased brother) 'drowned himself' (*O* 38). Despite the fact that the strange noises are later found to emanate from Theodore (a peasant who is revealed to be the legitimate heir to Otranto) in the apartment below, Bianca proposes that the ghosts of the astrologer and the young prince 'are now met in the chamber below' (*O* 39). Uninhibited by the manuscript's writer and translator, the reader is granted full access not only to Bianca's superstitious attitude, but to the superstitious beliefs that formed such an integral part of the age in which Walpole lived. Even Matilda, a member of the upper class and thus traditionally expected to possess more refined views, is revealed to be in the grips of superstition. Building on Bianca's theory, she proposes, firstly, that if the 'spirits' below are in pain, they may 'ease their suffering by questioning them' and, secondly, that such spirits can mean no harm to either herself or Bianca because they 'have not injured them' (*O* 39). Indeed, the entire cast of *Otranto* are revealed to be superstitious, and, in contrast to Hume's history, such beliefs are given full expression.

Countering Hume's negative attitude towards superstition and propensity for letting the present inform the past, religious and superstitious beliefs proliferate in Walpole's Gothic novel: from the widely feared prophecy that 'the castle and lordship of Otranto' will pass 'from the present family' whenever 'the real owner should be grown too large to inhabit it' (*O* 17) to the creed that '*the sins of fathers are visited on their children to the third and fourth generation*' (*O* 6). As Scott aptly points out (1829, 232), it is the object of

Walpole's Gothic novel 'to draw such a picture of domestic life and manners, during the feudal times, as might actually have existed' and to 'paint it chequered and agitated by the action of supernatural machinery, such as the superstition of the period received as matter of devout credulity'. Walpole's Gothic novel comprehensively rejects the cultural supremacy assumed by Hume in *The History of England*. For Walpole, the writing of history should not (at least deliberately) be coloured by the dominant (Enlightened) values and politics of the present. *Otranto* (and particularly its preface) illuminates that all historical writing is subjective in the sense that it inevitably encapsulates elements of the present. However, Walpole's Gothic novel effectively acts as a foil to *The History of England* by recounting the belief systems of former ages: the very act of inclusion draws attention to the distorting effects that Hume's excess subjectivity and (sometimes) deliberate encoding and implementation of personal and political attitudes can bring to bear on the past. In fact, one of the reasons that Scott (in agreement with Walpole himself) perceives *Otranto* as a 'new species' of literary composition and as a forerunner to the historical novel is because of the 'purity' of the language maintained throughout and the care taken to avoid (deliberate) references to the present (1829, 239–40).

Assuming that *Otranto* is (at least in part) a response to *The History of England*, it is important to consider the wider extent of Walpole's reaction to Hume's assumed cultural imperiousness. Hume's comments in his essay, 'Of the Study of History', are of interest here. Contemplating the pleasure of reading history, Hume argues that there are few things more enjoyable than observing 'all the human race, from the beginning of time, pass, as it were, in review before us, appearing in their true colours, without any of those disguises which, during their lifetime, so much perplexed the judgment of the beholders' (1854, 510). Such a comment inculcates the belief that the past can be studied objectively from the present; Hume fails to recognise that the values of the present colour interpretations of the past. This is certainly the case with *The History of England*. As I discussed a moment ago, Hume's history (especially for the contemporary reader) conveys the distinct impression that the age in which he is writing and judging the past is one free from primitive beliefs. By including superstitious beliefs, not judging them and exploiting their narrative potential, Walpole is not only being (historically) faithful to a former age, but is further satirising Hume's position. *Otranto* reveals that superstitious beliefs have formed an integral part of human history and, even in an 'Enlightened' (and Protestant) age, continue to hold sway. Eighteenth-century England was gripped by superstition and the invocation of such beliefs in *Otranto* was, arguably, one of the reasons for its immense success. When read alongside *The History of England*, therefore, *Otranto* reveals that Hume's supposedly realistic account of the past actually generates a fictional impression of the present. There is a great deal of irony in all this: the 'Enlightened' age that Hume affects throughout his historiography is in fact as fictional as the one Walpole represents in his Gothic novel. In response to dominant modes of historiography, the Gothic exposes the historian's tendency to not only disfigure the past, but to falsify the present. *Otranto* reveals that Hume's strategy of deriding or omitting superstitious beliefs that are still very much part of the present is absurd and, moreover, illuminates the constructed nature of history. By including elements that eighteenth-century historiography ignores, the Gothic reveals that, similarly to the writing of fiction, the writing of history 'involves a selection of detail, a determination of emphasis, a narrational shaping' (Cowart 1989, 17).

An imaginative revolt

To adapt Walpole's words in a letter to Lady Hervey dated 20 February 1759, *Otranto* 'contains many of those important truths that history is too proud to tell, and too dull from not telling' (1937–83, 31: 12). In addition to including the formerly neglected popular beliefs of previous ages, Walpole employs another means to write those aspects of the past that Hume excludes: the human imagination. Walpole's invocation of this faculty can be read as a profound reaction to Hume's philosophical speculations. Throughout Hume's philosophical works, the imagination has an ambivalent status. In contrast to Enlightenment thinkers such as John Locke, Hume is largely in opposition to the rationalist portrayal of humanity. 'Reason is, and ought only to be', writes Hume in *A Treatise of Human Nature*, 'the slave of the passions and can never pretend to any other office than to serve and obey them' (1911, 2: 127). Indeed, as John Biro points out (1993, 43), Hume's anatomy of the mind posits a divide between reason, a reflective faculty for making judgements based on evidence, and the imagination, a non-rational faculty that automatically shifts from experience to belief. Whilst reason and memory preserve 'the original order and position' of ideas, the imagination is a force of liberty in the sense that it 'transposes and changes' such ideas 'as it pleases' (Hume 1911, 1: 87). The imagination is a vital part of human nature for Hume: it is a creative faculty that saves individuals from the scepticism and doubts engendered by reason. However, despite lauding the creative potential of the human imagination and illuminating its importance in terms of human survival, it is a faculty that deeply unsettles Hume and complicates his professed rejection of certain Enlightenment beliefs.

A sense of ambiguity and menace surrounds Hume's reflections on the imagination. Whilst never undermining the importance of this most powerful of faculties, it is represented as a constant threat to order, especially in *A Treatise of Human Nature*. 'The imagination', writes Hume, has the 'command' over all ideas and 'can join, and mix, and vary them in all the ways possible' (1911, 1: 99–100). So powerful is the imagination, in fact, that it is a 'custom' that operates 'before we have time for reflection' (1: 106) and is frequently overactive: it continues to function 'even after the reason has ceased, which first determined it to begin' (1: 54). Hume's reflections intimate that the imagination possesses a propensity for anarchy and disorder. 'The imagination, when set into any train of thinking', writes Hume later on in *A Treatise*, 'is apt to continue even when its object fails it, and, like a galley put in motion by the oars, carries on its course without any new impulse' (1: 192). Hume's representation suggests that the individual has very little willed control over the imagination and that, moreover, this faculty is in constant need of restraint. Hume's reflections on reason, a force of order, are not as threatening as his deliberations concerning the imagination, a force of disorder. Despite his anti-rationalist affinities, Hume betrays a preference for the order instilled by reason. When it comes to past events in particular, Hume suggests that imagination is inferior to reason: where the latter can maintain the order of events over a long duration, the former cannot, 'without difficulty', preserve coherence and uniformity for 'any considerable time' (1: 18). *The History of England* embodies Hume's preference for reason and disinclination towards the 'natural infirmity and unsteadiness' of the imagination (1: 48). Bleached of figurative language and replete with sobering images and remarks, Hume's historiography makes little use of the imagination and succeeds in stifling its creative potential. Next to the fact that such beliefs violate his own values and those of the Enlightenment, Hume may avoid going into details about superstition, the supernatural and other phenomena because such subjects resist reason (cause and effect) and stimulate the imagination (a non-rational faculty). Throughout *The History of England* imagination is very limited and viewed as a threat to historical coherence and integrity.

As the following comments Walpole makes in a letter to Madame Du Deffand intimate, *Otranto* may be considered as a strong reaction to Hume's latent fear of the imagination and inclination towards reason in *The History of England*: 'I have not written the book for the present age, which will endure nothing but cold common sense ... this is the only one of my books with which I am myself pleased; I have given reins to my imagination till I became on fire with those visions and feelings which it excited' (Walpole 1767). Throughout his Gothic novel, Walpole rejects reason as the governing principle of historiography and invokes the human imagination (both his own and that of the reader) as a way of writing history and of liberating the past from the ideologies of the present. In contrast to Hume, Walpole demonstrates that imagination should not be seen as a threat to reason and historical accounts. He illustrates that the imagination should be embraced as a valuable tool for making the past 'live': making it something to which readers (of all historical ages) can relate. This is especially the case with the supernatural, attitudes towards which form an integral part of cultures throughout the ages. As I discussed previously, Hume's preference for reason results in a filtering of the past through the present in *The History of England*. He rarely enters into details concerning preternatural events and, when they are mentioned, they are always portrayed as a failure of reasoning, as the following quotation regarding the Saxons exemplifies: 'The knowledge of natural causes was neglected from the universal belief of miraculous interpositions and judgements' (*HE* 1: 51). In *Otranto*, Walpole radically readdresses *The History of England*'s exorcism of imagination and, by doing so, writes about a subject that pervades all ages and yet one that is neglected by Hume and his preference for reason: the supernatural. By not only *recounting* superstitious beliefs, but imaginatively *manifesting* them throughout his narrative, Walpole draws further attention to Hume's contempt and even omission of ancient beliefs.

In opposition to Hume's philosophy, Walpole's Gothic novel demonstrates that the imagination *can* be sustained long enough to write past events and that we have far more control over this faculty than Hume suggests. Indeed, *Otranto* is essentially an imaginative revolt against the subjugation of the imagination in *The History of England*. Imaginative, supernatural events manifest themselves everywhere in Walpole's Gothic novel. A portrait of Manfred's grandfather (Ricardo) comes to life, leaves its frame and walks around with a 'grave and melancholy air' (*O* 24–5). Conrad is killed by a giant 'helmet' that appears to 'fall from the moon' (*O* 41), the 'sable plumes' of which move as if 'bowed by some invisible wearer' (*O* 53). A 'gigantic sword' falls opposite to this helmet and remains 'immoveable' (*O* 59). With designs to marry Matilda, Frederic (Isabella's father) is warned against such a course of action by a deceased hermit who earlier aided his discovery of the gigantic sabre. Turning around and revealing to Frederic the 'fleshless jaws and empty sockets of a skeleton', the ghostly hermit warns him against the pursuit of 'carnal delights' (*O* 93). 'Three drops of blood' fall inexplicably 'from the nose of Alfonso's statue' (*O* 85). Alfonso the Good was the original master of Otranto, but was poisoned and usurped by Manfred's grandfather, Ricardo. In a series of supernatural occurrences, gigantic parts of Alfonso's body are sighted around the castle: 'it is a giant, I believe; he is all clad in armour, for I saw his foot and part of his leg, and they are as large as the helmet below in the court' (*O* 32). At the end of the novel, a 'vision' of Alfonso, 'dilated to an immense magnitude', appears in the centre of the (now) ruined castle to declare that Theodore is 'the true heir of Alfonso!' (*O* 98). Walpole does not only use his own imagination: he stimulates those of his readers and attempts to bring them into a closer relationship with the beliefs of former ages. The invocation of the imagination and presence of elements of the fantastic in *Otranto* subverts the 'normative ways' of perceiving reality and thus the past endorsed by Hume's rational historiography (Howard 2001, 43).

In this sense, perhaps the most significant quasi-supernatural incident to occur in *Otranto* involves Manfred and his (supposed) exclusive sighting of Alfonso's ghost: 'My dearest, gracious lord, cried Hippolita, clasping him in her arms, what is it you see? Why do you fix your eye-balls thus? – What! Cried Manfred breathless – dost thou see nothing, Hippolita? Is this ghastly phantom sent to me alone' (*O* 73). As a result of this uncanny physical resemblance, Manfred believes he is staring at Alfonso's ghost when, in reality, he is looking at Theodore. The 'delirium' of Manfred's brain unhinges him: he is genuinely at a loss to know whether the vision presented to him is 'Theodore, or a phantom' (*O* 74). Such an occurrence radically undermines the existence of a common phenomenological reality and negates even the possibility of viewing the past objectively. The Gothic problematises the very conception of reality that underpins Hume's historiography.

As Walter Scott so aptly observes (1829, 226–7), the author of *Otranto* 'is not a mere collector of dry and minute facts': Walpole 'brings with him the torch of genius', his imagination, to 'illuminate the ruins' of the past 'through which he loves to wander'. Of course, the obvious question that arises here concerns historical accuracy and coherence: surely Walpole's embodiment of imaginative and supernatural fears of former ages does, as Hume would argue, disorganise the past. The short answer to this question is yes: the imagination *is* a force of disorder in *Otranto*. Supernatural events erupt at random intervals and twist and turn the narrative. However, Walpole's position is this: the human imagination may well be a disorganising power, but this is no reason for it to be banished from the realm of historical writing. Its merits, its ability to grab the attention of the reader and to make one aware of formerly ignored (or omitted) parts of the past far outweigh its organisational disadvantages. This aspect of Walpole's response to Hume's aversion to the imagination is really quite profound. Underlying *The History of England* is the belief that only reason, not the imagination, can order and essentially (re)construct the past. Behind *Otranto* is the idea that reason and order can never effectively capture the past and that the imagination, an unstable, explosive and disorganised faculty, is the most effective means of writing a past (and a reality) that is by its very nature similarly unstable, disjointed and incoherent. *Otranto* proposes that the imagination brings us closer to the actual essence of reality and the past and, by doing so, suggests that historical accounts written entirely on the basis of reason are only ever a façade: histories such as Hume's use reason to mask the vast discontinuities that comprise the past. Histories bereft of imagination and oriented towards reason impose a false order on the past. *Otranto* carries with it the implicit suggestion that the reasoning of eminent eighteenth-century historians such as Hume is as fictional and imaginative as the preternatural occurrences it records. Furthermore, the imaginative, disorganised nature of *Otranto* draws attention to the formulaic nature of Hume's historiography, its predisposition to recount the events that eminent figures were involved in during their lives and to examine their characters in detail after their deaths. The Gothic highlights that the past simply does not take such a structured form. Walpole's utilisation of the creative potential of the human imagination also further undermines Hume's restrictive frameworks of reasoning. In terms of the Gothic, the imagination is not eighteenth-century history's enemy: it brings one into closer contact with the past and should thus be one of historiography's allies.

Writing the past, writing the uncivilised

In many respects, the Gothic is history's other: it includes elements that Enlightenment historiography omits and problematises our relationship to the past. This brings me to another important characteristic of Hume's historiography. *The History of England* is notable for its suppression of violent events; the bloody deeds and transgressions that formed an integral part of England's past are generally softened or omitted. Hume argues that the 'sudden, violent, and unprepared revolutions, incident to Barbarians' are 'so much guided by caprice, and terminate so often in cruelty' that 'they disgust us by the uniformity of their appearance' (*HE* 1: 3–4). It is 'rather fortunate for letters' and historiography, observes Hume, that such deeds are often 'buried in silence and oblivion' (*HE* 1: 4). Writing from an 'Enlightened' perspective, Hume argues that 'the adventures of barbarous nations, even if they were recorded, could afford little or no entertainment to men born in a more cultivated age' (*HE* 1: 3). Moreover, it would be 'almost impossible' and certainly 'tedious' to 'relate particularly all the miseries to which the English were thenceforth exposed' (*HE* 1: 117–18). Such an enterprise, he argues, would be sickening and teach us nothing. We would 'hear of nothing but the sacking and burning of towns; the devastation of the open country; the appearance of the enemy in every quarter of the kingdom; their cruel diligence in discovering any corner, which had not been ransacked by their former violence' (*HE* 1: 118). For Hume, such bloody events are simply not the province of Enlightenment historiography. The question we ask as readers though is, why? Surely the violent aspects of England's past are just as important and have as much claim to coverage as its particular characters and laws? The answer to this question is manifold.

In an interesting comment, Hume argues that the recording of bloody deeds is suited to older forms of historiography: the 'broken and disjointed narration of the antient historians' is 'well adapted to the nature of the war' (*HE* 1: 118), he argues.[12] Indeed, this comment suggests that the horrific and bloody battles that punctuate England's past jeopardise the coherence of his historical account. Such events are softened or omitted because they 'endanger the writer's authority', historical frameworks and, moreover, the validity of his rational conclusions (McIntosh-Varjabédian 2006, 113). Writing of the battle of Mearcredes-Burn, Hume keeps mention of bloodshed and violence to a minimum: 'though the Saxons seem to have obtained the victory, they suffered so considerable a loss, as somewhat retarded the progress of their conquests' (*HE* 1: 20). This example demonstrates that when it comes to dealing with traumatic events in England's past, they must be interpreted and contained within a wider framework. The details surrounding the violent battle that took place at Mearcredes-Burn are absent; it is the greater context of the 'progress' of the Saxons that is important to Hume. As McIntosh-Varjabédian highlights (2006, 113), in Hume's historiography, horror and crimes must be encompassed by a causal chain (in this example, Saxon progress) in which one factor reinforces the next. Violent, 'unnatural practices' that resist causal reasoning are simply 'not fit to be named' (*HE* 6: 337) and are consequently omitted. The best way to write history, argues Hume, is to pass over violent, discontinuous events and to focus primarily on the developing 'language, manners, and customs' of our 'ancestors' (*HE* 1: 4).

As Hume's analysis of eminent figures and prominent laws reveals, *The History of England* focuses almost exclusively on the evolution of civilised forms of society. Hume's remarks towards the end of volume 2 are quite telling in this respect and reveal a great deal about what he believed history should achieve: 'Thus have we pursued the history of England through a series of many barbarous ages; till we have at last reached the dawn of civility and sciences, and have the prospect, both of greater certainty in our historical narrations, and of being able to present to the reader a spectacle more worthy of his attention' (*HE* 2: 518). A greater respect and focus is given for more 'cultivated age[s]' (*HE* 1: 3) and the continuity of civil society is given preference to the barbaric events that comprise England's past in Hume's history. As Braudy notes (1970, 83), instead of 'contemplating the record of irrationality and cruelty', Hume seeks 'the materials of continuity and the growth of community interest'. For Hume, history should survey 'manners, finances, arms, commerce, arts and sciences' (*HE* 6: 140). In the rare instances that he does recount violence, it is used to accentuate a distance between a civilised present and a barbaric past. Aspects of the past that are 'horrid and deformed' teach us to cherish 'science and civility' (*HE* 2: 518–19). The nearer Hume gets to his own age, the fewer the references to violence. Recounting the reign of terror conducted by Hengist, a Saxon general, Hume notes how the 'private and public edifices of the Britons were reduced to ashes', how 'priests were slaughtered' on their altars and how people were 'intercepted and butchered in heaps' (*HE* 1: 19). He refers to such gratuitous acts of violence (especially in the medieval volumes) in order to demonstrate to the reader that contemporary society bears no resemblance to its primitive, gruesome past.

In his introductory remarks to 'Maddalena', Walpole identifies a trend in eighteenth-century historiography: historians such as Hume (and the educated members of the public who read such histories) tend to look back on 'the dark ages' with a 'fond enthusiasm' for its 'brighter' and more positive aspects, whilst steeping into 'a willing forgetfulness of its darker and more repugnant shapes' (1973, 23). In *Otranto*, Walpole radically readdresses this balance. Whereas Hume's history shines a spotlight on the history of civilised society, the Gothic probes the uncivilised aspects of the past that remain in shadow. For example, *Otranto* is pervaded by one of the vilest acts humans can commit as the threat of incest literally haunts the novel. Manfred pursues an 'incestuous design' by attempting to marry his 'contracted daughter' (*O* 45), Isabella, the young woman that Manfred's son, Conrad, was to marry shortly before his violent and premature end. Furthermore, in a bid to persuade Father Jerome to aid the proceedings of his divorce, Manfred claims that he and his wife, Hippolita, are related in 'the fourth degree' (*O* 46).[13] Manfred's description of Conrad as 'a sickly puny child' (*O* 23) only strengthens this suggestion. Subjects that would be strictly taboo in Hume's history are, nevertheless, an integral part of history (as they are in the present) and therefore considered eligible for discussion. Impulsive, pugnatory acts receive the same treatment.

In contrast to *The History of England*, Walpole's Gothic novel is not only punctuated by, but dwells on violent events. 'The valour that had so long been smothered in his breast' (*O* 69) breaking forth, Theodore brutally attacks a knight who he believes is in league with Manfred. Much to his dismay he discovers that the knight is in fact Isabella's father, Frederic, an enemy of Manfred. Despite the vast amount of 'blood that flowed from his wounds' (*O* 69), however, Frederic survives. Mistaking Matilda for Isabella, Manfred mistakenly murders his own daughter, plunging his dagger into her bosom: 'heaven directed my bloody hand to the heart of my child!' cries Manfred shortly after attempting 'to recover his dagger from Theodore to dispatch himself' (*O* 95–6). Indeed, *Otranto* draws attention not only to acts of violence in history, but to illogical and impulsive actions that punctuate the past. The Gothic focuses on the irrational nature of humankind and the past. In this respect Walpole (rather ironically) achieves what Hume originally set out to do in *The History of England*: to reveal aspects of the human species that remain the same in all times and all places. Hume loses track of his original philosophical aim in the course of his history by creating a vast gulf between 'civilised' (post-medieval) and 'uncivilised' (medieval) humans. By revealing the irrational actions of humanity and the impact that such impulsive, spontaneous acts have on the outcome of certain historical events, Walpole not only draws attention to the historian's role as editor of the past, but reveals how contemporary humans are not all that different from their medieval ancestors. The Gothic explodes the barrier between humankind past and present and, as a result, makes the (contemporary) reader contemplate the uncivilised human instincts that have determined (and continue to determine) historical events throughout the ages.

The following remark that the 'modern editor' makes in the preface to *Otranto* is quite telling: the principal arguments of the narrative may have occurred in 'the darkest ages of Christianity', he writes, but the 'language and conduct have nothing that savours of barbarism' (*O* 5). These comments represent what may be considered as a veiled attack on the emphasis Hume places on the barbarity of medieval man. A certain amount of barbarism determines humankind both past and present: it is an inherent part of the human condition. Perhaps the most irrational, violent and gruesome incident in *Otranto* is the death of Conrad, Manfred's son and heir: 'But what a sight for a father's eyes! – He beheld his child dashed to pieces, and almost buried under an enormous helmet, an hundred times more large than any casque ever made for human being, and shaded with a proportionable quantity of black feathers' (*O* 18). Rather than suppressing the violence of Conrad's death, Walpole accentuates it. Whether it is the 'bleeding mangled remains', the 'disfigured corpse' or the 'dashed out' brains of the 'young prince', Walpole spares the reader few details (*O* 19–20). The Gothic is effectively the negative of Enlightenment historiography; it records the darker aspects of human history. The foreign setting of Walpole's novel reflects the foreignness of the past: it is radically different and far more violent and uncivilised than Hume's structured, coherent and civilised historical account suggests. Walpole makes a sustained effort to capture violent events in the past and, by doing so, exposes the artificial and constructed nature of Hume's (and much eighteenth-century) historiography. Where eighteenth-century historians such as Hume and writers such as Henry Fielding are concerned with the continuity of human nature and civilised forms of society throughout the ages, the Gothic focuses on the volatility of human nature and the uncivilised acts that comprise past, present and future.[14] In this sense, *Otranto* marks a return of the repressed. It embodies the macabre elements of human nature and history that eighteenth-century historiography represses. The Gothic forces the children of the Enlightenment to contemplate the sinister nature of their own pasts and the bloody deeds upon which their present age is founded. Moreover, as the incidents mentioned above indicate, such events are not placed in a causal chain or narrative framework in Walpole's Gothic novel: they appear to be completely random and, by their unexpected nature, resist traditional historiographical frameworks of understanding.

The Gothic and chance

To adapt the words Walpole uses in the postscript to his play, *The Mysterious Mother*, *Otranto* is governed by chance and is 'more apt to produce improbable situations than to remove them' (1791, 91). Theodore accidentally wounds Frederic and, even though the deaths of Matilda and Conrad can be interpreted within the frame of '*the sins of the fathers are visited on their children to the third and fourth generation*' (a moral that Walpole undermines, *O* 6–7), their violent demises occur suddenly and unexpectedly. The past is never as ordered and teleological as Hume's historiography suggests. The sightings of Alfonso's limbs occur at random intervals, whilst Manfred's attempt to follow the ghost of his grandfather into a chamber is inexplicably foiled when the door is 'clapped-to with violence by an invisible hand' (O 25). The occurrence of such events resists rational explanation. It is arguably only by chance that the original Italian manuscript written by Onuphrio Muralto is found in a library in the north of England in the first place.

In response to Hume's negation of contingency in *The History of England*, events governed by chance dominate *Otranto*. Because all events share a 'species of unity' (Hume 1826, 27), Hume argues that there is 'no such thing as *Chance* in the world' (67). Consequently, *The History of England* recounts very few events that are of a contingent nature. Chance, Hume argues, is 'nothing real in itself': it is 'the negation of a cause' (1911, 1: 127) or 'nothing but a secret and concealed cause' (1: 131). Due to the fact that in 'every part of nature' there is 'contained a vast variety of springs and principles, which are hid, by reason of their minuteness or remoteness' (1: 133), historiography that recounts events seemingly determined by chance really exhibit 'ignorance of the real cause of any event' (Hume 1826, 67). For Hume, this is simply not the premise of historical writing. Walpole firmly rejects such philosophical speculations regarding chance. Conrad's abrupt death by means of a giant, supernatural helmet is particularly telling in this respect: the very absurdity of such a sudden and bizarre occurrence can be read as an attack against the omission of chance in Hume's history. The helmet is also an artefact of war and draws attention to the repression of violent incidents in Enlightenment historical writing. The occurrence of accidents, natural or supernatural, illuminates how far removed from reality Hume's historiography really is. As Walpole remarks in the postscript to *The Mysterious Mother*, he is more interested in the 'sudden and unforeseen strokes' of human life and bringing historic events 'nearer to the imagination' (1791, 84).

Moreover, it is not only violent and supernatural events that occur out of the blue and defy rational explanation in *Otranto*. Although supernatural agency ultimately determines the outcome of the novel, it is pervaded by miscommunication, chance and contingency. In the labyrinthine passages of Otranto, Theodore mistakes Matilda for Isabella: 'What! Said Theodore, was it another, and not thy lovely self, that I assisted to find the subterraneous passage?' (*O* 65). Through an act of miscommunication, Hippolita, who is very much alive and well, is presumed dead; hearing Bianca cry out 'the princess is dead!' when Matilda faints, Martelli (a friar) presumes she means Hippolita and communicates his news to the convent (*O* 77). It is completely by chance that Father Jerome (or the Count of Falconara, as it turns out) meets his son in Manfred's court: 'Gracious heaven! Cried the holy man starting, what do I see! It is my child! My Theodore!' (*O* 51). Presumed to be a peasant boy with an uncanny 'resemblance' to 'Alfonso's portrait' (*O* 87), Theodore turns out to be the 'true heir of Alfonso!' (*O* 98). The presence of chance in Walpole's novel complicates the chains of simple causality manifested in Hume's history. Although *The History of England* does not completely ignore the role of contingency in the past (as the very concept of the field of probability underlines), it is sacrificed to an emphasis on continuity, chronology and coherence. *Otranto* exaggerates the contingent nature of reality and thus the past and, by doing so, creates suspense and reveals the reductionism inherent in Hume's historical work. Again, narrative frameworks create a false impression of reality and the past. Indeed, the Gothic is effectively an attempt to emancipate the reader from the unnatural structures imposed on reality and the past by Hume's historiography. *Otranto* reveals the past in all its obscurity, partiality and discontinuity. Where eighteenth-century Enlightenment historiography emphasises coherence, chronology and order, the Gothic demonstrates that such effects are merely illusions created by historians.

The Gothic, domestication and defamiliarisation

From its inception then, the Gothic has been actively involved in defamiliarising the past. In contrast to *The History of England*, *Otranto* makes a sustained effort to impart a sense of the past as it is perceived, not as it is 'known' (Shklovsky 2004, 16). A past that is seemingly *heimliche* in Hume's historiography is ever so *unheimliche* in Walpole's Gothic novel. To adapt Viktor Shklovsky's words (2004, 16), the Gothic removes the past from the automatism of perception: eighteenth-century historiography's conception of the past as something inherently knowable and familiar is comprehensively negated. To a much greater extent than Hume's *The History of England* (and Enlightenment history in general), the Gothic conveys a sense of the 'epistemological uncertainty' in which humanity, pre- and post-Enlightenment, has existed (Braudy 1970, 176). Fiction suggests revisions for historiography. Championing the use of imagination in the writing of history, Walpole attempts to release the past from the shackles of dominant, reductive modes of historiography.

Despite being set in a foreign location, *Otranto* also marks a domestication of the past: in contrast to Hume's history, the home and the family become subjects eligible for historical analysis. The reader learns not only of the dark secret that literally haunts Manfred, but of the effect of this on the ordinary lives of his family, servants and individuals present within his household at the time (for example, Theodore). In his preface to the first edition of *Otranto*, Walpole highlights the importance of members of the lower classes (such as Bianca) in the events that take place; through their 'naïveté and simplicity', they 'discover many passages essential' to the action (O 6). *Otranto* helps to alter the focus of history from the public to the private, from the upper classes to the lower classes. The Gothic illuminates *The History of England*'s (and to a certain extent Enlightenment historiography's) propensity for exclusion.

Developing themes such as the dysfunctional family and a focus on violent deeds, Walpole's Gothic novel draws attention to aspects of the past that Enlightenment history neglects. While *The History of England* attempts to convey a sense of national historical consciousness, the Gothic endeavours to stimulate an awareness of the historically conditioned nature of one's own existence. The Gothic is not an alternative mode of historiography in its own right; it is an imaginative protest against rational, reductive historiographical techniques. As Walpole himself notes (1768, 94), despite convicting historians of 'partiality, absurdities, contradictions, and falsehoods' (and generally undermining their 'credit'), he has not ventured to establish any abiding historiographical theory or 'peremptory conclusion' of his own. As opposed to providing solutions, the Gothic revels in its propensity for dismantling established epistemic systems and creating fear and unease. As I have already mentioned in this chapter, between his rational, authoritative deductions and organisational frameworks, Hume offers the reader occasional glimpses of a multi-dimensional past in *The History of England*. It is out of these cracks, these glimmers of a multifarious past, that the Gothic grows and begins to flourish. Emerging out of the shadows of Enlightenment historiography, the Gothic highlights the need for a more flexible, elastic method of writing the past: one that can more effectively accommodate imagination, violence and contingency.

As *Sinister Histories* demonstrates, in its later manifestations, the Gothic continues to probe the nature of historical knowledge and to react to Enlightenment conceptions of history. However, in a more marked way than *Otranto*, Gothic pasts are increasingly used as vehicles to comment on anxieties in the present and engage more closely with their immediate historical contexts. Indeed, even though Walpole was the son of Whig Prime Minister, Robert Walpole, and served as an MP, his political attitudes in *Otranto* remain somewhat ambiguous. As I mentioned earlier, Walpole argued that his Gothic novel was essentially an act of 'defiance' against his own time (Walpole 1767). *Otranto* is concerned with historico-political subjects that were debated intensely during the eighteenth century, such as lineage, inheritance and the power of the aristocracy, but, as Andrew Smith argues (2007, 22), Walpole's political attitudes towards such subjects remain unclear and it is difficult to assess the extent to which his eighteenth-century political attitudes shape the past in *Otranto*.[15] As this book reveals, later Gothic writers – and particularly female authors – give the Gothic a more distinctive political edge. This is certainly the case with the Gothic's next incarnation: Clara Reeve's *The Old English Baron* (1778). As I discuss in the next chapter, the fifteenth-century past of Reeve's novel is heavily influenced by her Whig political beliefs and can be read as a reaction to the crisis of national identity engendered by the American Revolution. In Reeve's hands, the Gothic continues to probe the nature of the past and to react to Enlightenment conceptions of history. However, she takes particular issue with Walpole's use of the supernatural and redevelops a number of Gothic tropes in order to give the genre a firmer moral purpose.

Notes

1 Walpole's Strawberry Hill symbolised his interest in medieval history and his enchantment with the past. Adding cloisters, battlements, turrets, stained glass, and fireplaces to his house, Walpole helped to revive the Gothic style of architecture. The house became a celebrated attraction in the eighteenth century. Referring to the structure as his 'little Gothic Castle' (1937–83, 20: 111), Strawberry Hill is intricately connected with the composition of *Otranto*. Walpole even encouraged his readers to draw parallels between his Gothic narrative and house. 'When you read of the picture quitting its panel', he writes to a friend, 'did not you recollect the portrait of Lord Falkland all in white in my gallery?' (1: 88).

2 A number of critics have discussed how Walpole's historical attitudes in *Otranto* are shaped by eighteenth-century antiquarianism. For example, Ruth Mack considers how Walpole responds to the 'emergence of the object as a new kind of historical evidence' (Mack 2009, 112). Examining the appearance of Alfonso and the giant helmet, and Walpole's use of the Gothic trope of the discovered manuscript, she argues that *Otranto* probes the nature of history 'beyond empirical experience' (120) and contends that 'Walpole provides a theory of historical representation' (129). Sean R. Silver also discusses Walpole's fascination with historical artefacts. He contends that Walpole was interested in objects 'because of their potential to contradict the merely textual narratives of Enlightenment historiography'. Silver suggests that Walpole's 'Gothicism was interested in individual objects in what he found or considered to be their own terms, often as they violated the textual or traditional histories of early Enlightenment historians' (2009, 542). While the present chapter does consider aspects of the past that transcend language and narrative frameworks, it differentiates itself from Mack's and Silver's studies by focusing more on how *Otranto* engages with the epistemological problems of writing history in the eighteenth century.

3 Walpole was capable of serious historical work. In *Historic Doubts on the Life and Reign of King Richard the Third* (1768), he defends Richard III against the common belief that he murdered the Princes in the Tower. Walpole was a Ricardian and brought this ancient controversy back to public attention. There were numerous responses to his *Historic Doubts*. The President of the Antiquarian society, Jeremiah Milles, severely undermined Walpole's principal documentary evidence. Walpole was hurt by this and soon afterwards resigned his membership to the society. Walpole also reacted to Hume's thoughts on his *Historic Doubts* (see Note 9). Published from 1762, Walpole's *Anecdotes of Painting in England* – a work which details a number of English painters, sculptors and architects – also reveals his commitment to more serious historical work.

4 In his influential *Narrative Form in History and Fiction*, Leo Braudy argues that Hume's approach to history changes during the composition of *The History of England* (1970, 31–90). Throughout this section, I synthesise and develop a number of Braudy's thoughts regarding Hume's diverse historiographical strategies.

5 Hume's philosophy is sceptical in the sense that it undermines the rationalist perception of human nature by profoundly questioning the power and capacity of the human intellect. Hume described his own *A Treatise of Human Nature* as being 'very sceptical' in that it 'tends to give us a notion of the narrow limits of human understanding' (1938, 24).

6 Recording intriguing eighteenth-century sayings, fashions, incidents, and other events of a trifling nature, Walpole's letters themselves provide an alternative mode of historiography. Despite being one of his harshest critics, even Thomas Macaulay notes that Walpole's correspondence with Sir Horace Mann contains 'much information concerning the history of that time: the portion of English History of which common readers know the least' (Macaulay 1861, 269). The relationship between the Gothic, letters and the past will be discussed in more detail in the following chapters.

7 Hume actually wrote *The History of England* in reverse order, starting with the present and working backwards. Initially titled *The History of Great Britain*, the first volumes published contained the history of the Stuarts, followed by two Tudor volumes. Two medieval volumes followed these. It is plausible that Walpole had read all six volumes of Hume's historical work before writing *Otranto*, which was first published in 1764. Hume renamed his work *The History of England* after the publication of the medieval volumes and changed the chronology of the volumes: volume 1 now detailed the history of medieval England and volume 6 contained the history of the Stuarts.

8 Walpole is most likely referring to either the Stuart or Tudor volumes of *The History of England* in this letter.

9 Walpole knew Hume and corresponded with him. Early letters between the two date from around 1758. However, Walpole did not rate Hume's conversation, revealing that 'he understood nothing till he had written upon it' (1937–83, 16: 266). He also argues that, as a philosopher, Hume was a 'superficial mountebank' (42: 78). Walpole visited Paris at the time Hume was British Ambassador for France. In the winter of 1765–66, a popular subject of conversation in Paris was Jean-Jacques Rousseau, who had left Switzerland after public disputes. He believed himself to be the victim of an elaborate conspiracy, and sought congenial refuge, which Hume intended to provide by taking him to Britain. In the midst of these transactions, Walpole wrote a letter purportedly from Frederick II to Rousseau inviting him to take shelter in Prussia. The letter satirised Rousseau's paranoia, created a commotion in Paris

and provoked a furious reaction from the latter, who came to suspect that Hume himself had been involved. Walpole and Hume corresponded on the controversy and the latter (rather magnanimously) dismissed the episode 'as a piece of levity' (Hume 1932, 2: 10). In 1769, Hume wrote a critique of Walpole's *Historic Doubts* (1768) entitled 'Sixteen Notes on Walpole's Historic Doubts', which appeared in the French periodical *Mémoires littéraires de la Grande Bretagne*. Hume later integrated his 'Sixteen Notes' into a lengthy note to Chapter 26 of his *The History of England*. Walpole heard about (and maybe even read) Hume's forthcoming critique and was unhappy about it: he wrote to a friend, 'Mr. Hume shall publish a few remarks he has made on my book – they are very far from substantial, yet still better than any other trash that has been written against it, nothing of which deserves an answer (1937–83, 1: 133–4). However, once the work had been published, Walpole's reaction became very negative. In his *Supplement to the Historic doubts on the life and reign of King Richard III. With remarks on some answers that have been made to that Work* (1769), he defends his original arguments against all of Hume's contentions. Moreover, he describes Hume's contentions as 'vague, unfair, and void of argument' (Walpole 1829, 197) and accuses him of relying too heavily on questionable historical sources (particularly those by Thomas More and Francis Bacon).

10 Walpole was opposed to the recent, eighteenth-century trend towards Catholic emancipation, as his comment in a letter to Mann in 1784 indicates: 'You know I have ever been averse to toleration of an intolerant religion' (1937–83, 25: 541). However, one must be careful about reading such a view into *Otranto* or generalising about the Gothic's representations of the Catholic faith. As Robert Miles points out, the Gothic's relationship with Catholicism is complex and cannot be reduced to a single binary opposition of Protestant and Catholic, British and European. Gothic representations of Catholicism frequently prey on the insecurities of Protestant readers and it is inaccurate to suggest that all Gothic fiction enacts a 'chronic anti-Catholicism' (Miles 2002, 86). In terms of Walpole's Gothic novel, Miles argues that it 'is not about, is not a defence of, or an attack on, Catholicism' (93). Citing the political controversy surrounding Walpole's father and allusions to the Reformation in the prefaces to *Otranto*, Miles argues that, rather than criticising Catholicism, the novel is 'really about legitimacy, or rather lack of it' (93). For an overview of critical attitudes towards the Gothic's representations of Catholicism, see Angela Wright's *Gothic Fiction* (2007, 74–96). Throughout this book, I will note the Gothic's varied responses to Catholicism.

11 As Chapter 3 points out, the conflicting first person accounts that comprise Lee's *The Recess* have profound implications for Enlightenment historiography and the nature of historical knowledge.

12 Hume is most likely referring to historians such as Thucydides, Herodotus and Gaius Cornelius Tacitus here. Tacitus' *The Annals of Imperial Rome* was, in particular, a large influence on Hume, providing him with a model for working backwards, instead of forwards, in time. See Hicks's *Neoclassical History and English Culture: From Clarendon to Hume* (1996, 170–209) for further discussion of how Hume was influenced by classical historians.

13 As I discuss in the following chapters, the lack of social and economic power experienced by women in *Otranto* becomes a subject of intense scrutiny in future Gothic works. This is particularly the case with the Female Gothic novels of Lee and Radcliffe.

14 History, how it is written and what it should achieve, is a particular concern in Fielding's writings. For example, in the aptly named *The History of Tom Jones* (1749), Fielding conducts an extended meditation on the nature of history and, moreover, considers the complex relationship between history and literature (2005, 73–4). However, in contrast to the Gothic, Fielding's writings focus predominantly on the perennial goodness of humanity.

15 Walpole was a Whig and an aristocrat. As this book shows in the forthcoming chapters, the term 'Gothic' was a highly charged political term throughout the eighteenth century. As a Whig, Walpole believed in the myth of the ancient, Saxon or Gothic constitution: 'I have for five and forty years acted upon the principles of the constitution as it was settled at the Revolution, the best form of government that I know of in the world, and which made us a free people, a rich people, and a victorious people, by diffusing liberty, protecting property and encouraging commerce' (1937–83, 29: 351). However, the extent to which such political beliefs influence the past in his Gothic novel remains questionable. There have been numerous studies that examine the politics of the past in *Otranto*. For example, Miles reads *Otranto* as a response to the political plight of his father, Whig Prime Minister Robert Walpole (2003, 60–3). Andrew Smith contends that Walpole's novel can be read 'in the context of the economic upheavals which characterised Britain in the eighteenth century, ones in which aristocratic power was progressively replaced by the economies largely generated through international trade which were controlled by, and helped to consolidate, the new middle classes' (2007, 23). While this is certainly true and issues of political legitimacy loom large in the narrative, the foreign and Catholic setting of Walpole's novel

makes it difficult to identify distinctive Whig political beliefs. As Smith argues, although the novel 'illustrates some historically specific concerns relating to the aristocracy' (23), *Otranto*'s political stance on such issues remains 'ambivalent' (22). In the following chapter, I will discuss Whig notions of the Gothic constitution in more detail and show how Reeve's *The Old English Baron* has a much firmer political stance.

2

'[B]ringing this deed of darkness to light': representations of the past in Clara Reeve's *The Old English Baron* (1778)

The disastrous times do not inspire expense … We are returning to our state of islandhood, and shall have little, I believe, to boast, but of what we have been!

> Horace Walpole to William Cole (12 August 1779)

This is a dark story

> Clara Reeve, *The Old English Baron* (1778)

How many usurpations of provinces and kingdoms do we meet with in history without any miracle interposing to punish the usurpers?

> Paul M. Rapin de Thoyras, *History of England* (1726–32)

Thirteen years would elapse between *The Castle of Otranto* and the emergence of the next Gothic novel.[1] Originally published anonymously as *The Champion of Virtue: A Gothic Story* in 1777, Clara Reeve revised and republished her novel as the *The Old English Baron: A Gothic Story* in 1778. Featuring tropes such as fragmented manuscripts, violent pasts, repressed histories, usurpation, imprisonment, confused ancestry, female persecution, suspenseful sequences of action, and supernatural phenomena, Reeve set out to tame what she perceived as *Otranto*'s excesses. In the preface to *The Old English Baron*, she declares that her story is the 'literary offspring of the Castle of Otranto, written upon the same plan, with a design to unite the most attractive and interesting circumstances of the ancient Romance and modern Novel' (*OEB* 2). Walpole's novel may 'excite the attention' and 'engage the heart', she argues, but, with its relentless violent and supernatural occurrences, the novel is not kept within the 'utmost *verge* of probability' and 'palls upon the mind' (*OEB* 3–4). By locating her own Gothic novel in England rather than abroad, setting the action in an actual historical period – the early reign of Henry VI – and limiting supernatural occurrences, Reeve endeavours to avoid such 'defects' (*OEB* 4). Adapting *Otranto*'s plot of usurpation, disinheritance and restoration, Reeve's novel traces the reinstatement of a virtuous peasant, Edmund Twyford, as the heir of Lovel Castle and the exposure and punishment of the usurping murderer, Sir Walter Lovel, Edmund's kinsman. Edmund clearly follows in the path of *Otranto*'s Theodore. However, as I will discuss in more detail later, Reeve focuses as much on Edmund's virtues as his right to reclaim his social position. It is only after numerous testing trials and with the help of a noble knight, Sir Philip Harclay, and a virtuous master, the Baron Fitz-Owen, that the terrible history that haunts the novel's present is unearthed and Edmund is restored to his rightful place.

Walpole was unimpressed with Reeve's reworking of his Gothic novel. 'Have you seen *The Old Baron*', he writes in a letter to Reverend William Mason in April 1778, 'a Gothic story, professedly written in imitation of *Otranto*, but reduced to reason and probability! It is so probable, that any trial for murder at the Old Bailey would make a more interesting story!' (1937–83, 28: 381–2). Writing to William Cole in August 1778, he dismisses Reeve's novel as a work so 'stripped of the marvellous … except in one awkward attempt at a ghost or two, that it is the most insipid dull nothing you ever saw'. '[W]hat makes one doze', he adds, 'seldom makes one merry' (2: 110). Sir Walter Scott held a similar opinion.[2] Nevertheless, in spite of such harsh criticism, *The Old English Baron* proved to be a popular and enduring success. Between 1778 and 1786, Reeve's Gothic novel went through thirteen editions. It was translated into French twice (1787 and 1800), German once (1789), adapted for the stage by John Broster in his (never acted) *Edmond, Orphan of the Castle* (1799), and abridged in chapbooks. Moreover, in recent decades, Reeve's long-maligned work has been identified as far more than merely 'a footnote in literary history' (Spector 1984, 81). It is now widely acknowledged that Reeve's showcasing of dreams, providential agency, the restrained supernatural, a haunted apartment with mouldering furniture, an unrepentant villain, secret doors behind tapestries, themes of guilt, and her attitude towards history, influenced Gothic writers such as William

Beckford, Sophia Lee, Ann Radcliffe, and beyond. Exhibiting a very different, but no less important, attitude towards history compared to Walpole's *Otranto* (and many later tales of terror, for that matter), Reeve's novel marks a significant development in the genesis of Gothic fiction and reveals the diversity of the genre in the eighteenth century.

With interest in Reeve's life and works having grown in recent years, there is now an extensive body of scholarship on *The Old English Baron*.[3] This chapter seeks to both develop existing scholarship and forge new directions for Reeve criticism. Developing the notion that the Gothic responds to Enlightenment strategies of historical representation, the forthcoming discussion examines the relationship between Reeve's *The Old English Baron* and Paul M. Rapin de Thoyras's *History of England*. As this chapter reveals, Reeve was very familiar with this proto-Enlightenment work of historiography. Identifying elements of history that disturb Rapin, I will argue that such fears gained a new, frightening significance in the context of the American Revolution and that such anxieties are manifest in Reeve's novel. A number of questions will be posed: how do Reeve's own politico-religious attitudes shape the past in *The Old English Baron*, how significant is the revolt of the Thirteen Colonies in terms of the history she writes, and to what extent do Whig historical representational strategies inform the Gothic?

Throughout this chapter, I will discuss *The Old English Baron* as a response to *Otranto* and emphasise how Reeve's attitude towards the past differs from Walpole's. What is 'Gothic' for Reeve, what aspects of the past does she portray as particularly terrifying and how does her use of the supernatural differ from Walpole's? Exploring themes such as the family, ancestry, chivalry, violence, the law, and female oppression, the forthcoming discussion will show how definitions and conceptions of the 'Gothic' are fiercely contested in the eighteenth century. Marking a new direction for Gothic literature, Reeve's fictional novel is set in an actual historical period. What is the significance of this, why would she choose to set a Gothic novel in the early reign of Henry VI and to what extent is the past featured in the novel shaped by the present? The prefaces to the first and second editions of *The Old English Baron* reveal a great deal about Reeve's notion of the complex relationship between the Gothic, literature and history,

and will be employed as a means of examining the construction of the past in the novel. As the first preface discloses, *The
Old English Baron* is presented as a translated script. How does
Reeve's use of the Gothic device of the discovered manuscript
differ from Walpole's and what does it reveal about her attitude
towards the past? Before I begin to answer such questions, it is
necessary to examine James Watt's thoughts on Reeve's novel and
his notion of the Loyalist Gothic.

The Loyalist Gothic and the American Revolution

In his influential study, *Contesting the Gothic* (1999), Watt identifies *The Old English Baron* as an example of what he calls the
Loyalist Gothic: an often critically neglected yet significant strain of
Gothic works which were particularly prominent in the 1790s and
early 1800s. Dating from around the time of the British defeat in
America, but growing in popularity once the French Revolution had
turned violent in the mid-1790s, he argues that these 'little-known
works rely upon an English medieval setting', serve 'an unambigu-
ous moral and patriotic agenda' and 'privilege the didactic potential of romance' (1999, 7). These Gothic works centre on glorious,
English Protestant histories rather than on backward European,
Catholic pasts. Such Gothic tales are usually set in actual historical periods, rather than in the vague historical setting employed
by Walpole in *Otranto*, and tend to explore a different aspect of
the 'Gothic'. Rather than conjuring up images of barbarism and
savagery, these authors use it to take one back to 'the "dark ages"
of the English medieval period' and viewed it as a 'purer expression
of English national identity than the neo-classical present' (Heiland
2004, 4). Citing the significance of the American Revolution
(1775–83) and the crisis of British patriotism and national identity
that it triggered, Watt contends that *The Old English Baron* is a
'prototype of the Loyalist Gothic' (1999, 50).[4] This chapter supports this notion.[5] A prominent theme of Loyalist Gothic narratives
that Watt identifies – and one that, as the forthcoming discussion
will reveal, features prominently in *The Old English Baron* – is the
fear of '*constitutional* degeneration' (1999, 59). This is linked with
the chaotic cultural context in which the novel was written.

The revolt of the Thirteen Colonies, which was in full swing by
the writing of *The Old English Baron*, rocked Britain's colonial

power and asked awkward questions about Britain's own political and constitutional makeup. National insecurities were only exacerbated when the old enemy, France, joined the American revolt in 1777. Linda Colley eloquently conveys the sense of political, constitutional and religious angst triggered by events taking place across the Atlantic when she argues that the American Revolution caused Britons 'to look anxiously and inquiringly inwards' (2005, 4) and left many 'with the sense that part of their history and collective identity had been brutally amputated' (141). A particular point of conflict for the Americans was the relationship between Parliament and the monarchy. As Colley points out, the colonies questioned Parliament's right to tax them: their allegiance was owing to the King of England alone and, in terms of taxation, only their own elected colonial assemblies had the right to demand it of them (136). The revolt of the Thirteen Colonies brutally exposed Britain's failure to 'build an effective structure of royal authority and administration in their American colonies' and revealed fissures in Britain's constitutional monarchy (136). Indeed, the American Revolution drew a clear distinction between royal authority and parliamentary authority; a division that did not sit well with the British (and particularly Whigs) on the other side of the Atlantic (136). As Walpole's epigraph to this chapter demonstrates, with the time-honoured or 'Gothic' constitution brutally undermined by the transgressions taking place across the Atlantic, there were widespread fears that Britain could regress into insignificant islandhood and internal conflict. The turbulent cultural context at home only heightened such fears.

Debates about British national identity raged before and during the time that Reeve was writing *The Old English Baron*. As Colley points out (2005, 112), men and women struggled to come to terms with the unprecedented and expensive victory and new imperial responsibilities in the wake of the turbulent aftermath of the Seven Years' War (1756–63). Gary Kelly notes how issues over the imperial administration of India, dissenters' campaigns for full citizenship and religious toleration, economic reform of government, and the reduction of the crown and court's powers of patronage destabilised conceptions of national identity (1999, 1: xiii). As well as these anxieties, the American Revolution threatened political stability, contributed to domestic division and debate, and 'compelled different groups of Britons to re-examine the nature and boundaries of their patriotism' (Colley 2005, 141). In England, some English patriots felt under threat from Scottish ambition and Protestant beliefs in England's destiny as a nation and world power were shaken. A particularly notable response to this was the tumultuous campaign launched by John Wilkes and his supporters, who fought for the reinstatement of ancient English liberties and new English rights during the 1760s and beyond. 'Wilkes and Liberty' became a slogan for his campaign and, as Colley points out, he 'functioned as an English nationalist administering comfort to people in a flux' (117). Wilkes's campaign supported the notion that England was an exceptional nation, blessed by God with a unique degree of freedom.[6]

Arguing that Reeve's Gothic novel can be read not only as a retort to Wapole's *Otranto*, but as a response to Rapin's *History of England* – the themes of which became more resonant with the political situation at home and abroad – the forthcoming discussion will show how the fifteenth-century past of Reeve's Gothic novel also represents a complex reaction to its tumultuous cultural context. This chapter will argue that Reeve focuses on certain aspects of the past not only to bolster English patriotism, but to heal divisions at home and to create a more united sense of Britain by drawing attention to shared beliefs, principles and values.[7] I will begin with an examination of two Gothic themes that are central to Reeve's fictional past: religion and the supernatural. Before doing so, it is necessary to examine Rapin's history and its religious views.

Rapin, Walpole and Reeve: the Gothic, providence and the past

As I discussed in the Introduction, Rapin's *History of England* was very popular in the eighteenth century and, with its critical treatment of primary sources and simple style of narration, contributed to the development of Enlightenment historiography.[8] A particularly notable aspect of Rapin's proto-Enlightenment history is its aversion to and general disinterest in religious and ecclesiastical history. As Laird Okie notes, Rapin possessed a 'secular, anti-clerical tone, which distinguished it from the theistic, super-historical themes of previous histories' (1991, 47). More interested in political and constitutional history, religion plays a relatively small part in the *History of England*. As Okie points out, in his history of Tudor England, Rapin says almost nothing about the ecclesiastical and theological problems that divided various religious groups (60). Moreover, what Rapin has to say about the clergy is usually critical and, in the course of his history, there is very little discussion of the religious disputes between Puritans and Arminians, Presbyterians and Anglicans, Low Church and High Church (60). Perhaps the most significant aspect of the *History of England* is Rapin's reluctance to appeal to providential or divine agency for explanations of certain historical events. This is not to say that he did not believe in providence or that the *History of England* rejects divine agency altogether. For example, speaking of the death of Henry V, Rapin argues that it was probably the 'particular direction of divine providence' (*H* 5: 207). Furthermore, Rapin was a Huguenot and certainly believed that human history was preordained by God. However, throughout the *History of England*, references to providence are infrequent and, as the following quotation exemplifies, he is sceptical of histories based entirely on religious and supernatural grounds: 'can it be affirmed that it concerns God's honour to punish in an exemplary and supernatural manner the heinous acts of injustice committed in the world? How many usurpations of provinces and kingdoms do we meet with in history without any miracle interposing to punish the usurpers?' (*H* 5: 472–3). Despite believing in God and appealing to providence at certain intervals in his history, Rapin does not believe that 'history should or could be written' to highlight (exclusively) the workings of divine providence (Okie 1991, 60). Miracles, providential interventions and supernatural displays of divine power are not considered fit for historical discussion. For Rapin, history should demonstrate a sharper awareness of historical change by recording long-term developments such as the growing power of Parliament and the rise of political parties. Indeed, it is Rapin's secularisation of the historical cause that proved so influential for future Enlightenment, philosophical historians such as David Hume. As Okie points out (64), by reducing the omnipresence of God and the Church in the historical domain, the *History of England* cleared a path for future Enlightenment historians to examine social, economic and political change. More significantly in terms of the current discussion, however, Rapin's historical attitudes had a significant impact on Reeve, the Gothic and the past constructed in *The Old English Baron*.

Reeve had certainly read Rapin's history. At 'an age when few people of either sex can read', writes Reeve in a letter to a friend, '[m]y father ... made me read Rapin's *History of England*' (Reeve 1829).[9] However, similarly to Walpole's attitude towards Hume's *The History of England*, Reeve was not exactly enamoured with Rapin's work: 'the information it gave, made amends for its dryness', she writes (Reeve 1829). From a very early age, Reeve's historical views were shaped by Tindal's popular translation of Rapin's history. Furthermore, it is beyond doubt that her reading of Rapin shaped her creative works. At the beginning of her later historical novel, *Memoirs of Sir Roger de Clarendon* (1793), Reeve acknowledges him in a list of 'historians consulted in this work' (1793, 1: xxiv). *The Old English Baron* can be read as a complex response not only to Walpole's *Otranto*, but to Rapin's proto-Enlightenment historical attitudes in the *History of England*.

Since its inception, the Gothic has been transfixed with the supernatural and divine agency. *Otranto* proliferates with such occurrences. As I discussed in the previous chapter, Walpole reacted to Hume's excision of the supernatural, divine intervention and miracles from the historical realm by filling his Gothic novel with such instances. As Reeve notes in her preface to the second edition of *The Old English Baron*, such examples include a 'sword so large as to require an hundred men to lift it', a 'helmet that by its own weight forces a passage through a court-yard into an arched vault', a 'picture that walks out of its frame' and a 'skeleton ghost in a hermit's cowl' (*OEB* 3). Long-held religious prophecies, such as the notion that the '*sins of fathers are visited on their children to the third and fourth generation*' (*O* 6), are seemingly fulfilled in *Otranto* and human actors are manipulated by forces outside of their control. It is also important to note that the past Walpole constructs in his Gothic novel is Catholic; the proliferation of paranormal occurrences serve to undermine and castigate what many eighteenth-century Protestants perceived as a backward, superstitious religious order that dominated southern Europe. Set in fifteenth-century England and translated from a manuscript originally written in old English (or so Reeve would have us believe), *The Old English Baron* utilises the Gothic's focus on divine agency for a different purpose. As the above quotation suggests, Reeve disapproves of Walpole's frequent use of the supernatural. Even though the past constructed in Walpole's novel is Catholic, it is aimed at a Protestant audience and poses questions about God and divine agency in history and human life. The random nature of supernatural occurrences and acts of divine intervention in *Otranto* conflict with elements of Christian teachings and providential models of human history.

In *The Old English Baron*, there is a dual movement against the secularisation of the historical cause in Rapin's history and the religious ambiguity that surrounds the past featured in *Otranto*. Writing at a time when the American Revolution challenged deeply held Protestant beliefs that England was an elect nation marked out by God and that its destiny was shaped by an overruling providence, the secularisation of the historical cause in Rapin's history was brought into sharper focus. Believing that strong Christian faith is vital to England (and Britain) at a time of national crisis, Reeve writes a past that is governed by providence. Exploiting the Gothic's focus on the supernatural, divine Christian intervention dominates the fifteenth-century past constructed in Reeve's Loyalist Gothic novel. In what is a short novel, there are approximately twelve references to providence, twenty-eight references to God and forty-nine references to heaven in *The Old English Baron*. Harclay declares that Edmund, the novel's hero, is the 'child of providence! – the beloved of heaven!' (*OEB* 75) and believes that he is an 'instrument of justice in the hand of Heaven!' (*OEB* 90). 'Heaven has in its own way made him the instrument to discover the death of his parents', he adds (*OEB* 89). The Baron Fitz-Owen argues that 'Heaven effects its purposes in its own time and manner' (*OEB* 98), whilst even the villain of the novel, Sir Walter Lovel, comes to recognise that 'nothing can be concealed from the eye of Heaven' (*OEB* 92). After exhuming the body of Lord Lovel, Father Oswald (a religious servant of the Baron Fitz-Owen) declares that the discovery is the work of providence: 'Behold the day of retribution! of triumph to the innocent, of shame and confusion to the wicked' (*OEB* 116). Using Gothic fiction as an imaginative protest against increasingly secular eighteenth-century historiography, Reeve restores religion and Christian, providential agency to the past. This is underscored at the end of the novel when Reeve states that the events of the novel function as a 'striking lesson to posterity, of the over-ruling hand of Providence, and the certainty of RETRIBUTION' (*OEB* 136).

In contrast to *Otranto*'s superstitious past and Rapin's secular history, the past constructed in *The Old English Baron* reflects a 'Christian universe' (Ehlers 1978, 76). As Leigh Ehlers points out, the 'characters in *The Old English Baron* replay the Christian history of man; the Lovel family moves in a linear or straightforward fashion through a three-stage progression, with no significant digressions, from "glory," to "ruin" to "restoration"' (1978, 65). The past in *The Old English Baron* follows a providential pattern and takes the hero, Edmund, from a position of initial security, to a period of hardship where his faith is severely tested, to a phase of purgation of weakness and sin. He is then rewarded with a position of restored security and victory over his enemies (65). Reeve directs the mystery and awe that surrounds the supernatural occurrences in Walpole's Catholic Gothic past towards contemplations of God and the workings of Christian providence. For example, whilst sleeping at Wyatt's cottage, Harclay is awestruck by 'many strange and incoherent dreams' (*OEB* 11). His old friend, Arthur Lovel, appears to speak to him and leads him to a 'dark and frightful cave' where 'dismal groans' are heard and Harclay beholds 'a complete suit of armour stained with blood' (*OEB* 11). This dream turns out to be prophetic and an example of divine intervention. Reeve counters the increasingly secular nature of Enlightenment historiography by ensuring that it is the light of religious revelation, rather than the light of reason, that helps to solve the mysteries of the past. At various points in the narrative, Oswald declares that the 'ways of providence are wonderful' (*OEB* 45). Harclay exclaims, 'Praise be to God for his wonderful doings towards the children of men!' (*OEB* 76), whilst, in a letter, Lord Clifford compels his addressee to 'unite with us in wondering at the ways of providence' (*OEB* 96). Since its genesis with the publication of *Otranto*, the Gothic has been obsessed with the mystery of being and the seemingly irrational forces that drive human history. Reeve hijacks this aspect of the Gothic for strictly Christian ends and to encourage readers to contemplate the wonders of Christian providence. Drawing a parallel between Edmund's struggles and England's current plight at home and abroad, Reeve shows how, throughout history, England has avoided a succession of disasters and escapes; she reminds English readers of who they are and reassures them of their privileged place in God's providential scheme.

To use the words of Aubrey Williams, history in *The Old English Baron* is controlled by providence and, in marked contrast to Rapin's proto-Enlightenment *History of England*, works 'in and through human choices and natural events, through chance encounters and strange accidents, through improbable mishaps and fantastic coincidences' (1971, 284). As Ehlers points out (1978,

69), similarly to *Otranto*, Reeve's Gothic novel is replete with seemingly random occurrences. For example, with his (foster) father, Andrew Twyford, weary of supporting his adopted child, Edmund is taken into the Baron Fitz-Owen's service 'just in the nick' (*OEB* 53). This is just one of many 'seemingly accidental circumstances' that leads the hero 'imperceptibly towards the crisis of his fate' (*OEB* 27). It is fortunate that Margery Twyford (Edmund's foster mother) preserves the ear-rings, necklace and locket worn by Edmund's mother (*OEB* 54). These mementos function as 'strong and indisputable' proofs of his identity (*OEB* 54). When Edmund has to spend a night in the haunted apartment, he just happens to discover and gain access to two hidden rooms which contain vital clues to his identity and the bloody misdeeds that led to his father's death (*OEB* 36). As I discussed in the previous chapter, Walpole's *Otranto* focused on fortuitous discoveries and random occurrences to reject the role of chance in Hume's *The History of England*. Such events serve an entirely different purpose in *The Old English Baron*. Events in Reeve's Loyalist Gothic novel may appear to be random acts of chance, but throughout they turn out to be instances of the foreknowing and protective care of God, who shapes the past and ensures that Edmund is restored to his rightful place. As Edmund declares, even though God's ways may seem mysterious at first, 'Providence will in its own time vindicate its ways to man' (*OEB* 30). Reeve adopts the Gothic's obsession with complex plots and acts of chance to underscore the mysterious, complex workings of Christian providence in human life and history. Rebelling against the marginalisation of God in Rapin's *History of England*, Reeve exploits the Gothic's fascination with chance in order to imaginatively reunite history and theology. Furthermore, the past constructed in *The Old English Baron* has a strong moral purpose, as will be demonstrated.

Supernatural pasts: providence and Reeve's didactic Gothic

The providential past constructed in *The Old English Baron* is a reflection not only of Reeve's own, deeply held Christian beliefs, but her attitude towards romance. Reeve's later work, *The Progress of Romance* (1785), is useful here. In this remarkable work of literary history and criticism, Reeve traces the romance to its origins and defends it against the Augustan Age's tendency to 'decry and ridicule them' (1785, 1: 105). She raises the profile of this much-derided form of literature by showing how the 'modern Novel sprung out of its ruins' (1: 8) and by concluding that 'Epic Poetry is the parent of Romance' (1: 25); she criticises those who 'despise and ridicule Romances, as the most contemptible of all kinds of writing, and yet expatiate in raptures … on stories far more wild and extravagant' when those stories are written by ancient poets (1: 21). However, championing this often ridiculed form of literature, Reeve has reservations concerning some types of romance. She is particularly alarmed by ones that utilise historical detail. 'In the days of Gothic ignorance', she writes, 'these Romances might, perhaps, be read by many persons as true Histories, and might therefore more easily affect their manners' (1: 57). In Reeve's view, such tales are potentially harmful to society. Romances should have a didactic purpose and possess a strong 'moral tendency' (1: 97).

Indulging in aesthetic excess, imaginative flights of fancy and resisting moral frameworks of understanding, it is not difficult to see how Walpole's *Otranto* conflicts with Reeve's religious beliefs and aesthetic values. Vague in its religious attitudes and morality, Reeve disapproved of Walpole's Gothic past; it is an example of a romance that can 'become an instrument to corrupt the manners and morals of mankind' (*OEB* 2). However, despite such reservations, Reeve did not entirely condemn Walpole's 'attempt to unite the various merits and graces of the ancient Romance and modern Novel' (*OEB* 3). It is the religious ambiguity and lack of a clear moral message that disturbs Reeve above all else. Her aim in *The Old English Baron* is to construct a past which still 'excite[s] the attention', but, in contrast to the reckless extravagance of *Otranto*, directs the Gothic to 'some useful, or at least innocent, end' (*OEB* 3). This would become a key aspect of future Loyalist Gothic works. Richardsonian in tone, the Gothic takes a turn towards didacticism in Reeve's hands.[10] In Reeve's view, all romances – including the Gothic – must have a strong social purpose and promote virtue and morality.

As this section has contended so far, Reeve's Loyalist Gothic novel can be read as a reaction to both *Otranto* and Rapin's *History of England*. Before I examine how her religious, didactic principles shape the past constructed in *The Old English Baron*, it is important to consider the moral implications of Rapin's *History of England*. As I discussed previously, throughout Rapin's work, religious history is neglected in favour of political analysis. For example, in his discussion of Henry VI's reign, Rapin cites the effects of the unscrupulous behaviour of certain individuals and political conflict for his downfall: 'After the death of the Duke of Bedford, Henry suffered himself to be guided by the Cardinal of Winchester and the Duke of Suffolk, who ... minding only their own affairs, completed his ruin' (*H* 5: 449). Possessed of 'uncommon abilities', Queen Margaret has the opportunity to 'put his affairs again in a flourishing condition' (*H* 5: 449). However, uninterested in the 'honour of the King, and welfare of the nation', her 'sole view was to engross all the power, and make use of the King's name to justify her passions', writes Rapin (*H* 5: 449). Indeed, human nature is often presented at its worst and most immoral in the *History of England*, particularly in Rapin's discussion of the political wrangling of Henry VI's government during his minority. Furthermore, as Rapin's quotation from earlier demonstrates, acts of usurpation in the historical domain often happen 'without any miracle interposing to punish the usurpers' (*H* 5: 472–3). Anticipating future Enlightenment works of history, Rapin's *History of England* destabilises the traditional role of history. History may still teach valuable lessons in statecraft, but, by focusing on political rather than religious issues, its role as a teacher of morality was cast into doubt. This has significant implications for *The Old English Baron*. Reeve's remarks in the preface can be read as a response to Rapin's work of historiography: 'History represents human nature as it is in real life; alas, too often a melancholy retrospect!' she laments (*OEB* 2). Contrasting with Walpole's use of Gothic romance to focus on the aspects of humankind that Enlightenment historiography represses, Reeve sees it as an opportunity to exhibit the more benevolent aspects of humanity: 'Romance displays only the amiable side of the picture, it shews the pleasing features, and throws a veil over the blemishes' (*OEB* 2). Utilising tropes such as the supernatural and divine intervention, *The Old English Baron* aims to direct the Gothic to 'good and useful purposes' (*OEB* 2) and to defy Rapin's proto-Enlightenment work of historiography by making the past a teacher of key Christian values such as humility, endurance, modesty, compassion, justice, forgiveness, and reverence. Bolstering English national identity at a troubled time, Reeve constructs a past that portrays England as a free and distinctive country; a nation which, strong in Christian faith, is able to keep alien and arbitrary rule at bay. Her use of the supernatural is telling here.

Concerned with the frequency of ghostly instances in *Otranto*, Reeve deliberately limits her use of the supernatural in *The Old English Baron*. Nevertheless, there are numerous paranormal instances in Reeve's fictional past and they are very significant in terms of understanding her Loyalist Gothic construction of history. A particularly notable example involves the Baron Fitz-Owen's kinsmen, Wenlock and Markham. After Edmund's mysterious disappearance from a ruinous room in an abandoned wing of the Castle Lovel, the Baron Fitz-Owen compels them to spend a night in the same apartment. Before examining this paranormal episode, it is important to note that, prior to this event, these two resent Edmund's virtue and the consequent praise and attention he receives from the Baron Fitz-Owen. Jealous of the preference Emma (the Baron Fitz-Owen's daughter) shows for Edmund, Wenlock spreads disparaging rumours about him and seeks to sully his character with the 'sin of ingratitude' (*OEB* 20). Wenlock is the chief offender. During their military exploits in France, he hatches a plan to have Edmund killed and, when this fails and Edmund is about to be awarded a knighthood for his valiant actions, he is sure to remind the Regent that such an honour 'cannot be conferred on a peasant' (*OEB* 25). He also attempts to lower Edmund in the Baron Fitz-Owen's estimation (*OEB* 27). As the action progresses, Wenlock's and Markham's relationship becomes increasingly fraught and reaches breaking point during their enforced stay in the haunted apartment. Shortly after entering the room, they both rise 'with the resolution to fight', but, just as they are about to do so, they hear 'a dismal groan from the room underneath' (*OEB* 68). Both men stand 'like statues petrified by fear, yet listening with trembling expectation' (*OEB* 68). A few moments later, all the doors 'flew open, a pale glimmering light appeared at the door from the staircase, and a man in compleat armour, entered the room' (*OEB* 68). The phantom points to the door and they crawl away 'as fast as fear would let them' (*OEB* 68). Having escaped, Wenlock is described as 'half dead' and Markham as 'half distracted' (*OEB* 69). In the past constructed in *The Old English Baron*, those who do not live good Christian lives are subject to the terror of the supernatural. Those who fail to live up to Christian values are punished.

This supernatural scene is in stark contrast to Edmund's first experience in the haunted apartment. During his first night in the chamber, Edmund hears a 'hollow rustling noise like that of a person coming through a narrow passage' (*OEB* 36). Similarly to his enemies, Wenlock and Markham, he is initially struck with 'fear'; 'all the concurrent circumstances of his situation struck upon his heart', writes Reeve, 'and gave him a new disagreeable sensation' (*OEB* 36). However, recollecting his virtuosity and Christian values, Edmund puts his faith in God: 'What should I fear? I have not wilfully offended God or man; why then should I doubt protection?' (*OEB* 36). In contrast to the malevolent actions of his enemies, Edmund does not react in terror; he gains courage by staying strong in his Christian faith and 'resigning himself wholly to the will of Heaven' (*OEB* 36). During the second night in the haunted apartment, Edmund, Joseph and Father Oswald descend to the lower rooms of the castle's abandoned wing. Edmund discovers his father's bloodstained armour and, shortly after surmising that the person that owned this armour lies buried under the floorboards, a 'dismal hollow groan was heard as if from underneath' (*OEB* 46). 'A solemn silence ensued, and marks of fear were visible upon all three; the groan was thrice heard', writes Reeve (*OEB* 46). However, following Oswald's example, all three kneel, praying for the direction of heaven and for the 'soul of the departed' (*OEB* 46). As a result, the groaning ceases, their fears subside and they are able to continue their endeavours to restore Edmund to his rightful place. In the medieval past depicted in *The Old English Baron*, those who lack virtue feel the fear and wrath of the supernatural whilst those who live virtuous Christian lives and remain constant in their beliefs do not.

Exploiting the imaginative potential of the Gothic and directing the supernatural for didactic ends, Reeve tightens the loose moral framework of Walpole's *Otranto*. Those that reject Christian values and are consumed by jealousy, hatred and revenge (such as Wenlock) are hindered by the supernatural whilst those who remain virtuous, even during times of immense hardship (such as Edmund), are aided by it. For example, whilst sleeping in the haunted apartment, Edmund is visited by his dead parents in a dream: a 'Warrior, leading a Lady by the hand' seemingly enters his apartment and declare that he is their child (*OEB* 38). This quasi-supernatural experience enables him to realise his true identity. When Edmund returns to

Lovel Castle as the rightful master, the 'great folding doors into the hall' are 'opened without any assistance' (*OEB* 115). When he enters the hall, 'every door in the house flew open' (*OEB* 115). Whilst the servants are terrified by such an occurrence, Oswald reassures everyone that this is an act of divine intervention and that the doors have opened of their own accord 'to receive their master' (*OEB* 115). As Ehlers notes, 'ghosts work to Edmund's providential advantage' in *The Old English Baron* (1978, 69). Revolting against Rapin's history, an act of usurpation *is* punished with providentially orchestrated ghosts and miracles 'interposing to punish' the usurpers (*H* 5: 473).

Utilising the imaginative and historical potential of the Gothic and placing its supernatural tropes into a strictly Protestant framework, Reeve combats the increasingly secular nature of eighteenth-century historiography by restoring history to one of its most traditional, pre-Enlightenment roles: as a teacher of Christian morality. In contrast to *Otranto*, *The Old English Baron* is very concerned with the morality of history and features a number of exemplary Christians. Throughout the novel, Harclay acts as a 'Christian soldier' (*OEB* 10), the Baron Fitz-Owen is predominantly noble in his actions, William is steadfast in his belief in providence, and Edmund is a model of Christian virtue. Furthermore, as Ehlers points out, Reeve allows her most virtuous characters the fullest and most sentimental development in *The Old English Baron* (1978, 72).[11] For example, Harclay and Edmund are often described as shedding 'tears of affection' (*OEB* 129) whilst her villains remain unrepentant; when offered a chance of salvation, Walter Lovel (the novel's villain) still attempts to escape (*OEB* 118), whilst Wenlock is described as a 'serpent' and is furious when he is exiled (*OEB* 83–4). Not only are responses to the supernatural an index of characters' Christian faith, but, as Ehlers notes, Reeve's 'appeal to sentiment coexists with the appeal to providence' (1978, 72). Indeed, in Reeve's fictional fifteenth-century past, Christian values such as humility, piety, endurance, thankfulness, compassion, forgiveness, and justice triumph over ignorance, fear and vice. By the novel's end, Christian grace and magnanimity have been bestowed on the undeserving sinner, Walter, who is exiled to a 'very distant part of the world' (*OEB* 119) rather than executed, and the virtuous, namely Edmund, Harclay and the Baron Fitz-Owen, are rewarded with long and happy lives. Defying Rapin's history and

Walpole's ambivalent, fictional past, Reeve utilises Gothic romance as a means of writing a past that is worthy of imitation. To use Reeve's words from elsewhere, her primary aim in *The Old English Baron* is to 'support the cause of morality, to reprove vice, and to promote all the social and domestic virtues' (1788, 1: xiii). Writing in a time of national crisis and responding to what she perceives as a corrupt political regime at home, Reeve writes a Loyalist Gothic past that provides a good model of Protestant, Christian behaviour and government.

Conflicted pasts: Rapin and Whig history

Now that I have discussed the religious aspects of Reeve's novel, I will focus on the politics of the past in *The Old English Baron*. Before doing so, it is requisite to examine Rapin's political orientations in the *History of England*. Whilst Rapin's history reveals strong, proto-Enlightenment historiographical methodologies, it is also a significant work of Whig historiography. As Okie remarks, with its anti-clerical emphasis, Whig history played a major role in the development of Enlightenment historiography (1991, 6). Having fought with William III in Ireland, Rapin was pensioned by the crown and served as tutor to the son of William's Dutch favourite, the Duke of Portland. Portland was a diplomat and ally of the Whigs and owned a vast collection of historical works. Rapin was heavily influenced by these histories and published his *Dissertation sur les Whigs et les Torys (An Historical Dissertation upon Whig and Tory)* in 1717; a political treatise based on his close observation of court politics in William's reign.[12] As Okie argues, although Rapin was 'able to step back from the party fray and deliver verdicts on previous historians with relative detachment', his *History of England* has a 'clear Whig slant' (57).[13] Indeed, Rapin's work is Whiggish in several of the ways outlined by Herbert Butterfield in *The Whig Interpretation of History* (1931). Conforming to Whig political principles, Rapin refutes Tory historians by advocating the power of Parliament rather than the king and stressing the rise of constitutional government, personal freedom and liberty. One of the main characteristics of Whig history is the identification of the past as a site of conflict. This is certainly the case with Rapin's *History of England*, where representatives of the modern and progressive are constantly fighting against archaic and reactionary forces.

Rapin's representation of the conflict between the Magna Carta barons and King John serves to illustrate this point. Taxed heavily by John, the barons 'saw him daily usurping an arbitrary power, which made them apprehensive of his having formed a design against their liberties' (*H* 3: 166). Fighting a tyrannical leader in an archaic context, Rapin identifies the barons as modernisers. Frustrated by John's injustice towards them, they form designs to curtail his power and 'bound themselves by oath, to exert their utmost endeavours to obtain the re-establishment of their ancient privileges, and mutually to stand by one another' (*H* 3: 211). The barons' political stance accords with Rapin's Whig politics and he heralds their cause: '[t]his is the first league or confederacy which was ever made in England against the King, in defence of the liberties of the nation' (*H* 3: 211). 'This charter', lauds Rapin, 'contained in substance the liberties which the people of England enjoyed during the dominion of the Saxon Kings' (*H* 3: 217). Treasuring the constitutional monarchy in the present, Rapin heaps praise on the barons' refusal to 'submit to an absolute power' (*H* 3: 166) and heralds the Magna Carta (he even attaches a copy of it to the end of volume 3). Despite John's (and a number of his successors') attempts to get them annulled, from 'that time forward these two charters have been the basis and foundation of the English Liberties', argues Rapin (*H* 3: 224). To adapt Butterfield's words, Rapin reads the past through the present and 'seizes upon those personages and parties in the past whose ideas seem more analogous' to his own (1951, 29). The historical personages that Rapin admires are ones whom he perceives to have furthered progress by spreading liberty and ensuring the survival of ancient freedoms. Indeed, Rapin speaks approvingly of the Magna Carta barons because these figures from the past are seen to hold present political values. The same applies to certain historical personages in the early reign of Henry VI. Seeking to maintain order and political stability, Rapin praises the Dukes of Bedford and Gloucester for their 'valour, experience, and wisdom' (*H* 5: 208).

In Butterfield's words, the fervour of Rapin's work of Whig historiography comes from 'what is really the transference into the past of an enthusiasm for something in the present, an enthusiasm for democracy or freedom of thought or the liberal tradition' (1951, 96). The corollary of this is to identify and stigmatise aspects of the past that do not accord with political ideals held in the present. As Butterfield argues, by writing the past through immediate reference to the present, historical figures become classified into two groups: those personages who 'furthered progress' and those who 'tried to hinder it' (11). The Magna Carta barons belong to the former category; Rapin places King John, the enemy of these men, in the latter group. Extorting money, raising taxes, confiscating properties, and violating ancient freedoms in order to fund wars in France, Rapin argues that it cannot 'be denied but that during this time, his subjects had a mortal hatred against him' (*H* 3: 242). We learn that John keeps the barons in a 'wretched state' (*H* 3: 222), seizing their lands and 'ravaging the kingdom' (*H* 3: 230). 'Instead of regaining their privileges', writes Rapin, they 'beheld their estates plundered and given to foreigners whilst the king was glutting himself with the pleasure of revenge' (*H* 3: 230). Crafting a distinctly Whig historical narrative, John is the force of anachronism in Rapin's history of this period; ruling absolute, he views himself as above the law and threatens to drag the barons – agents of liberty and progression – back into the unenlightened, tyrannous past. Although Rapin treats previous histories sceptically and acknowledges that John has been 'drawn' in 'blacker colours than he deserved' (*H* 3: 240), he argues that John had 'scarce any one valuable qualification' (*H* 3: 250) and 'had great faults' (*H* 3: 240). Although John does sign the Magna Carta, we learn that he only does so because he 'had no other course to take' (*H* 3: 222) and 'made as if he willingly granted what in reality was extorted by force' (*H* 3: 223). It is the valiant endeavours of the barons that force the King to respect their historic rights and privileges, making him subject, rather than superior, to the law. Almost immediately after signing the document, John is 'eager to find out the means to disentangle himself from a yoke which seemed intolerable' and he and the barons are soon afterwards at war (*H* 3: 225). Conforming to Whig notions of history, John is presented in a negative light largely because his reign is unconstitutional, repressing freedom and liberal thought in England. The same applies to Rapin's treatment of certain historical personages during the reign of Henry VI. Henry's wife, Margaret, is castigated for acting in violation of the constitution and not helping to save her husband and not caring about the 'welfare of the nation' (*H* 5: 449). Indeed, Rapin writes a past that endorses the Whig values he cherishes in the present.

Historical perils: Whig history, Reeve and the Gothic

In the same letter in which Reeve reveals that she has read Rapin's *History of England*, she speaks of her father's political orientations: 'My father was an Old Whig; from him I have learned all that I know; he was my oracle', she writes (Reeve 1829). It is no coincidence that Reeve's father urged her to read Rapin's *History of England*, a work which Caroline Robbins describes as 'Whig republican in tone' (2004, 268). Reeve's political persuasions are very similar to Rapin's. She also reveals that her father used to make her read 'Parliamentary debates' (Reeve 1829). 'I gaped and yawned over them at the time', writes Reeve, 'but, unawares to myself, they fixed my principles once and forever' (Reeve 1829). In political terms, Reeve was an Old Whig. In the sense that Reeve employs it, the term 'Old Whig' denotes those Whigs who became disillusioned with Sir Robert Walpole – Horace Walpole's father and British Prime Minister between 1721 and 1742 – and the means he took to maintain political power. Reeve's political persuasions have significant implications for the past she constructs in *The Old English Baron*. In contrast to the aristocrat, Walpole, Reeve came from an educated middle-class background, her father being a curate in Ipswich. Indeed, all of Reeve's works have strong political persuasions.[14] As Kelly notes, in *The Old English Baron*, Reeve 'aimed to displace Walpole's work and its aristocratic and elitist Whig ideology with the more bourgeois-democratic politics she promoted in all her fiction' (2002, 1: xxxii). The political intent of Walpole's *Otranto* is ambiguous; by the end of the novel, the social order, symbolised by the castle, is destroyed. Furthermore, Walpole merely recognises the legitimacy of the novel's hero, Theodore. In contrast to this, Reeve gives the Gothic a firm Old Whig political stance. At a time when the nation was collectively assessing its own political makeup in the wake of rapid colonial expansion and the American Revolution, Reeve – similarly to Rapin – constructs a past that privileges the political values she holds in the present.

The relationship between Whig history and the Gothic has long been recognised.[15] However, because *The Old English Baron* does not stage a conflict between a progressive Protestantism and a regressive Catholicism, many critics have neglected to examine the impact of such historiography on Reeve's fiction. This is quite surprising considering her overt Whig political beliefs. Indeed, *The*

Old English Baron is governed by Whig codes of historical representation. However, in contrast to Rapin, who constructs a progressive narrative and identifies his political counterparts in real historical figures who have furthered progress, Reeve creates 'an imaginary past of domestic [and] ancestral conflict' (Mighall 1999, 10). Utilising the Gothic's focus on dysfunctional families and using the home as a means of commenting on the state, Reeve depicts the heroes and villains of the domestic realm. Similarly to Rapin's *History of England*, she locates the past as a site of conflict in *The Old English Baron*. From the outset of the novel, Edmund – who is still thought to be the son of a labourer – is marked out by his extraordinary 'merit', 'good qualities', and 'extraordinary genius and disposition' (*OEB* 14). Even though he possesses 'that inward consciousness that always attends superior qualities', he constantly reminds himself of his 'low birth and dependant station' and controls 'the flames of ambition' (*OEB* 21). As Kelly notes, such meritocratic characteristics accord more with late eighteenth-century professional middle-class values than aristocratic qualities of the fifteenth century (2002, 1: lxxvii). Edmund is a model of modesty and virtue and his conduct is exemplary. Indeed, Edmund demonstrates the admirable middle-class virtues of self-reliance and independence: 'words are all my inheritance', he declares (*OEB* 21), before arguing that he had 'nothing but my character to depend upon' (*OEB* 30). Embodying a fusion of Old Whig and bourgeois values treasured by Reeve in the present and conforming to patterns of Whig history, Edmund is identified as the key progressive protagonist in *The Old English Baron*. It is the villainous Walter Lovel who opposes Edmund and functions as the enemy of liberty.

Reminiscent of Manfred in *Otranto*, Walter is a wicked aristocrat and is the root cause of evil in Reeve's fictional fifteenth-century past. Akin to all the Gothic pasts discussed in this book, a macabre history is unearthed in *The Old English Baron*. Many years previously to the novel's action, Walter commissions the murder of Arthur Lovel, his brother and Edmund's father. This is the 'deed of darkness' that is 'brought to light' in the novel (*OEB* 115). Walter's motivation for having Edmund's father murdered is particularly illuminating. 'My kinsman excelled me in every kind of merit, in the graces of person and mind, in all his exercises, and in every accomplishment', Walter recounts bitterly (*OEB* 91). 'I was totally eclipsed by him, and I hated to be in his company', he adds (*OEB*

91). Overcome with 'bitter hatred' and 'revenge', he exults in the 'prospect of possessing' his brother's 'title, fortune, and his Lady' (*OEB* 92). Earlier in the narrative, Arthur is described as a 'gentleman of eminent virtues and accomplishments' (*OEB* 5). Walter is the antithesis of Edmund (and his father); conforming to Gothic stereotypes of hero and villain he is profoundly corrupt, hateful, revengeful, unrepentant, and plays a large part in the death of Edmund's mother, as his advances towards her compel her to escape from his clutches. Whilst doing so, she slips and falls to her death and, in an attempt to cover up her disappearance, he conducts a 'fictitious funeral' (*OEB* 91). Indeed, Walter shows no remorse for the deaths of either of Edmund's parents. He denies the charges levelled at him by Harclay and tries to escape when he has been made a generous offer to answer to his crimes. Harclay variously calls him a 'treacherous kinsman', an 'assassin of his nearest relation' and an 'inhuman monster' (*OEB* 78). Walter is a symbol of the corrupt and elitist aristocracy that Reeve perceives as so harmful to her own eighteenth-century social order and the nation's future and she uses the past as a means to comment on the present and subvert Walpole's Whig elitism.

Similarly to Rapin's Whiggish historical work, Reeve maps the present onto the past and places a modern representative in an archaic context. Edmund, the progressive force and hero of liberty in the novel, is pitched against Walter; an enemy of freedom and symbol of the old, elite, corrupt aristocracy. Reeve fuses Whig representational strategies with Gothic conventions in order to present a vision of an aristocracy that is not based on greed or corruption, but one that has assimilated the values of the increasingly mobile eighteenth-century professional middle classes. These include principles of inward merit, moral and intellectual integrity, self-discipline, social responsibility, and philanthropy. Subverting Walpole's *Otranto*, Reeve focuses not solely on the hero's lawful *right* to rule the Castle Lovel, but the extent to which he *deserves* such a station. Edmund is fighting against the past and for freedom in the future. Walter – a symbol of the corrupt, old aristocracy – is a symbol of the past and all its evils. Indeed, Walter threatens to drag Edmund – and all the other virtuous characters in the novel – back into the corrupt, violent and unenlightened past. What is particularly striking about the representation of Walter is not only his profound corruption, but the violent means by which he usurps Edmund's inheritance. Walter relates how his men 'killed' Edmund's father and 'drew him aside out of the highway', before recounting how he then sent them back 'to fetch the dead body, which they brought privately into the castle' (*OEB* 92). The gruesome details do not stop here. 'They tied it neck and heels, and put it into a trunk', he adds, 'which they buried under the floor in the closet' in the abandoned wing of the castle (*OEB* 92). For a Loyalist Gothic novel that does not intend to dwell on violence or gruesome acts, this is quite a surprising level of detail. Constructing a past that assimilates Whig codes of historical representation, Reeve uses Gothic tropes – such as scenes of violence, the unearthing of horrible histories and the focus on inherently evil villains – to emphasise the gulf between the progressive forces of history and the regressive and anachronistic forces that threaten them.

Old Whig reform: class and female persecution

Written at a time of national anxiety and focusing on the evil deeds of Walter (the Gothic villain), *The Old English Baron* encapsulates the worst fears of Old Whigs by depicting the survival of corrupt, barbaric, anachronistic customs and attitudes in the Enlightened present. The corrupt and elitist aristocracy which threatens Edmund in the fifteenth century still persists in Reeve's own age and threatens national stability at a particularly precarious moment. Throughout *The Old English Baron*, the past and the present are intertwined. However, even though Reeve's medieval past is a site of conflict and is pervaded by eighteenth-century middle-class notions of virtue and merit, the novel still endorses a hierarchic social class system. In a later work of historical fiction, Reeve writes that 'the best government and most likely to be permanent' is one that 'makes different ranks and degrees of men necessary to each other, and leads them to co-operate together in order to promote the good of the whole' (1793, 1: xvii–xviii). Citing the example of Rome and its 'gradation of ranks during her republican state', Reeve argues that a 'form of government founded upon levelling principles, never did, nor ever can continue' (1793, 1: xviii). Utilising the Gothic theme of female persecution, Reeve's fifteenth-century past depicts the horror of deviation from a hierarchical class structure and ends with the reinstatement of hierarchy in Edmund's rule as Baron.

By murdering Arthur, Walter disrupts the existing class system and sets in motion a series of disastrous events which have a particularly devastating impact on the lives of the novel's female characters. Compelled to escape as a result of Walter's ambition to marry her, Lady Lovel meets a tragic end: on her way to find help during a dark night, her 'foot slipped, and she fell into the river and was drowned' (*OEB* 51). Her body is discovered 'floating upon the water' under a foot bridge (*OEB* 51). Walter tells everyone that she died of madness and, as mentioned previously, conducts a fictional funeral for her (*OEB* 29). It is only with the discovery of Walter's involvement in Arthur's death that this additional 'deed of darkness' is unearthed (*OEB* 115). Edmund is born shortly before his mother's tragic death and is adopted by a surrogate family. Bitter that the socially displaced Edmund is draining his family resources and is not naturally disposed for manual labour, Andrew (Edmund's surrogate father) takes out his frustrations on his wife, Margery. We learn that, after Edmund has been taken into the Baron Fitz-Owen's service, Margery's attempts to speak to her adopted son are foiled by her husband, Andrew, who physically abuses her: 'Andrew beat me the last time I spoke to Edmund; and told me he would break every bone in my skin if ever I spoke to him again' (*OEB* 50). When the rigid class structure is compromised, the worst of human nature is in evidence and it is women who generally suffer.

As an Old Whig with increasingly bourgeois values, Reeve is not totally averse to the aristocracy. Edmund is, after all, revealed to have been an aristocrat all along. Rather, Reeve calls for a more responsible aristocracy and, as Watt argues, she 'presents an aristocracy which is redeemable *because* it is possessed of merit' and 'uphold[s] a rigid and hierarchical, if harmonious, system of class relations' (1999, 48). There are numerous examples of agreeable, yet distinct, class relations in *The Old English Baron*; whether it is the assistance the peasant John Wyatt gives Harclay (*OEB* 8–10), the servants' delight for their true master's return to the Castle Lovel (*OEB* 115) or Harclay's care home for aging soldiers (*OEB* 130). As Sue Chaplin astutely points out, even though the novel posits meritocracy as the key to domestic and political order, 'social class nevertheless reasserts itself as a highly significant organising principle and is clearly shown ultimately to retain a link with "worth" which undermines earlier intimations of the existence of a universal moral sense' (2007, 48). To use Abby Coykendall's words, Reeve depicts the 'miraculous rise of meritorious virtue, while all the time insisting that such virtues arise in only the most ancient or most aristocratic families' (2005, 470). Moreover, when Edmund is restored to Lovel Castle and the hierarchic class structure is reasserted, the lives of the female protagonists improve. At the end of the novel, Andrew is repentant and Margery can visit her adopted son again (*OEB* 132). After Edmund's noble birth is confirmed, Emma (the Baron Fitz-Owen's daughter) no longer has to contemplate marrying a man she does not love. Along with his father, Lady Lovel (Edmund's mother) is also afforded a proper burial (*OEB* 127). Allied with an increasingly democratised aristocracy is a benevolent patriarchy; women do not suffer when the status quo is restored. However, even though Walter ultimately fails to drag Edmund and the female protagonists back into the barbarous past, the crimes he commits remain concealed for decades and, without help from noble friends such as Harclay, they come close to remaining in suffering and obscurity. The aristocratic, elitist Whig greed and corruption of Walter comes close to destroying the progressive, liberating social order that is established at the end of *The Old English Baron* and is the real element of danger in this Gothic novel. Utilising Whig models of historiography, Reeve writes a fictional past to show not only what has been gained in the present, but what can so easily be lost. Such a message has an even greater resonance in the context of Britain's recent defeat in America.

Historical nightmares: Rapin and the 'Gothic' constitution

As my previous discussion of Rapin's representation of the Magna Carta barons highlights, a significant aspect of his history – and a major facet of Whig historiography – is an emphasis on ancient freedoms and the English constitution. In his *Dissertation*, Rapin contends that England has had a 'mixt government', with power shared between the King and Parliament, since the Anglo-Saxon conquest (1717, 2). This system continued until the seventeenth century, when James I attempted to roll back the power of Parliament. These political ideas reverberate in the *History of England*. Rapin may resist the traditional Whig view of Parliamentary powers by highlighting the late origins of the House of Commons, but, as Okie argues, he was really an ancient constitutionalist; his 'entire work rests upon the proposition that English liberty could be traced back to the Saxon constitution' (1991, 57). In the *History of England*, Rapin argues that the English constitution and English freedoms are at least as old as the Saxon constitution: 'The maxim, that no laws are binding but what the whole nation has consented to, has all along been looked upon in England, as the foundation of liberty, and the basis of government' (*H* 2: 176). It is the preservation of these ancient liberties that the Magna Carta barons fight so hard to preserve against the tyrannical rule of John. For Rapin, the unwritten English constitution embodies unique, ancient English freedoms; liberties that need to be adhered to in all historical ages. According with many eighteenth-century debates on the subject, Rapin's history conveys the notion of a 'Gothic', ancient constitution and perceives England as an inherently free nation. As an ancient constitutionalist, Rapin sees a unity and continuity behind the vicissitudes of history and the differences of constitutional forms.[16] In highlighting the vulnerabilities and dangers to the constitution in diverse historical periods, Rapin 'makes no distinction between the fifteenth, sixteenth and eighteenth centuries' (Forbes 1985, 240). Indeed, throughout the *History of England*, Rapin glorifies English polity and betrays fears surrounding the survival of the constitution and Gothic (ancient) freedoms. Rapin's worst fear is the ever present threat of constitutional degeneration, as his following general remarks on Kings of England demonstrate:

> The pride therefore and insatiable avarice of favourites and ministers are the only things that make him lose sometimes the advantages he may naturally draw from the constitution of the government. These men, impatient of seeing any bounds set to their unlawful ambition of governing with an absolute sway, seek all possible means to instill into their master a desire to set himself above the laws, and to become like other princes. That is, they do all that lies in their power to change the King's true and solid happiness into real misery. For supposing a King of England should render himself absolute, he would never be able by oppression and violence to get from his people what he may draw from them with their consent, by submitting to the laws and constitution of the government. We have seen in the two late reigns of William III, and Queen Ann, and we daily see in that of the Prince now on the throne, such undeniable proofs of what I am saying, that I think it needless to add any thing farther.
>
> (*H* 10: 230)

In the *History of England*, Rapin emphasises the perennial danger that the English constitution will be subverted by factionalism. The

Whig historical narrative of liberty versus faction pervades every page and every historical period of Rapin's history. Throughout his account, he highlights the frighteningly precarious nature of the constitution; comparable to a Gothic heroine, it is terrifyingly vulnerable and needs protecting by the friends of liberty and the enemies of faction. As my earlier discussion of the Magna Carta barons revealed, justice needs to be vigorously defended and corrupt leaders (such as John) brought to account. The pride and avarice of courtiers continually threatens to divert reigning monarchs away from the liberating tenets of the treasured English constitution. Court influence threatens the corruption of Parliament, which has the potential to result in Rapin's worst nightmare: the dissolution of Gothic (ancient and time-honoured) freedoms.

The Old English Baron **and fears of constitutional degeneration**

Heightened by the traumatic cultural context of the American Revolution, the long-held Whig anxieties that manifest themselves in Rapin's *History of England* assumed a new resonance in the 1770s. The fears surrounding the constitution in Rapin's historiography manifest themselves in Reeve's Loyalist Gothic novel. Rapin's history demonstrates that the perpetuation of the ancient, Gothic constitution is central to Whig historical and political beliefs. As an Old Whig, Reeve believed in the Gothic, ancient origins of the constitution and perceived its survival as paramount to England's (and Britain's) future. H. T. Dickinson points out that, to Old Whigs and classical republicans such as Reeve and her father, the 'constitution could only be safeguarded by men of property who cherished their independence and were prepared to put the public good before private gain' (1977, 103). As Rapin's *History of England* attests, this constitution 'could be tracked back to a Gothic and Anglo-Saxon past', but it had been – and continued to be – threatened by a combination of increased royal power and patronage, large monied interests and the growth of corruption as a means used to maintain the power of the crown and associated privileged interests (Dickinson 1977, 104). With the American Colonies highlighting problems with the nature of Britain's constitutional monarchy and trying to drive a wedge between the monarchy and Parliament, the values of the constitution seemed more vulnerable than ever.[17]

Old Whig fears of constitutional degeneration haunt the pages of *The Old English Baron*. Reeve exploits the Gothic's focus on

dysfunctional families as a vehicle to examine the wider threats facing Britain's prosperity at a difficult historical moment. The Baron
Fitz-Owen's household is particularly significant. At the beginning
of the novel, the Baron Fitz-Owen is ruler of Castle Lovel and, unin-
fluenced by his charges (Wenlock, Markham and Robert), rules as
he sees fit. Recognising the innate nobility of Edmund, the Baron
Fitz-Owen takes him into his care and, for a time, the newly created
'family' all live peacefully under the same roof. The Baron Fitz-Owen
enjoys 'the true happiness of a parent' (*OEB* 14), whilst Edmund
is awed by the Baron's goodness towards him and his 'uncommon
bounty' (*OEB* 16). However, as Harclay predicts, Edward's 'good
qualities' begin to 'excite envy and create him enemies' (*OEB* 19).
Indeed, the 'sons and kinsmen' begin to 'find fault with him, and
to depreciate him with others' (*OEB* 19). As I suggested earlier,
Markham and Wenlock are particularly averse to Edmund's 'fine
qualities' (*OEB* 19). They manage to excite a 'dislike in Master
Robert', which, in 'time was fixed into habit, and fell little short
of aversion' (*OEB* 19). More significantly, however, they strive to
'lessen him in the esteem of the Baron and his family' (*OEB* 19).
With Wenlock and Markham having 'insinuated a thousand things
against' Edmund, the Baron Fitz-Owen 'perceived that his kinsmen
disliked Edmund' (*OEB* 27). However, we learn that 'his own good
heart hindered him from seeing the baseness of theirs' (*OEB* 27).
'It is said', writes Reeve, 'that continual dropping will wear away a
stone; so did their incessant reports, by insensible degrees, produce
a coolness in his patron's behaviour towards him' (*OEB* 27).

The Old English Baron resonates with the Whig fears manifest
in Rapin's *History of England*; namely, the corruption of leaders (or
monarchs) by insidious court cultures and anxieties surrounding
the perversion of the English constitution. Comparable to the figure
of a reigning monarch, the Baron Fitz-Owen is manipulated by his
charges, who can be read as ambitious and deceitful courtiers. To
use Rapin's words, the 'pride' and 'insatiable avarice of favourites'
make the Baron Fitz-Owen lose the 'advantages he may naturally
draw from the constitution of government' (*H* 10: 230). Indeed,
in *The Old English Baron*, Rapin's Whig historical nightmares are
very nearly realised. We learn that if Edmund 'behaved with manly
spirit, it was misconstrued into pride and arrogance; his generosity
was imprudence; his humility was hypocrisy, the better to cover
his ambition' (*OEB* 27). Alienated in the Baron Fitz-Owen's favour

by jealous enemies, Edmund is compelled to flee the Castle Lovel; in order to regain his credibility, he has to prove his own ancestry and show the Baron Fitz-Owen how he has been misled by his jealous, scheming charges. Ambition and greed threaten to overturn the spirit of liberty that has governed Lovel Castle for so many years. The founding tenets of the English constitution – liberty and the rule of law – become warped and corrupt. Edmund comes perilously close to spending his life wronged and in total obscurity. In perhaps the most striking parallel with Rapin's history, the Baron Fitz-Owen highlights the very real threat of constitutional degeneration and the frightening vulnerability of its liberating tenets: 'It is no wonder that princes should be so frequently deceived, when I, a private man, could be so much imposed upon within the circle of my own family' (*OEB* 84). Using the Baron Fitz-Owen's 'family' as a means of commenting on the state of Britain towards the end of the eighteenth century, Reeve (similarly to Rapin) highlights the fragility of law and order.

Justice is a particularly prominent feature of the past constructed in *The Old English Baron*. Writing in a period where the colonised (the Thirteen Colonies) had recently revolted against the colonisers (Britain), contemporary fears surrounding law and order manifest themselves throughout Reeve's fictional fifteenth-century past. Since its inception, the Gothic has been fixated with the law and transgressions of established social customs. Focusing on the machinations of Manfred and the usurpation of Theodore's estate, Walpole's *Otranto* raises issues concerning government and succession. Reeve exploits the Gothic's focus on the law and, by doing so, the past she writes in *The Old English Baron* refracts contemporary concerns surrounding the survival of Gothic (time-honoured) English liberties. This brings me back to the Baron Fitz-Owen's manipulation by his charges and his unfair (and unconstitutional) treatment of Edmund during this time. Blind to the schemes of Wenlock and Markham, the Baron Fitz-Owen judges Edmund and changes his behaviour towards him. He accuses him of speaking ill of him and sentences him to spend a night in an abandoned wing of the castle (*OEB* 33). Indeed, in *The Old English Baron*, one of the most cherished maxims of the English constitution – the presumption that a person is considered innocent until proven guilty – is very nearly subverted. As Robert Miles points out, since its genesis, the Gothic has functioned as a form that draws attention to the 'law's fragility' (2001, 62).

This is certainly the case in Reeve's Loyalist Gothic novel where the law – and, by implication, the English constitution – is constantly tested and under threat. Having lost the duel with Harclay and confessed to usurping Edmund's fortune, Walter is given the very generous offer of either retiring 'into a religious house' or else quitting 'the kingdom in three months time' (*OEB* 107). He is also offered a 'decent annuity, that he may not want the comforts of life' (*OEB* 107). Throughout this entire episode, there is a strong emphasis on legal proceedings; Lord Clifford is appointed 'arbitrator' for Edmund's claim and keeps records of events as they unfold (*OEB* 80). Despite such rigorous legal proceedings, Walter comes very close to transgressing the law and affecting an escape (*OEB* 118). Without the watchful eye of Zadisky (a servant loyal to Sir Philip Harclay), Walter may well have defied the law and left Edmund in obscurity. The rightful line of succession for the governance of Lovel Castle comes frighteningly close to being subverted forever. In line with Whig historical divisions, those who uphold the law and, thus, promote the most cherished values of the constitution, are celebrated whilst those who transgress it are villainised.

Shaped by the Whig mode of historical writing, a founding, progressive element of the English constitution and a social mechanism treasured in the present – the law – is a subject of intense scrutiny in the fifteenth-century past of Reeve's Gothic novel. There is a particular emphasis on juridical proceedings. Throughout the episode where Walter admits to murdering Edmund's brother, Lord Clifford and Lord Graham – the appointed 'Commissioners' for the case – make sure that they are 'entirely satisfied with the justice of Edmund's pretensions' and keep 'an account in writing of all that they had been eye-witness to' (*OEB* 121). Despite Walter's testimony and, indeed, his own, Edmund is still compelled to present evidence of his true ancestry: 'I can see nothing to make us doubt the truth of it: But let us examine the proofs. Edmund gave into their hands the necklace and ear-rings' (*OEB* 106). Once Walter's escape has been foiled and Edmund's ancestry is finally confirmed, attention quickly switches to financial settlements: 'Who is to pay the arrears of my ward's estate, which he had unjustly been kept out of these one and twenty years?', questions Harclay (*OEB* 108). For all the emphasis on a 'democratising sensibility' (Chaplin 2007, 78) in this Gothic novel, strict legal procedures and customs ultimately settle disputes concerning property and ancestry. As Chaplin points out, law enforcement and 'financial settlements remain central to the restoration of social, legal and moral norms at the end of the text' (2007, 78). Echoing Whig historical writing, the past and present become difficult to demarcate; the lengthy legal and financial dispute that takes place in the fifteenth century is more reminiscent of contemporary, eighteenth-century procedures. With notions of English (and British) national identity shaken by recent events at home and abroad, Reeve's fictional past reveals not only anxieties concerning the force of the law and its perpetuation, but the importance of judicial processes to the nation's stability. In order to maintain the law and fend off threats of constitutional degeneration, ancient Gothic customs do not only need to be practised in times of crisis; they need to be vigorously defended.

'Gothic times and manners': Reeve, Rapin and military history

This brings me back to Rapin's *History of England*. Even though he was a professional soldier by trade, Rapin's historical work is uninterested in martial conflicts. Anticipating Hume's Enlightenment aversion to violence in history, Rapin argues that the historian should only record 'the causes and grounds ... the interests, motives and artifices of the parties' involved in battles rather than focusing on 'warlike exploits' (*H* 12: 55). Speaking of sieges during the reign of Henry VI, he argues that to relate the particulars of such violent events would lead one into a 'thousand circumstances which few people would think worth notice'; the best method, continues Rapin, is to 'only mark in two words the beginnings and issues' of such conflicts (*H* 5: 227). *The Old English Baron* can be read as an imaginative response to the suppression of fighting and heroic martial deeds in Rapin's history. However, in comparison to Walpole, Reeve exploits the Gothic's concern with violence and conflict for very different ends. Focusing on Gothic savageness and backwardness, Walpole's *Otranto* exhibits numerous violent events and conflicts as a means of revolting against the suppression of such occurrences in Hume's historiography. Exploiting the term 'Gothic' to denote old-fashioned and ancient values, Reeve takes the Gothic's preoccupation with conflict and violence and uses it to bolster Britain's glorious, military past at a time when the country's martial might and time-honoured liberties were severely challenged.

In the introduction to *The Old English Baron*, Reeve speaks of her novel as 'being a picture of Gothic times and manners' (*OEB* 2). Indeed, she constructs a medieval past that stages the hostile defence of ancient, Gothic freedoms and where martial endeavours and chivalry feature prominently. Perhaps the most notable example of this is Harclay's duel with Walter. The duel conforms to very strict social customs: Lord Clifford and Lord Graham are installed as judges of the field, Harclay declares the 'cause of his quarrel', Walter is required to answer the charges levelled against him, both combatants are presented with their weapons, and are then allowed to fight (*OEB* 86–7). Sweating with the 'violence of the exercise', Harclay sets out to 'wound but not kill Walter' (*OEB* 88). He thrusts his 'sword through his left arm' and then 'passed the sword through his body twice' (*OEB* 88). With Walter 'slain', Harclay removes the villain's weapon and demands an 'honest confession' (*OEB* 88). After some resistance, Walter obliges, thus ensuring the restoration of Edmund as master of the Castle Lovel. Walpole's Gothic novel focuses on superstition and Catholicism; Reeve's Loyalist Gothic work cultivates Protestant images of glory, heroism and chivalry. As Richard Hurd argues in his influential *Letters on Chivalry and Romance* (1762), chivalry is a 'military institution' (7); 'PROWESS, GENEROSITY, GALLANTRY, and RELIGION', he argues, are the 'peculiar and vaunted characteristics of the purer ages of chivalry' (14). Harclay's chivalric actions serve to reaffirm the importance of custom, hierarchy and rank. The historical accuracy of the duel is of little importance to Reeve. Conforming to Maurice Keen's theory of chivalry, she holds up an idealised historical image of armed conflict in defiance of the harsh realities of actual warfare (1984, 237). Individual heroism comes over strongly with sword fighting, as combat is at close quarters. In an age where political corruption is rife and the nation's future uncertain, Reeve looks back to a purer (albeit fictional) past in order to rouse patriotism in the troubled present.

In *The Old English Baron*, threats of constitutional degeneration are dispelled by a forceful adherence to time honoured social customs and a commitment to law enforcement. By the end of the novel, Walter is brought to justice, Edmund (deservedly) regains his estate and all the main protagonists (including Harclay and the Baron Fitz-Owen) go on to live long and happy lives. Throughout Reeve's Gothic novel, Harclay is an exemplary patriot; he always acts in the interest of the constitution, upholds its values and enforces justice. Communicating more to Reeve's own generation than the medieval past of which she writes, Harclay is a champion of virtue; he is a model of how to act in times of national and constitutional crisis. 'When we read of our glorious ancestors', writes Reeve in *Memoirs of Sir Roger de Clarendon*, 'their actions ought to stimulate us to equal them, to support and maintain the honour of our country: to be ashamed to degenerate from our forefathers, to sit down in indolence and effeminacy, and bring reproach upon them' (Reeve 1793, xii). In Harclay, Reeve presents a defender of the realm and a figure worthy of imitation in the present; remembrance of him is designed to encourage future generations to 'emulate his virtues' and 'be ashamed to degenerate from their ancestor' (*OEB* 135).[18] Against the threat of hostile enemies, Harclay forcefully defends the innocent and fights for liberty. Influenced by Whig history, Reeve presents a fifteenth-century past where treasured English freedoms are constantly under threat but are ultimately defended and perpetuated. Reeve cultivates a cohesive sense of English (and British) national identity by exhibiting ancestral heroes and the purity of the Gothic, Saxon democratic tradition.

The historical setting of Reeve's novel is telling in this respect. Indeed, she chooses to set *The Old English Baron* in 'the minority of Henry the Sixth, King of England, when the renowned John Duke of Bedford was a Regent of France, and Humphrey the good Duke of Gloucester was Protector of England' (*OEB* 5). Published after *Otranto* and bearing the words, 'A Gothic Story' (*OEB* 5), on its title page, this would not seem the most obvious place to set a suspenseful novel. As I discussed in the previous chapter, Walpole constructs a strange, vague and medieval history in order to reveal the unfamiliarity of the past and to heighten superstitious fears. Although Reeve is not overly concerned with historical accuracy and her novel is more fiction than fact, she opts for quite a precise historical period where real historical figures are in evidence, albeit marginally.[19] Rapin's *History of England* is useful for understanding Reeve's choice of historical setting. Indeed, she sets her novel at a very specific historical moment; after the hugely successful reign of Henry V and in the very early reign of Henry VI, when Humphrey the Duke of Gloucester was protector of the realm between 1422 and 1437. Rapin's history is particularly notable for its focus on England's colonial relationship with France. As Rapin's

history records, this was a turbulent time, but a generally successful one (*H* 5: 207–16). Due to aggressive foreign policy, England
secured a 'long-awaited hiatus in the civil wars as well as an absolute sovereignty over a sizeable portion of France' (Coykendall
2005, 452). Indeed, the action of *The Old English Baron* is set on
something of a historical cusp; it is set in a time of martial success, in the afterglow of Henry V's valorous deeds and just before
the disastrous rule of Henry VI (he takes to the throne in 1437).
Proliferating with instances of usurpation, treachery, scheming,
manipulation, ancestral conflicts, and domestic tensions, Rapin's
history highlights how Henry's later reign becomes a series of disastrous events and instances of poor government, with the monarchy
becoming increasingly unpopular due to a breakdown of law and
order, corruption, court favouritism, and the steady loss of territories to France (*H* 5: 449–50). Rapin argues that Henry comes to
be 'looked upon only as the shadow of a king' and as 'incapable of
retrieving the honour of the nation, and restoring the affairs of the
kingdom to a flourishing state' (*H* 5: 409).

In *The Old English Baron*, Reeve's fifteenth-century past functions as an analogue for her own age. Offering a historical parallel to the glorious, expansionist reign of Henry V before the later
disastrous, contracting rule of Henry VI, Britain had recently
defeated France in the Seven Years War (1756–63) and consolidated an American empire. However, echoing the loss of territories in Henry VI's reign, Britain seemed about to lose all this
in a 'widely unpopular war, imposed by royal will, against the
American colonies, which were allied to the old enemy, France'
(Kelly 2002, 1: lxviii). Political division at home, doubts about the
effectiveness of a constitutional monarchy and concerns about the
growth of royal power raised doubts about the progress of civil
society and Britain's future as a world power. As Toni Wein writes,
in *The Old English Baron*, the reader is 'invited into a space that is
simultaneously the distant past and the immediate present' (2002,
7). At the time in which Reeve is writing, Britain seems alarmingly
close to following the nationally destructive times of Henry VI's
reign, where division and unconstitutional behaviour have a cor-
rosive effect on the nation's prosperity and expansion. Countering
the suppression of martial conflict in Rapin's *History of England*,
Reeve adapts the Gothic for a patriotic agenda, reaffirming Gothic,
ancient values and rousing memories of England's glorious military

past. In a deeply troubled present, Reeve calls for the preservation of ancient and unique English liberties and believes that they are vital to Britain's future prosperity.

The Old English Baron and the nature of the past

Reeve appeals to a Gothic (ancient, chivalrous) past in order to provide models of good, imitable behaviour in the present. The manner in which she represents the past in *The Old English Baron* tells us much about her attitude towards history. Akin to *Otranto*, Reeve's Gothic novel is presented as a discovered manuscript. Although Reeve dropped this device in the second edition (as Walpole did), when she first published her work as *The Champion of Virtue* in 1777, her 'address to the reader' describes the text's origin. '[I]t occurred to my remembrance', writes Reeve, 'that a certain friend of mine was in possession of a manuscript in the old English language' (*OEB* 139). If 'it were to be modernised', she exclaims, it 'might afford entertainment' (*OEB* 139). Assuming the role of an editor, Reeve describes how, with her 'friend's permission', she 'transcribed, or rather translated a few sheets' of the script (*OEB* 139). Having read it to a 'circle of friends of approved judgement' who gave her the 'warmest encouragement to proceed', she is compelled to 'finish it' (*OEB* 139). Furthermore, Reeve uses the Gothic trope of the discovered manuscript not only as a framing device, but as a theme throughout her novel. Even though she chose to drop this frame in the second edition, the novel still has the appearance of a manuscript. For example, a short way into the narrative, Reeve (retaining the role of editor) interdicts: '*From this place the characters in the manuscript are effaced by time and damp. Here and there some sentences are legible, but not sufficient to pursue the thread of the story*' (OEB 23). '*The following incidents are clear enough to be transcribed*', continues Reeve, before describing how '*the beginning of the next succeeding pages is obliterated*' (*OEB* 23). She suggests that '*we may guess at the beginning by what remains*' and then uses a series of asterisks to denote an absence in the script (*OEB* 23). Indeed, Reeve innovates the Gothic trope of the discovered manuscript by introducing the notion of historical mutability. The early parts of the script are replete with missing sections, signs of decay and absences; dimensions of the past that

Rapin's (and Hume's) history generally disregards. A little further on, Reeve declares that the 'manuscript is not legible for several pages', particularly surrounding the time of 'the death of Lady Fitz-Owen' (*OEB* 26). The text resumes for a short paragraph before she tells us that the *'manuscript is again defaced for many leaves'* (*OEB* 26). Reeve highlights the fragile nature of the past and our convoluted access to it in the present.

Building on Walpole's *Otranto*, Reeve adds a narrative complexity to the Gothic and its representations of the past. She invests the Gothic trope of the discovered manuscript with historical chasms and lapses in time: *'Here follows an interval of four years, as by the manuscript and this omission seems intended by the Writer'* (*OEB* 19). Indeed, *The Old English Baron* is deceptive; when scrutinised and considered alongside the preface to the first edition (where Reeve assumes the role of editor), its structure is far more complicated than it initially appears. Not only do years elapse in the writing of the manuscript (or so Reeve would have us believe), but it shows evidence of multiple authorship: *'What follows is in a different hand, and the character is more modern'* (*OEB* 19). Rewriting *Otranto*, Reeve develops the Gothic's emphasis on the textual nature of history, our troubled access to it in the present and the complexity of historical transmission; aspects of the past that Hume's and Rapin's (proto-)Enlightenment historiography belies. The representation of the past in *The Old English Baron* is further complicated by discussions surrounding the recording of historical events in the narrative and the external structure of the novel is sophisticated by its internal discussion. For example, after Walter's crime is revealed and Edmund takes over as rightful master of the Castle Lovel, Lord Graham's priest suggests 'that an account be written of this discovery, and signed by all the witnesses present' (*OEB* 116). Furthermore, he requests that 'an attested copy be left in the hands of this gentleman, and the original be sent to the Barons and Harclay, to convince them of the truth of it' (*OEB* 116). It is not until the end of the novel, where Harclay 'caused the papers relating to his son's [Edmund's] history to be collected together', that we are informed that the 'first part' of the script was 'written under his [Harclay's] own eye in Yorkshire' and that 'the subsequent parts by Father Oswald at the Castle of Lovel' (*OEB* 135). However, as Fiona Robertson points out, although Reeve may highlight the incomplete and disjointed nature of history, the written version of the past in *The Old English Baron* 'provides all the information the reader needs' (1994, 89).

Indeed, it is important to note that the manuscript is only fragmented in the early parts of the narrative. After a certain point, *'the letters become more legible, and the remainder of it is quite perfect'* (*OEB* 26). True to her word, there are no more breaks in the text for the remainder of the narrative. Although Reeve does use the Gothic trope of the discovered manuscript to highlight the truncated and fragile nature of history and to heighten anxiety and suspense, she does not do so to the extent that Walpole does (or any of the other authors discussed in this book do). The past is still a site of conflict and anxiety for Reeve, but she focuses predominantly on the *familiarity* of the past rather than on our alien, disembodied relationship with history. Watt phrases this quite elegantly when he argues that Reeve's Loyalist Gothic story and the past that it recounts emphasise 'familiarity rather than a distant alterity' (2003, xix). As this chapter has highlighted, Reeve dwells less on the nature of the past and more on the relevance of the past to the present and the didactic role of history. In many ways, the structure of Reeve's historic Gothic novel resembles the English constitution; it is a disparate collection of documents written by multiple authors and consisting of various legal decisions and conventions. Similarly to Rapin's Whig conception of the English constitution, a spirit of justice and liberty suffuses every fragment and page of *The Old English Baron*. For Reeve, the fragmented nature of history only means that it is more important than ever to preserve ancient customs by adhering to them in the present. The complex textual tissue and multiple authorship of Reeve's work serves to underscore the unanimity of benevolent patriarchs and their commitment to fending off transgressors and preserving ancient liberties. The ultimate fear in *The Old English Baron* is that such fragile, Gothic liberties may not be transmitted to future generations because of internal and external threats to time-honoured, treasured social ideals. Even though the fifteenth-century past of Reeve's novel is precarious, fragile and wrought with its own perils, Reeve is generally comforted by it; it offers a valuable (not to mention timely) lesson for the present by exhibiting the valiant defence of embattled freedoms and rouses patriotic pride in England's glorious past.

The Gothic authoress and history

As this chapter has demonstrated, *The Old English Baron* represents a very different direction for the Gothic in the eighteenth century. In Reeve's novel, the Gothic continues to react to (proto-) Enlightenment modes of historical writing. Assessed alongside Rapin's *History of England*, *The Old English Baron* exhibits the Gothic both rejecting and assimilating elements of dominant modes of eighteenth-century history. Reeve gives the past a much firmer moral purpose than Rapin, but is also heavily influenced by his Whig codes of historical representation and the political themes that form an integral part of this. The relationship between literature, the Gothic and history becomes increasingly complicated in *The Old English Baron*. Rather than following the dictates of *Otranto* by constructing a narrative that focuses exclusively on gruesome histories, acts of treachery and supernatural occurrences, Reeve writes a more congenial past; one which, although it features disturbing moments, provides models of good personal and political conduct. As an early example of the Loyalist Gothic – a form that would not reach its peak until the French Revolution turned violent in the 1790s – Reeve utilises the Gothic to cultivate patriotism in a period where Britain's future was cast into question by the revolt of the American Colonies.

The Old English Baron has traditionally been neglected on the grounds that it presents something of an awkward fit in the genesis of a normative, homogeneous Gothic genre. However, as this chapter (and this book) demonstrates, the Gothic is a site of conflict and contested ideologies. A study of Gothic representations of the past would simply be incomplete without discussing Reeve's contribution; as I will show, so much of what follows is a reaction to *The Old English Baron*. For a Gothic novel written by a woman in the eighteenth century, it is perhaps surprising that women and the politics of female identity do not play a larger part in the narrative. Reeve's novel does focus on masculine behaviour and inculcate a code of manliness: benevolent, courageous and respectful towards women, Edmund and Harclay are historical figures that Reeve presents as role models for men in the eighteenth century. However, as this chapter has suggested, women have a rather marginal role in the narrative and there is little emphasis on female subjectivity. If the 'Female Gothic' is defined as a form of fiction that focuses on the heroine and the house, *The Old English Baron* cannot be classified as an example (or even an early prototype) of such a work. Nevertheless, the fact that the novel engages with history and is clearly penned by a politically motivated authoress is significant. In the eighteenth century, women were encouraged to read history as an antidote to 'poisonous' novels, but they were not granted the privilege or, in many cases, the education, to write history. Catharine Macaulay did write a fully-fledged history that received considerable acclaim. However, behind the praise there was concern that a woman had transgressed into the male-dominated world of historiography.[20] As Kelly notes, because of the hybridity and generic openness of the Gothic novel, it 'could be used to appropriate and diffuse all kinds of discourses otherwise barred to women or difficult for them to engage in openly and directly' (2002, 1: xxix). As *The Old English Baron* demonstrates, the Gothic provides the perfect vehicle for women writers to access and have their say on prestigious, male-dominated subjects such as politics and history; subjects otherwise denied to them.[21]

Rewriting Walpole's *Otranto*, the fictional, politicised past of Reeve's novel showed future female writers the possibilities that the Gothic could afford. In a more striking way than Walpole's *Otranto*, *The Old English Baron* showed how fictional pasts can be used as a means of commenting on the present.[22] Whereas Reeve appealed to an ancient, Gothic history of benevolent patriarchs in order to cultivate a sense of united national identity during a time of national anxiety, writers such as Lee and Radcliffe would write pasts that engage explicitly with eighteenth-century gender politics. As this book will demonstrate, the 'Gothic' continued to be a fiercely contested term in the eighteenth century. The ways in which authors interpreted the term shaped the pasts they wrote. In Lee's *The Recess* – the next Gothic novel to be published after *The Old English Baron* – Reeve's emphasis on recorded history and actual historical periods would remain important. Countering Reeve's virtuous fifteenth-century past peopled by benevolent patriarchs, Lee constructs a complex sixteenth-century past characterised by fear and oppression. The absences and gaps that characterise the Gothic trope of the discovered manuscript (and that did not particularly trouble Reeve) would become very significant for Lee. Changing the direction of the Gothic once more, Lee focuses more on gender politics than on party politics. Morbid and tragic female histories remain on the periphery of Reeve's novel; in Lee's *The Recess*, such repressed and macabre female pasts loom much larger in the Gothic imagination.

Notes

1 A notable Gothic work to be published in the interim between *Otranto* and *The Old English Baron* was John Aikin's *Sir Bertrand, a Fragment* (1773). This 'Fragment' is often wrongfully ascribed to his more famous sister, Anna Laetitia Aikin (later Mrs Barbauld), due to the fact that it was published in their joint collection of *Miscellaneous Pieces* (1773). The work is a literary realisation of the principles outlined in his sister's prefatory essay, 'On the Pleasure Derived from Objects of Terror' (1773). Walpole approved highly of the fragment; he argued that its author 'showed her talent for imprinting terror' (1937–83, 41: 410). Many of the images contained in the *Fragment* found their way into later Gothic works. These include doors creaking on hinges, seemingly endless stairways, vaunted halls in ancient mansions, the touch of a cold dead hand, deep hollow groans, a mysterious light, and the protagonist's sensation of terror. As I will show in the next two chapters, the figure of the fragment itself became very important for future Gothic writers and their representations of the past.

2 In his brief memoir of Reeve that he contributed to the Novelist's Library Edition of her work, Sir Walter Scott argues that, despite a 'competent command of those qualities which constitute a good romance' (1829, 243), *The Old English Baron* is 'tame and tedious, not to say mean and tiresome' (248). Furthermore, he describes Reeve as a secluded 'authoress', whose 'acquaintance of events and characters derived from books alone' (248). Scott also acknowledges that Reeve was acquainted with Rapin's historical work (246).

3 In the last decade, a number of extended studies of *The Old English Baron* have been published. Notable examples of books that dedicate chapters to Reeve's Gothic novel include Toni Wein's *British Identities* (2002), Donna Heiland's *Gothic and Gender: An Introduction* (2004) and Sue Chaplin's *The Gothic and the Rule of Law 1764–1820* (2007). Volume 1 of Kelly's *Varieties of Female Gothic* (2002) and Abby Coykendall's essay, 'Gothic Genealogies, the Family Romance, and Clara Reeve's *The Old English Baron*' (2005), also discuss Reeve's Gothic novel at length.

4 Wein also examines the impact of the American Revolution on *The Old English Baron* in *British Identities* (2002). Focusing on the family

as a cipher for the nation and arguing that the private comments on the public, Wein contends that Reeve's Gothic novel 'thematizes the American Revolution and its aftermath, first by telling multilayered stories of betrayal, and then by accommodating individual and social rights' (2002, 74–6).

5 Throughout the forthcoming discussion the terms 'Gothic' and 'Loyalist Gothic' will both be used. The term Gothic will be used to denote aspects that are common to the genre; it will often be used in the context of discussing how Reeve adapts the conventions set out by Walpole in *Otranto*. The term Loyalist Gothic will be used to highlight how Reeve's novel – a prototype of this strain of fiction – differentiates itself from other Gothic works (primarily *Otranto*). When discussing contested political definitions of the 'Gothic', such distinctions will be made clear in the relevant sections.

6 Wilkes was a patriot, heralded a strictly Whig interpretation of English history and celebrated Whig ancient constitutionalism. As this chapter discusses, Reeve held similar beliefs and such notions can be detected in the fictional fifteenth-century past that she represents in *The Old English Baron*, which attempts to cultivate a strong sense of national purpose in a challenging cultural context.

7 England and Britain are distinct terms yet have been used interchangeably owing to England's historically dominant position in the British Isles. Britain refers to three nations – England, Scotland and Wales – that make up the largest of the islands and were constituted as a sovereign state in 1707 with the creation of Great Britain. As I am concerned primarily with histories of England and English historical writing (and the influence of such writings on Gothic novels published in England), I refer mainly to England throughout this book. However, as numerous commentators have pointed out, Reeve's novel is particularly concerned with English and British national identities, and so I will refer to both entities in this chapter. For example, Watt argues that the restoration of Edmund is significant not only for preserving justice in England, but 'implicitly heralds a larger process of national reconciliation' and 'the emergence of a new and inclusive Britishness' (2003, xix–xiv). Wein draws attention to the 'copious marital alliances' at the end of the novel and how these marriages 'draw together families from the marches of Scotland with inhabitants of Yorkshire, Cumberland, the west of England, and Wales'. Ancient English freedoms have been preserved but, as Wein argues, far more than this has been achieved: the 'characters' marriages discover that interests cross local borders, at the same time that they testify to the forging of an identity that is specifically British' (2002, 94–5). For more information on the Gothic novel and British national identity, see Wein's *British Identities* (2002).

8 It is widely acknowledged that Rapin's historiography had a large influence on Hume. For example, Laird Okie points out that the 'influence of Rapin can be detected in David Hume's analysis of the rise of political parties and in his picture of the "moderate men" from both parties ejecting James II' (1991, 56). The anti-clericalism of Rapin's account also appealed to Hume. However, he rejected the Whig bias of Rapin's account and contested his notion of an ancient, 'Gothic' constitution (see Note 16).

9 In the same letter, she also reveals that she had 'read *Cato's Letters*, by Trenchard and Gordon … the Greek and Roman Histories, and *Plutarch's Lives*' (Reeve 1829). As critics such as Kelly have noted (2003, 117), by showing how history can be used to teach civic virtue and social responsibility, Plutarch's historically inflected work had a particularly significant influence on Reeve.

10 The novels of Samuel Richardson had a strong impact on Reeve's fiction. In her history of prose fiction, *The Progress of Romance* (1785), Reeve heaps praise on Richardson, and especially *Pamela* (1740–41). She was particularly influenced by his appropriation of fiction for didactic ends and Richardsonian themes (such as virtue in distress and the certainty of retribution) manifest themselves throughout her fiction. E. J. Clery goes as far as to describe *The Old English Baron* as Reeve's 'rewriting of *Otranto* as *Pamela* in fancy-dress with the spice of the paranormal, an illustrative conduct-book for the proper correlation of wealth and virtue' (1995, 86). Furthermore, in a telling gesture, Reeve prefaced the 1780 edition of her Gothic work with a dedication to Martha Bridgen, daughter of Richardson. She acknowledges the influence of her 'patronage and protection' and credits her with correcting 'the errors of the first impression' (*OEB* 140).

11 *The Old English Baron*'s relationship with sensibility is complex. As I mentioned previously, the situation of the story – that of virtue in distress – is clearly influenced by novels of sensibility (primarily Richardson's). Numerous critics have discussed this aspect of Reeve's work. Watt highlights how, rather than functioning as a fifteenth-century character, Edmund is shown to be 'possessed of a modern, eighteenth-century sensibility' and bonds with others 'in an expressive, sentimental fashion, in such a way as to temper differences of rank' (2003, xvi). Sue Chaplin notes that the virtuous characters in *The Old English Baron* are not only imbued with a greater range of emotions; their actions present an 'alternative economy of justice that is dependent on the promptings of the heart', which 'supplements legally proper claims to property and power' (2007, 77). However, as she notes, social class is still rigidly asserted at the end of the novel. I will examine this in more detail when I discuss the role of the law in

Reeve's fictional fifteenth-century past. For a thorough discussion of the role of sensibility in *The Old English Baron* (and particularly its relationship with social rank) see Chaplin's *The Gothic and the Rule of Law, 1764–1820* (2007, 76–82). In her later novel, *The School for Widows* (published 1791), Reeve would express fears concerning sensibility, and what she refers to as 'false sensibility' (1791a, viii). I discuss the relationship between Lee's *The Recess*, the Gothic and sensibility in the following chapter.

12 Published in 1717, Rapin's *Dissertation sur les Whigs et les Tories* describes the English political party system and represents his first attempt to formulate a pattern of English history. Although it was written for continental Europeans, in England it became a standard, post-revolution (if Whig-biased) account of the national past. Tindal attached a translation of Rapin's *Dissertation* – which he entitled as a *Dissertation on the Origin of the Government of England. And on the Rise, Progress, Views, Strengths, Interests, and Characters of the two Parties of Whigs and Tories* – to his popular translation of the *History of England* (H 14: 367–438).

13 Rapin's critics were quick to react to the clear Whig slant of his *History of England*. In 1734, the *Defence of English History Against the Misrepresentations of M. de Rapin-Thoyras* (1734) was published. This work criticised the *History of England* as anti-monarchical, anti-Church, and accused Rapin of promoting levelling and anarchism.

14 Reeve's politics informed her works from the outset. In 1772, she published her first work of fiction, *The Phoenix; or The History of Polyarchus and Argenis*. This work translates and adapts John Barclay's Latin *Argenis* (1621), a political allegory on France's religious and civil wars of the late sixteenth and early seventeenth centuries. Attracted to the work because of its relevance to her own age, Reeve describes *The Phoenix* as 'a romance, an allegory, and a system of politics' (1772, 1: i). Indeed, it is this political and didactic dimension of Reeve's fiction that has led Gary Kelly to discuss Reeve as a Bluestocking writer. Although there is little evidence to suggest that Reeve was in contact with the metropolitan Bluestocking Circle, he argues that Reeve can be perceived as a 'provincial Bluestocking' (2003, 105). Citing her Old Whig values, Kelly argues that her fiction shares a Bluestocking agenda in the sense that it is interested in 'modernisation in state, economy, society and culture' and alliances 'between progressive gentry and professional people' in order to increase 'prosperity in an economy still largely agrarian' and dominated by 'gentry wealth, status, and power' (1999, 1: xlv). For Kelly, Reeve's didactic fiction – and particularly her later works – aim 'to secure a more prominent role within modernisation for women of the classes whose interests modernisation served'

(xlv). However, Kelly's study focuses almost exclusively on the social utility of *The Old English Baron* and limits discussion of her use of Gothic tropes and the fears that are manifest in her novel. This chapter seeks to cultivate an image of Reeve as a Gothic authoress. For more information on Reeve's status as a writer with Bluestocking affinities, see Kelly's *Bluestocking Feminism* (1999) and his essay, 'Clara Reeve, Provincial Bluestocking: From the Old Whigs to the Modern Liberal State' (2003).

15 Perhaps the most influential discussion of the relationship between Whig history and Gothic fiction is conducted by Robert Mighall in the first chapter of his *A Geography of Victorian Gothic Fiction* (1999, 1–26). Concentrating on Radcliffe's Gothic fiction, Mighall discusses the Whig notion of the past as a site of conflict and identifies the struggles that take place between those representing modernity and those fighting for the tyranny of the past. He also focuses on the Whig associations of Protestantism with progressivism and Catholicism with backwardness. With his attention directed more towards Victorian Gothic fiction, Mighall does not discuss Reeve or the possible impact of Whig history on the past represented in *The Old English Baron*.

16 Hume objected to the Whig political slant of the *History of England*. He criticised both the style and content of Rapin's history and waged war against Whig orthodoxy by radically revising theories of ancient constitutionalism. Challenging notions of a constitution that has remained essentially the same throughout diverse historical periods, Hume argues that the 'English constitution, like all others, has been in a state of continual fluctuation' (*HE* 4: 355). Hume sets about destroying what he perceives as the Whig myth of the ancient constitution. As Forbes points out (1985, 267), for Hume, the 'more ancient the constitution, the more primitive and barbaric and unworthy of imitation it is'. Indeed, it was the less political and more philosophical and literary bent of Hume's *The History of England* that appealed to the later Georgian readership and that helped it to supersede Rapin's history.

17 Although discussions concerning the origins and future of the English constitution came into sharper focus with the outbreak of the American Revolution and, later, the French Revolution, such debates raged throughout the eighteenth century. Two notable contributions to such debates are Charles Louis de Secondat de Montesquieu's *Spirit of the Laws* (composed in 1748 and translated into English in 1750) and William Blackstone's *Commentaries on the Laws of England* (1765–69). Both of these writers argue that the English constitution has ancient, Gothic, Germanic roots. Blackstone's study is particularly interesting in terms of eighteenth-century Gothic literature in the sense that he famously likens the English constitution to a Gothic castle that needs only a few minor modifications to make it relevant and efficient

within a modern context. For a detailed study of the implications of Blackstone's work on early Gothic literature, see Sue Chaplin's *The Gothic and the Rule of Law, 1764–1820* (2007, 39–47).

18 These words are actually spoken about the Baron Fitz-Owen. However, as early critics demonstrate, the identity of the title character of Reeve's novel provokes debate. When she decides to revise her novel, Reeve argues that she changes the 'title from the *Champion of Virtue* to the *Old English Baron*: – as that character is thought to be the principal one in the story' (*OEB* 4). As Scott notes, however, the Baron Fitz-Owen is quite a marginal and 'passive' figure in the narrative and is 'only acted upon by others' (1829, 242). Anna Laetitia Barbauld argues that Harclay is 'a fine character' and that he is the 'old baron' of the title (1810, ii).

19 The historical figure of Richard of Plantagenet features briefly in Reeve's Gothic novel. Reeve describes him as a man 'whose pride of birth equalled that of any man living or dead' (*OEB* 25). This mixing of real historical figures with fictional characters represents an important moment for Gothic fiction and would prove significant for Lee's *The Recess* (see Chapter 3).

20 Embarking on the remarkable task of writing an eight volume historical work, Catharine Macaulay had her *History of England* published between 1763 and 1783. It was initially received positively, especially by Whigs, who identified it as an antidote to Hume's Tory-biased *The History of England*. However, the *Monthly Review* focused more on the fact that a woman had written such a work than on the merits of Macaulay's history. Indeed, the *Review*'s tone is quite condescending, referring to her as 'the fair Macaulay' (*Monthly Review* 1763, 372) and 'our fair historian' (374). Although the *Review* offers mild praise for her work, it expresses a wish that 'the same degree of genius and application had been exerted in more suitable pursuits', because writing history is not recommended 'to the practice of our lovely countrywomen' (372–3). Macaulay's sympathy with the American colonists also diminished her in the eyes of many Whigs.

21 Reeve's fascination with history remained undimmed throughout her writing career. In the preface to her semi-historical *Memoirs of Sir Roger de Clarendon* (1793), she speaks of having attempted to write a history of all the great men who lived in the reign of Edward III. However, having filled several sheets of paper with names, she realised the task was beyond her powers (1793, xvi). She elects instead to write the aforementioned novel; a work which uses the past to urge Britain to adhere to a strict subordination of ranks in the wake of revolutionary events taking place in France. Reeve's last known work was a fictionalised history entitled *Edwin, King of Northumberland: A Story of the Seventh Century* (published 1802). Written for young readers, it

pursues the Plutarchan agenda of using the lives of great men of history to educate youths in civic virtues.

22 *The Old English Baron* was not supposed to be Reeve's last foray into Gothic fiction. In the preface to her novel, *The Exiles* (1788), she speaks of writing a '*Ghost* Story' (1788, xviii) entitled '*Castle Connor – an Irish Story*' (xix). Reeve completed the work in 1786 and sent it to London by the Ipswich blue coach in May 1787, but it was lost in transit. There is speculation that the story is contained in *Fatherless Fanny*, a novel attributed to Reeve and published in 1819. However, Reeve believed that the Castle Connor tale was stolen and the story that appeared in *Fatherless Fanny* is unlikely to be hers. No further evidence has come to light.

3

'Entombed alive': Sophia Lee's *The Recess* (1783–85), the Gothic and history

This Recess could not be called a cave, because it was composed of various rooms ... every room was distinct, and divided from the rest by a vaulted passage with many stairs, while our light proceeded from small casements of painted glass, so infinitely above our reach that we could never seek a world beyond.

Sophia Lee, *The Recess* (1783–85)

The impatient assassins, regardless of her efforts, rushed upon their prey, and by overturning every thing which stood in their way, encreased the horror and confusion of the scene. Douglas, seizing Henry's dagger, struck it in the body of Rizzio, who, screaming with fear and agony, was torn from Mary by the other conspirators, and pushed into the antichamber, where he was dispatched with fifty-six wounds. The unhappy princess, informed of his fate, immediately dried her tears, and said, she would weep no more; she would now think of revenge.

David Hume, *The History of England* (1754–62)

The historical specificity that Clara Reeve introduced to the genre remained important in the next major work of Gothic fiction to be published after *The Old English Baron*. Based around the reign of Elizabeth I and the tragic history of Mary, Queen of Scots, Sophia Lee's *The Recess; or, A Tale of Other Times* features two female narrators, Matilda and Ellinor; the (fictional) twin daughters of Mary by a secret marriage to the Duke of Norfolk. The twins are raised in an isolated, underground chamber known as 'the Recess', and Lee's novel recounts their diverse and traumatic experiences of the outside world as fictional characters, circumstances and events collide with those of recorded history. Published between 1783 and 1785 – approximately five years after the appearance of *The Old English Baron – The Recess* was heralded as an extraordinary development in English fiction, and, due to its similarity to certain accounts of England's past, was frequently likened to both David Hume's *The History of England* (1754–62) and William Robertson's *The History of Scotland during the Reigns of Queen Mary and James VI* (1759). *The Recess* builds substantially on the level of historical detail contained in *The Old English Baron*. A wealth of real historical figures populate Lee's late sixteenth-century past, the novel's (fictional) heroines find themselves caught in the middle of numerous major historical events and, as a whole, the novel draws on the scandal and conspiracy that surrounds Elizabeth I's reign. Historically inflected and utilising numerous Gothic conventions, Lee's novel proved immensely popular in the eighteenth century and beyond.[1]

In contrast to Horace Walpole's *The Castle of Otranto* and Reeve's *The Old English Baron*, *The Recess* does not bear the words 'a Gothic story' on its title page. This has led literary critics to dispute the classification and Gothic nature of Lee's novel.[2] However, debates about the genre of the novel aside, *The Recess*'s influence on the development of Gothic fiction is indisputable. Lee's novel is packed with Gothic themes and tropes; it encompasses decaying edifices, confused ancestry, incest, usurpation, motherless women, dreams, villains, family paintings, violence, and anxieties surrounding Catholicism.[3] As this chapter will demonstrate, Gothic themes of repressed histories, madness, entrapment, irrationality, and acts of female persecution also feature prominently throughout *The Recess*. The very title of Lee's novel has Gothic connotations. In the *Oxford English Dictionary*, the word 'Recess' has a number of unsettling and sinister meanings: 'A place of retirement, a remote and secluded spot, a secret or private place', 'A departure from some state or standard', 'A dark resource, a secret'. Like *The Old English Baron, The Recess* is a novel that has been critically neglected over the years, but has witnessed a resurgence of interest in the last decade or so. Lee's novel is now discussed routinely in histories of Gothic fiction; rather than being mentioned briefly in passing, it has begun to receive chapter-length examinations, particularly in recent years.[4] It is the intention of this chapter to further this trend by examining representations of the past in *The Recess*.

Beginning with an analysis of Lee's attitude towards history, this discussion poses a number of questions. Why does Lee choose to set her Gothic novel during the reign of Elizabeth I? What does the marginalised Recess symbolise, and what is the significance of the novel's emphasis on female experience? This chapter will demonstrate how Lee's use of the Gothic varies from both Walpole's and Reeve's works by focusing more on gender issues and discussing subjects as diverse as concealed writings, the figure of the absent mother, women's role in history, female inheritance, sensibility, and the epistolary novel. *The Recess* represents a unique variant of the epistolary form in the sense that there is a complete lack of consensus; the memoir-letter written by Matilda (the elder twin and primary narrator) is counterpointed, contradicted and fragmented by her sister Ellinor's letter. What is 'Gothic' for Lee? What contemporary anxieties does her novel betray? What are the implications of her novel for historical writing, and what does her use of the epistolary say about the nature of the past? Throughout this chapter, I will show how Lee utilises the Gothic metaphor of entombment to comment on woman's plight in the past and present. Due to the fact that knowledge of Lee's life and reading habits is limited, we cannot be absolutely certain that she had read Hume's *The History of England*, William Robertson's *The History of Scotland* or Tindal's popular translation of Rapin's *History of England*. However, as critics such as April Alliston and Anne H. Stevens have pointed out, certain passages of *The Recess* have remarkable similarities to Hume's and Robertson's accounts of the reign of Elizabeth I.[5] Contending that *The Recess* represents a complex response to male dominated historical writing, this chapter endeavours to highlight the continuing importance of eighteenth-century historiography to the development of early Gothic literature. Before exploring such issues, I will begin with an examination of the historical context of *The Recess* and Lee's decision to set her Gothic novel in the late sixteenth century.

The reign of Elizabeth I: history, the Gothic and Lee

In contrast to Reeve's decision to set *The Old English Baron* during the minority government of Henry VI, the reign of Elizabeth I is certainly a more obvious historical period within which to set a suspenseful Gothic novel. There are numerous aspects of this reign which have inherently 'Gothic' elements about them, with savage, mysterious and barbaric acts taking place. This chapter opened with an extract from Hume's description of the brutal murder of David Rizzio – Mary, Queen of Scots's secretary and adviser – in *The History of England*. Reminiscent of a scene from Renaissance drama, Hume's impassioned prose and focus on violent incident would not be out of place in one of the numerous Gothic novels produced in the later eighteenth century. Even to historians committed to strict epistemological systems of historical enquiry and calm, measured prose, the events of this historical period stirred their creative faculties. The machinations of Elizabeth I's reign fired the eighteenth century's historical imagination. As Hume's, Robertson's and Rapin's accounts of this period demonstrate, it was a time of protracted political conflict at home and abroad and a reign punctuated with instances of conflict, treachery, tragedy, and violence. Elizabeth battled against a predominantly Catholic Europe intent on overturning the Protestant faith, and presided over England's vast (and often bloody) expansion abroad. Uncompromising in her views and formidable in her actions, she did not hesitate to remove those deemed a risk to her government, even if they were close to her. For example, she had former royal favourite Robert Devereux (the Earl of Essex) executed for revolting against her regime. However, perhaps most significantly in terms of *The Recess*, this is a historical period dominated by the volatile relationship between two female figures: Elizabeth, and her mortal enemy, Mary, Queen of Scots. Mary was implicated in the murder of Lord Darnley (Mary's husband and claimant to the English throne) by a series of documents of dubious authenticity that became known as the Casket Letters.[6] Despite doubts about their probity, Elizabeth used them as an excuse to keep Mary as a prisoner in England and stain her reputation across Western Europe. Replete with conspiracies, repressed pasts, imprisonments, poisonings, bitter jealousies, threats of usurpation, tyrannical behaviour, and acts of revenge, the reign of Elizabeth has all the hallmarks of a romance.

Lee says as much in the advertisement to *The Recess*. 'A wonderful coincidence of events stamps the narration at least with probability', she writes, 'and the reign of Elizabeth was that of romance' (*R* 5). 'If this Lady was not the child of fancy', she continues, 'her fate can hardly be paralleled; and the line of which she came has been marked by an eminent historian, as one distinguished alike by splendor and misery' (*R* 5).[7] With the border between history and literature, fact and fiction, reason and romance, almost indistinguishable in discussions of the events of Elizabeth's reign, it is the perfect historical period in which to set a spellbinding Gothic novel. Akin to the rumours of forgotten, sinister histories that are central to eighteenth-century Gothic novels, England's recorded history during this period becomes a series of rumours, conjectures and conspiracy theories. Lee fashions a Gothic narrative out of the unsaid and unseen of history and draws on the themes of secrecy, persecution and betrayal that dominate historians' descriptions of this period. In Lee's hands, the Gothic continues to be fixated on violent and repressed pasts. She uses fiction to reveal the absences that are endemic of the historical record and to expose the weaknesses of Enlightenment historiography. Furthermore, it is important to note the renewed relevance of Elizabeth's reign – and the historical figure of Mary, Queen of Scots – towards the end of the eighteenth century. As E. J. Clery notes (2004, 40–1), in terms of colonial expansion and Catholic anxieties, the reign of Elizabeth bore a number of resemblances to the state of late eighteenth-century England.[8] Furthermore, with the publication of documents such as the Burghley State Papers in 1759, much of the contemporary source material concerning Mary was made available for the first time. Debates about Mary's character and her involvement in Darnley's murder became known as the 'Marian Controversy' and such discussions dominated the male world of eighteenth-century historiography. Historians such as Hume and Robertson employed their Enlightenment methods of historical enquiry to try and solve once and for all the mysterious events of Elizabeth's reign and the enigma of Mary's character. However, despite their endeavours, doubt and uncertainty continued to plague such subjects.

In *The History of England*, Hume asserts to the authenticity of the Casket Letters, describing them as 'incontestible proofs' of Mary's guilt (*HE* 4: 113). Objections made to their authenticity are of 'small force', he adds (*HE* 4: 114). Hume was so passionate about the genuineness of the Casket Letters that he endeavoured to convince his friend and fellow historian, Robertson, of their truth. In *The History of Scotland*, Robertson is not so confident and argues that 'none of the points in question could be decided with certainty' (1761, 2: iv). However, by November 1758, Robertson seems to have concurred with Hume (Hume 1932, 1: 287–90).

Meanwhile, apologists of Mary rejected such notions and intensified the debate. For example, Walter Goodall's *An Examination of the Letters said to be written by Mary Queen of Scots, to James Earl of Bothwell: Shewing By intrinsick and extrinsick Evidence, that they are Forgeries* (1754) sought to highlight the erroneous nature of the Casket Letters, whilst William Tytler's *Inquiry* (1760) directly confronted Hume's conclusions in *The History of England* and offered a vindication of Mary's character. Tytler's *Inquiry* rattled Hume and, in a letter to Alexander Dick in August 1760, he modifies his stance. He argues that Mary's guilt is 'far from resting solely on the Letters', targets flaws in her character, and cites her silence in regard to the evidence as a 'Proof of Guilt' (Hume 1954, 59–64). The widespread debate and fervour surrounding the validity of the Casket Letters in eighteenth-century culture more than likely proved the catalyst for Lee's ambitious rewriting of the enigmatic events of Elizabeth's I's reign. Lee challenges the androcentrism of such historical debates by writing a Gothic novel that offers an imaginative, alternative view on such subjects. Utilising the same means as Reeve, but for entirely different ends, the Gothic enables Lee to enter the forbidden realm of male dominated eighteenth-century historiography.

The Recess, the Female Gothic and history

Before I focus on Lee's use of the Gothic to access historical discourse, it is important to emphasise the prominent role of gender politics in *The Recess* and to discuss notions of the Female Gothic. *The Recess* represents a major innovation in the development of Gothic fiction in the sense that it is narrated in the first person by women. Gothic pasts have, of course, been concerned with gender issues, and particularly the subject of female persecution, since the beginning. At the start of *Otranto*, Manfred's son and Isabella's husband-to-be, Conrad, is killed shortly before his wedding. In an arranged meeting shortly after this tragic event, Manfred compels Isabella to forget his son and marry him, as he now requires a male heir. We learn that 'words cannot paint the horror of the princess's situation' and that Isabella's 'dread of Manfred soon outweighed every other terror' (O 26–7). Manfred's wife, Hippolita, also suffers badly as a result of her husband's tyrannical behaviour. Reeve's fictional fifteenth-century past in *The Old English Baron* is pervaded by a tragic female cast. Margery Twyford suffers a miscarriage and is violently abused by her husband, Emma is a pawn in a male power-struggle and Edmund's mother, the Baroness Lovel, meets a tragic end. However, in contrast to Walpole's Gothic novel and Reeve's Loyalist Gothic work, there is a much greater emphasis on female experience and subjectivity in *The Recess*. Using the intimate, first-person form of the epistolary, Lee adds psychological depth to *Otranto*'s detached descriptions of female fear and, in contrast to *The Old English Baron*, moves women from the margins to the centre of her work.

As I mentioned in the previous chapter, despite being written by a woman and alluding to marginal female histories, *The Old English Baron* cannot really be considered as an example of the Female Gothic. In keeping with its Loyalist Gothic agenda, Reeve's novel is more concerned with the actions of (fictional) great men of history and rousing patriotism than interrogating gender politics. Although Lee's novel engages with debates surrounding Britain's colonial expansion, its abiding concern is with gender issues. Indeed, it is Lee's female-centric *The Recess* that marks the first 'early statement' of the Female Gothic (Kelly 2002, xxxiii). The Female Gothic – a fiercely contested term – has a long and complex history, and, beyond the working definition outlined here, it is not the premise of this chapter to become embroiled in such debates.[9] Rather, as I have suggested, the Female Gothic can be read as a politically subversive branch of Gothic fiction, which privileges female subjectivity and which enables women writers to utilise certain Gothic tropes to express fears and anxieties about dominant patriarchal structures and women's marginalised role in society and history.[10] This chapter will show that, in contrast to previous Gothic texts, there is a much greater emphasis on female rights, inheritances and concealed writings in the pasts of Female Gothic fiction. The narrative lens is firmly on the persecuted heroines, their domestic imprisonment in castles and abbeys, and their larger historical plight.

In contrast to Reeve, Lee uses the Gothic not only to access the male-dominated realm of historiography, but to comment on and critique it. Pioneering the Female Gothic by writing about events through the eyes of her persecuted heroines, Lee utilises romance to provide a new, female angle of historical vision; a perspective which contrasts with Enlightenment histories written by the likes of Hume, Rapin and Robertson in cultivating a sentimental engagement with the past. In contrast to Reeve's interpretation of the 'Gothic' as something ancient, liberating and time-honoured, the term has a very different meaning for Lee. Harking back to Walpole's *Otranto*, the Gothic signifies anything oppressive, barbaric and superstitious in *The Recess*. Throughout the course of this chapter, I will show how Lee hijacks certain themes and tropes manifest in Walpole's and Reeve's fictions and adapts them in order to probe women's repression in the past and the present.

Historical entrapment: Gothic villains and persecuted heroines

Although ordinary women are excluded from history (as I will discuss in more detail later), eminent women feature prominently in eighteenth-century historiography. As I have already indicated, two female figures loomed particularly large in the eighteenth-century historical imagination: Elizabeth and Mary, Queen of Scots. Even though Robertson's and Rapin's histories show similar traits, and could have been usefully compared to Lee's *The Recess*, my discussion will use Hume's *The History of England* – the most popular work of eighteenth-century historiography and a probable source for Lee's historical information – to elucidate some of the ways she uses the Female Gothic to critique male history. After writing of Elizabeth's death, Hume conducts his habitual character assessment and presents her as a heroine. He is full of praise for this female monarch, arguing that there are fewer 'great personages in history' than Elizabeth (*HE* 4: 351). However, the characteristics he acclaims are predominantly those associated with ideals of manhood; Elizabeth is praised for her 'rigorous', 'imperious' nature and the 'vigour', 'vigilance', 'penetration', 'constancy', and 'heroism' that she exhibited during her reign (*HE* 4: 351–2). Hume recognises that a certain controversy surrounds Elizabeth in regards to a 'consideration of her sex' (*HE* 4: 352). He notes that, when contemplating her as a woman, one is simultaneously struck with her many (predominantly masculine) qualities and yet, is aware that she lacks 'some of those amiable weaknesses by which her sex is distinguished', such as 'softness of disposition' and a 'greater lenity of temper' (*HE* 4: 352). However, Hume dispels such thoughts, choosing to consider her as a sovereign, a 'rational being' entrusted 'with the government of mankind', rather than as 'a wife or mistress' (*HE* 4: 353).

Hume's analysis of Elizabeth's character betrays the gender-bias that pervades the historical values not only of *The History of England*, but much eighteenth-century history written by men. To use Bonnie G. Smith's words, Hume's language in *The History of England* (and much male-dominated eighteenth-century historiography) duplicates the 'language of a universalized masculinity' (1998, 141). The theoretical frameworks and paradigms that are employed to write the past in *The History of England* embody the ideals of eighteenth-century manhood: authority, self-regulation, confidence and a representation of universality; the requisition of the composed, coherent and distanced mind to transcend contingencies such as chance, nationality and race; and the need to complete hard work by adhering to strict methods (141). Eighteenth-century historiography written by historians such as Hume does not exclude eminent women from history; it judges them and represents them by using male values. Femininity is inherently weak and inferior in Hume's eyes and he is keen to spot what he perceives as woman's failings. It is almost as if, because Elizabeth exhibits more male qualities than so called 'weak' feminine traits, she is a source of perennial admiration.

Hume's representation of Elizabeth lays bare the gender politics that underpin eighteenth-century historiography. Such gendered historical representations are even more apparent when Hume's treatment of Elizabeth's bitter enemy, Mary, Queen of Scots, is examined. Despite doubts surrounding Mary's involvement in Darnley's murder, Hume is certain of 'her consent to the king's murder' (*HE* 4: 113) and, even though he acknowledges the bitter jealousy Elizabeth exhibits towards Mary, the emphasis is more on Mary's transgressions and inherent criminality than on the misery and suffering inflicted on her by England's reigning monarch. Hume highlights the many 'dangers, which arose from the character, principles, and pretensions of the queen of Scots' (*HE* 4: 222) and points out how her actions continually 'threatened the repose and authority of Elizabeth' (*HE* 4: 222–3). The Catholic unrest associated with Mary colours her representation and Hume condemns her involvement in numerous conspiracies to assassinate Elizabeth (*HE* 4: 227). In his concluding character analysis of Mary, Hume argues that an 'enumeration of her qualities might carry the appearance of panegyric; an account of her conduct must, in some parts, wear the aspect of severe satire and invective' (*HE* 4: 252). Although Hume does show sympathy towards her (particularly in his description of her execution), he continually suggests that there is something intrinsically villainous about Mary, and decides instead to focus on her physical appearance. Indeed, she becomes subject to Hume's male gaze. He commends the 'beauties' of Mary's person, her 'lovely form' and gentility, and applauds that 'she seemed to partake only so much of the male virtues as to render her estimable, without relinquishing those soft graces, which compose the proper ornament of her sex' (*HE* 4: 251). Hume may suggest that Elizabeth lacks such virtues, but, by focusing almost exclusively on these aspects of Mary's character, his account is voyeuristic and somewhat belittling. Refusing to comment on the motivations for her actions – and the dubious evidence that led to her imprisonment – Hume does not treat Mary as a historical figure who may have been greatly wronged; instead, she becomes merely an object of physical admiration for him. When describing her female qualities, Hume's tone is also quite condescending; using Elizabeth's ruthlessness, clear-sightedness and rationality (male ideals) as a yardstick to judge other female figures, he is quite patronising in his assessment of Mary being commendable for her 'polite', 'gentle', 'affable' (*HE* 4: 251), and warm manners (qualities traditionally associated with femininity).

In *The Recess*, Lee is acutely aware of such gendered readings of the past. Utilising Gothic tropology and the woman-centrism of the Female Gothic, she sets about subverting such male historical values. In contrast to Hume's representation of Elizabeth as a heroine, Lee presents her as a despotic figure: she is variously described as an 'inexorable tyrant' (*R* 81) in whom 'self-preservation' as opposed to compassion is an 'unconquerable principle' (*R* 33). 'The eye of Elizabeth became yet more dreadful to me', recalls Matilda; 'I fancied every moment it dived into my heart, and death for ever seemed to surround me in forms yet dearer to me than my own' (*R* 91). Reminiscent of the malicious Manfred in *Otranto* and the wicked Walter Lovel in *The Old English Baron*, Elizabeth is cast as an evil Gothic villain in *The Recess*. She terrorises the twin protagonists (particularly Ellinor) and tyrannises Mary, Queen of Scots. The enmity that Hume acknowledges Elizabeth felt for Mary – and that he deems of marginal importance in terms of her successful reign – consumes her in *The Recess*. Elizabeth is filled with 'jealousy and hatred' (*R* 24) of Mary and, whilst holding her prisoner, we learn that she 'cut her daily off from some comfort or convenience; frequently changed her keepers and prison; and by her severity, taught the captive Queen that hatred may be stronger than love' (*R* 34). Perhaps the most significant remark concerning Elizabeth comes from Mrs Marlow (the woman that raises Matilda and Ellinor in *The Recess*), who describes her as a woman whose 'heart was more full of policy than feeling' (*R* 26). To use Jane Spencer's words, Elizabeth is portrayed as a 'woman who has turned away from womanly values' (1986, 196). The very male ideals that underpin Hume's laudatory representation of Elizabeth – authority, ruthlessness and strength of mind – make her a figure of fear, horror and trepidation in Lee's novel.

If Elizabeth is the Gothic villain in *The Recess*, Mary plays the role of the persecuted female victim. Where Hume turns away from a consideration of Mary's actions in disgust and chooses, rather condescendingly, to focus solely on her physical appearance, *The Recess* draws attention to the horrific trials she has to endure at the hands of the tyrannical Elizabeth. Casting her as a typically beautiful Gothic female victim, Lee does acknowledge her physical attributes, but these are not the basis of her historical representation (*R* 10). The sense of innate criminality and Catholic distrust that typifies eighteenth-century historiographical responses to Mary are also absent. Mary may not always help herself and have a tendency to be ruled by her feelings, but it is her oppression by the formidable Elizabeth that drives her to desperation. 'Estranged from all society', writes Lee, 'the Queen of Scots gave herself up to the blackest despair; she had, alas! no hope to soften her captivity, no bosom to receive her tears' (*R* 34). Even though Hume and Robertson do express sympathy for Mary's plight, Lee amplifies it and focuses on her dire situation. In *The History of England*, Hume does not doubt the validity of the Casket Letters and Mary's guilt. Exploiting the historical ambiguity surrounding these artefacts, *The Recess* challenges this: Mary's 'innocence' (*R* 26) is referred to on a number of occasions and, at one point, she is referred to as a 'Queen, innocent at least in all that respected her' (*R* 35). Accused of being 'criminal' and forced to 'give herself up a prisoner to a government she had never offended' (*R* 25), she is movingly described as an 'exile from her country, a prisoner in another, a wife without a right to that name, and a mother, while a stranger to her children' (*R* 33).

Inverting the values and characterisations of these two famous historical women, Lee casts Elizabeth as a tyrannical Gothic villain and Mary as a persecuted victim in order to draw attention to the male ethics and ideals that shape eighteenth-century historiography. Her representations of these historical figures act as foils to Hume's *The History of England* and much male-centred eighteenth-century historiography. By presenting such radically different portraits of these two famous historical females, *The Recess* interrogates notions of historical accuracy and furthers the Gothic's obsession with tenuous connections to the past. Using the perspective afforded by the Female Gothic, Lee demonstrates that what eighteenth-century historiography records about women is 'refracted through the lens of men's observation' (Lerner 1981, 174). Exploiting the obscurity and uncertainty of the historical record and focusing on the villain's (Elizabeth's) persecution of a helpless female protagonist (Mary), Lee shows how women are essentially imprisoned within male codes of historical representation. Exploiting the Gothic's identification of the past as a site of conflict and transferring the figure of Mary from history to the realm of Gothic romance, Lee shows how eighteenth-century history does not ignore eminent women; it entraps them within male norms and criteria, and, as a result, has the potential to stain the reputations of women who do not conform to male ideals. When it comes to 'ordinary' women, the historical situation is even more disturbing. In terms of *The Recess*, Elizabeth and Mary are quite marginal presences; the focus is predominantly on the two female protagonists, Matilda and Ellinor. A key theme of the Female Gothic is the unwanted legacy of the mother, and, unfortunately for the 'twin heirs of misfortune' (*R* 270), they share a similar form of historical incarceration to their mother. Using a prominent Gothic trope, Lee transfers the sense of (male) historical distortion surrounding Mary onto her daughters and, by doing so, comments on the larger theme of women in history.

The Recess, history and ghostly women

The most identifiable Gothic element of Lee's novel is the ruined Recess itself. As the epigraph to this chapter indicates, it is in this underground chamber that Matilda and Ellinor are raised by Mrs Marlow, in 'total ignorance of their birth till able to know its inutility' (*R* 32). Fearing the reprisals that would accompany the discovery of the twins' identity, they are forced to endure a life of seclusion in this mouldering edifice, away from the sunlight and the world beyond. Serving as a substitute for Walpole's and Reeve's Gothic castles, the Recess contains various subterranean vaults and passages, as well as ancestral portraits. As Rictor Norton notes, this underground structure has a complex role in the novel: it is a place of concealment which functions simultaneously as 'a sanctuary and a prison, a place of refuge and a den of horror' (Norton 2000, 13). Once the twins have left the confines of the Recess and endure harrowing experiences in the wider world, they often look back on it as a 'calm retirement from the odious forms and cares of life' (*R* 34). However, despite such nostalgia, this underground chamber is the site of much of the novel's terror. It is here that Matilda and Ellinor are menaced by the evil Williams – a former servant of Lord Leicester's who betrays him – and his banditti. As Matilda vividly recalls, the Recess – a place 'sacred once to piety and innocence' – was now the 'shelter of rapine, perhaps murder' (*R* 99). Both twins are forcefully imprisoned and threatened by the prospect of violence and abuse. Before escaping, Leicester murders Williams within the Recess's walls (*R* 103). Throughout the novel, the Recess is frequently represented as a place of imprisonment: Matilda refers to it variously as a 'prison' (*R* 15), 'a horrible dungeon' (*R* 34) and speaks of feeling 'entombed alive' (*R* 10) within its confines.

This image of being buried alive is significant, especially when considered alongside the historical dimension that Lee attaches to the Recess. Mrs Marlow relates that this ancient edifice was formerly a convent 'inhabited by nuns of the order of St. Winifred', but was destroyed during the English Reformation (*R* 22). 'In this situation it remained many years, shunned by the country people', she adds, 'and devoutly visited by those travellers whom chance or curiosity brought this way' (*R* 22). During the Reformation and the oppression of Roman Catholics in England of Henry VIII's reign, it became a hiding place for monks (*R* 22–3). 'Thus, in a few years', relates Mrs Marlow, 'a monastery was hid among the ruins of the convent' (*R* 23). Once the final inhabitants had left, the existence of the Recess was kept a secret for many years. The historical aspect of the Recess does not end here. When the twins first go above ground, we learn that the entrance to it is hidden by a 'high-raised tomb' of a 'famous knight', surrounded by ensigns. Observing this memorial, Matilda notes that a 'meagre skeleton had struck an arrow through his shield into his heart; his eyes were turned to the cross which St. Winifred held before him' (*R* 37). The twins are surrounded by images of death, burial and entombment. Akin to their own exist-ence, they encounter material artefacts of a forgotten past; a secret history which is only remembered by those connected to the decay-ing convent. Surveying the ruins that surround the Recess, Matilda describes the scene as 'wild and awful to excess' and she is over-awed by the 'vast heaps of stones', the fragmented pillars, and the 'clusters and spires of ivy' which surround their 'mouldering' tops (*R* 37).

As the complex history of the Recess reveals, it is a structure that has multiple levels of meaning within the novel. Indeed, the images of concealment and burial that are associated with it work on literal, figurative and historical levels. With its links to the Reformation, the decaying Recess functions as a symbol of England's traumatic history. Written in the wake of the recent Gordon Riots (1780), this building serves as a timely material reminder of the historico-political upheaval from which 'the alliance of church and state of the eighteenth century had emerged' (Sweet 2004, 233). Perhaps more significantly in terms of the current discussion, how-ever, is the fact that the Recess used to be a convent. As Jane Spencer points out, as a former nunnery, the Recess is a powerful 'reminder of lost female communities and lost female power' (1986, 198). Though Anne H. Stevens describes the Recess as an 'ahistorical space' (2003, 270), Lee's detailed historical construction of this structure is more complex than this. In a strange paradox, the Recess is a building steeped in history and yet outside it; it is a pro-foundly historical structure, but below or on the margins of history. Drawing attention to an edifice that embodies female agency in the past – and a structure replete with the secret histories of nuns and monks – Lee continues the work Walpole started by using Gothic tropes to probe history's blind spots. Lee wants us to believe that the decaying nunnery is an important, and yet ignored, aspect of England's conflicted past. She employs the Gothic convention of the decaying edifice – in this instance, the ruined Recess – to highlight that, much like Ellinor and Matilda, women are 'entombed' in his-tory. Below ground and out of view, the Recess is synonymous with the oppression and general absence of ordinary women in history; it is a symbol of their historiographic marginalisation. Focusing on the tombs and memorials that surround Matilda and Ellinor, this ancient structure serves as a metaphor for the buried lives of ordi-nary women in history (or those sidelined by it).

The issue that Lee utilises the Gothic – and, more precisely, the Gothic trope of the decaying castle or building – to address is perhaps most clearly stated in Jane Austen's *Northanger Abbey* (1798–99). The novel's female protagonist, Catherine Morland, is thoroughly disillusioned with history's focus on 'the quarrels of popes and kings, with wars or pestilences, in every page; the men all so good for nothing, and hardly any women at all' (Austen 2003, 104).[11] Even though, as April Alliston points out, Lee rewrites history through 'female viewpoints unverifiable by a historiography that excludes such viewpoints' (1996, 122), women in the novel are still exterior to the historical events recounted. Like the Recess itself, Matilda and Ellinor remain strangely at the centre of history, but removed from it. The twins have a haunting presence throughout the novel. Pale and fatigued, Matilda refers to herself at one point as 'more like a spectre than myself' (*R* 60). In a similar vein, Ellinor describes her life as 'visionary'; 'seen without being known; adored, without being esteemed; punished without being guilty; applauded without being meritorious, we were all an illusion', she argues (*R* 157). Critics who have contested the Gothic nature of *The Recess*, such as Robert Hume, often point to the absence of the supernatural in the novel (1969, 283–4). Indeed, Lee is generally perceived as continuing Reeve's work by 'taming' the Gothic and removing some of its wilder, Walpolean excesses. However, Lee's Female Gothic novel is more complicated than this. Anticipating Ann Radcliffe's use of the 'explained supernatural', paranormal occurrences may be absent from the novel, but Lee nevertheless appropriates the Gothic's obsession with phantoms and images of death. During her imprisonment in the Arlington residence, Ellinor affects an escape by pretending to be the corpse of a recently deceased maid: 'when placing myself and treasure in the homely coffin, I was boldly conveyed like the Empress Maud through the midst of my enemies', she writes (*R* 218). As Jayne Elizabeth Lewis notes, gripped by madness, Ellinor 'becomes a ghost in the eyes of others' (*R* 180).

In one of the novel's most famous scenes, Ellinor (now mentally deranged due to her various sufferings) bursts into Queen Elizabeth's chamber. Presuming that she is dead, Elizabeth believes that the presence before her is a 'ghastly spectre' (*R* 266). Ellinor is described as a 'beauteous phantom' while her 'long garments of black flowed gracefully over the floor' (*R* 266). '[F]or surely never mortal looked so like an inhabitant of another world', writes Lady Pembroke (*R* 266). In this scene, a variety of circumstances combine to 'give this strange visitation the appearance of being supernatural' (*R* 268). For Lee, there is no need to feature ghosts and instances of the supernatural in her Female Gothic narrative; when it comes to history, women are always already spectres. Even though the narrative lens is fixed on the trials of Matilda and Ellinor, they are always outside of the male-dominated world of history; denied entry into this world, they haunt it instead. Matilda and Ellinor symbolise the women who populate the past, but have been forgotten by traditional modes of historiography; they represent fictional presences of real, ordinary historical females. Moreover, it is not only in the historical realm that women are depicted as unsubstantial or ghostly. Lee employs the lens of the Female Gothic and its propensity for using the past as a subterfuge to comment on the present in order to paint a deeply disturbing picture of the lives of eighteenth-century women.

Buried writings: women, history and civil death

Lee not only hijacks and adapts the Gothic trope of the remote, decaying edifice to comment on women's role in history, she also utilises the Gothic theme of concealed writings. As the previous two chapters of this book have demonstrated, the Gothic is fixated with secret histories and buried writings. The first editions of Walpole's *Otranto* and Reeve's *The Old English Baron* are presented as ancient, forgotten manuscripts. Furthermore, Reeve wants the reader to believe that the manuscript she has translated is a patchwork of legal proceedings and letters. Lee substantially develops this aspect of Gothic fiction. Not only are the twins effectively buried underground; Lee wants us to believe that the original documents detailing their history – and which she claims to have translated – are concealed in an obscure casket (*R* 326). At the end of the novel, Matilda bequeaths a casket to Adelaide Marie De Montmorenci, the person to whom her memoirs are addressed (*R* 326). The reader assumes that the memoir-letters that comprise *The Recess* are stored in this casket, which is later discovered – and its contents translated – in the eighteenth century (or so Lee would have us believe).[12] Moreover, concealed writings play a major role throughout Lee's Female Gothic novel; she uses them to critique both women's marginalisation in history and their repression in her own time.

A particularly notable episode that features buried writings involves Ellinor. During a confrontation, Queen Elizabeth throws a large book at Ellinor, rendering her senseless (*R* 119). When the laces on her dress are cut to aid her breathing, the 'eager eyes' of Elizabeth spot a 'small pacquet suspended to the black ribbon she always wore round her neck' (*R* 119). We learn that this 'pacquet' conceals the 'duplicate proof' of the twins' true ancestry; whilst Matilda keeps hers (at least at this stage in proceedings) treasured in a 'secret cabinet at Kenilworth' Castle, Ellinor keeps hers on her own person (*R* 120). Ravishing the document from Ellinor's body, Elizabeth immediately recognises its significance and promptly tears the document 'into atoms' (*R* 119). With the loss of these documents, Ellinor effectively loses her identity; she becomes unsure of who she is and eventually lapses into madness and insanity. Using the Gothic's focus on concealed writings and casting Elizabeth as a tyrannical Gothic villain, Lee demonstrates how women have been sidelined and, in this instance, completely erased from history. After her proof of birth is destroyed and she lapses into insanity, the only historical record that exists of Ellinor is via her own handwritten accounts and the other long-forgotten writings that comprise *The Recess*. This episode is just one of many in the novel that focuses on the relationship between female identity and documents. Such scenes have an even greater significance in the context of women's lives and legal status in the eighteenth century.

Reminiscent of *The Old English Baron*, the past is often the present in disguise in *The Recess*. Lee uses the Gothic's focus on concealed documents, the law and inheritance in order to critique the lives of women in her own century. In Lee's age, the male-dominated law meant that many women had no social and financial independence. William Blackstone's influential *Commentaries on the Laws of England* (1765–69) – the standard textbook for trainee lawyers in the eighteenth century – explains a woman's legal position once she is married: 'By marriage, the husband and wife are one person in law: that is, the very being or legal existence of the woman is suspended during the marriage, or at least is incorporated and consolidated into that of the husband: under whose wing, protection, and *cover*, she performs every thing' (1765–69, 1: 430). Blackstone's image of a woman's legal identity being 'suspended' during marriage is quite Gothic in itself. In Lee's eighteenth century, the patriarchal legal system meant that many females were denied autonomy and were rendered almost entirely dependent on their husbands. Due to primogeniture, many women were deprived of any inheritance when their husbands died; that privilege usually went to the eldest son, who, by law, was considered the head of the family. As Marcia Pointon highlights, once a woman was married she was 'considerably disadvantaged with regard to her legal status since common law regarded her as feme covert' (1997, 34). Utilising the emphasis on gender rights provided by the Female Gothic and exploiting the trope of buried writings, Lee examines the inheritance restrictions placed upon women in *The Recess*.

In this sense, another important incident involving concealed writings and female inheritance occurs when Matilda returns to Kenilworth Castle after the death of her husband, Lord Leicester. She recalls how one night she aided her late husband in placing 'several caskets, for which he seemed more than commonly anxious', in 'secure and unknown cabinets' located in the premises. Matilda notes how she also added 'Mrs Marlow's papers' and 'testimonials' of her birth (*R* 273). *The Recess* continues to exploit the Gothic's obsession with secret locations and hidden papers. With Mrs Arundel's help, Matilda has now returned to recover the 'well-remembered caskets' (*R* 275). In typical Gothic fashion, she locates the 'secret spring of the cabinet' (*R* 275) behind a bed, opens it and begins to explore the contents of the caskets:

> The largest was filled with family papers, bonds, contracts, mortgages, many of which were to me unintelligible, and all useless. The next contained letters and little ornaments, less precious from their intrinsic value, than their analogy to particular events – under these was a gilt casket filled with jewels of great value, and what was of infinitely more, the authenticated bonds and acknowledgements of all the sums Lord Leicester had informed me he had providently deposited in other countries; and of which I knew not any memorandum remained.
>
> (*R* 275–6)

Matilda's inheritance does not end here. 'The next casket was a gift from the fond mother to the darling of her heart', she writes, before explaining how it 'contained all the testimonials of the Queen of Scots, and other parties concerned, on the subject of my birth, with the contract of marriage between Lord Leicester and myself' (*R* 276). 'I felt rich in these recovered rights', pronounces Matilda.

Allied with Ellinor's experience, this episode serves to demonstrate how women are defined by documents in *The Recess*. Perhaps the most significant facet of this scene is her recognition of how important the recovery of the caskets is to the 'welfare' of her young daughter, Mary (*R* 273). As on many other occasions in *The Recess*, documents are more valuable than gold and jewellery. Matilda is aware that the manuscripts found in the caskets restore her own and, more importantly, her daughter's legitimacy, ancestry and legal identity. With these documents, young Mary will not suffer the same fate as her mother and will, in theory, be able to claim the life that she is entitled to. Matilda even dares to dream of one day claiming an alliance between herself, her daughter and King James I (*R* 276).

Matilda may believe that she has preserved a lasting legacy for her daughter, but it is cruelly snatched away from her. Attempting to turn her dream into a reality and to restore her own and her daughter's ancestral links to the monarchy, Matilda gathers the manuscripts found in the caskets at Kenilworth castle and reveals them to King James I. She takes literally 'every paper, and proof' that authenticates her rights, including the documents containing the 'unquestioned handwriting' of her mother, Mary, Queen of Scots (*R* 300–1). Although initially hospitable, the King betrays Matilda, imprisoning her and her daughter and destroying the legal documents. As in Ellinor's experience, Matilda realises, to her horror, that young Mary's (and, indeed, her own) identity is essentially terminated along with the documents:

> Rescued, in yet unconscious childhood, from slavery, neglect, and obscurity, fortune at one moment seemed willing to restore all the rights of your birth, when a weak, credulous mother assisted the cruel wretch who was pre-determined to entomb you, and annihilate every trace, every memorial, of our dear and honoured progenitors. – Nameless – dishonoured – your blooming youth must wither in an unknown prison – blighted by the tears of a parent who can never pardon herself the extravagant error produced by over-fondness. – I knew the King to be mean, base, subtle, yet I madly delivered into his treacherous hands every thing on which our hopes, nay, even our vindication must be grounded.
>
> (*R* 306)

Reminiscent of how Mary, Queen of Scots, may have been effectively destroyed through the male manipulation of the Casket

Letters, Matilda's and young Mary's social existence is virtually eradicated by the King's decision to destroy the documents. Young Mary is soon poisoned by the jealous wife of her lover, Lord Somerset (*R* 316), and, after witnessing the death of her beloved daughter, Matilda is forced to spend the rest of her days alone as an exile (*R* 325). Without documents, women are rendered powerless in Lee's novel.

The past communicates with the present in *The Recess* and Lee manipulates the Gothic's obsession with obscure papers to present a nightmare vision of a world where women's lives have been reduced to documents. There is a dialogue between the 1580s and the 1780s and, reminiscent of Blackstone's remarks, women in Lee's Female Gothic novel do not have an identity independent of marriage. When their husbands die and they are left to fend for themselves, they become even more invisible and ghostly. Whereas Reeve's Loyalist Gothic work upheld the law as a bastion of order and civility, Lee's Female Gothic novel presents it as something inherently misogynistic: as a male-driven, impersonal force that imprisons and socially suffocates women. Utilising Gothic tropology and focusing on the plight of women in the sixteenth century, *The Recess* conducts a bitter critique of eighteenth-century law, and, more specifically, marital law. Functioning as ciphers for women of her own time, Matilda's and Ellinor's tenuous and phantasmal existence through a series of secretive legal documents reveals how women are effectively 'dead' within dominant male power structures such as the law. To use Mary R. Beard's words, one of the abiding images of *The Recess* – and, for that matter, the Female Gothic – is that of woman, past and present, as 'being always and everywhere subject to *male* man or as a ghostly creature too shadowy to be even that real' (1946, 77). According with Blackstone's comments on women's suspension of identity when wedded, Matilda and Ellinor experience a form of civil death during and after marriage. Lee utilises the Gothic's focus on female persecution and concealed writings in order to highlight woman's perennial historiographic, legal and economic 'identitylessness' (Heller 1992, 2). Critiquing eighteenth-century gender ideology through her use of Gothic tropology, Lee reveals how patriarchy is maintained by depriving women of their inheritance and, ultimately, writing women out of society and history.

The curse of the mother: women and the perils of sensibility

As well as marital law, another source of unease for Lee is sensibility. When Walpole described *Otranto* as an 'attempt to blend the two kinds of romance, the ancient and the modern' (*O* 9), the Gothic became inextricably linked with novels of sensibility. By referring to 'modern' romances and comparing his work to 'drama' (*O* 6), Walpole motions towards (what is now called) the eighteenth-century novel and the sentimental works of Samuel Richardson.[13] In *Otranto*, Hippolita and Isabella are frequently shown crying and fainting. In the previous chapter, I commented on the tension between sensibility and ownership in *The Old English Baron* and how Reeve was influenced by Richardsonian didacticism. However, it is in the Female Gothic that the cult of sensibility, which had always been part of the Gothic, is at its most visible and where it receives its most incisive analysis. In *The Recess*, the cult of sensibility is a subject of intense scrutiny; eighteenth-century sensibility is mapped anachronistically onto the 1590s. Similarly to sentimental novels written by Richardson and Henry Mackenzie, the novel is replete with a variety of spontaneous emotional acts such as swooning, crying and embracing. As Janet Todd notes, differing from sentiment, the term sensibility came to denote spontaneous and 'delicate emotional and physical susceptibility'; it referred to 'the faculty of feeling, the capacity for extremely refined emotion and a quickness to display compassion for suffering' (1986, 7).[14] A particularly significant example of such spontaneous emotion occurs in the reclusive Recess when Matilda and Ellinor look upon an ancestral portrait – a staple Gothic device since *Otranto* – of a 'lady in the flower of youth, drest in mourning, and seeming in every feature to be marked by sorrow' (*R* 10). Although the twins do not know at this stage that they are looking at a portrait of their mother, Mary, Queen of Scots, Matilda relates how the poignant image 'seemed to call forth a thousand melting sensations; the tears rushed involuntarily into our eyes, and, clasping, we wept upon the bosoms of each other' (*R* 10). This display of sensibility over the absent mother is particularly significant. Intertwined with the subject of sensibility, the absent mother plays a major role in *The Recess*.[15] From Lee's novel onwards, motherless daughters loom large in the Female Gothic imagination.

Influenced by novels of sensibility, *The Recess* encourages readers to engage sympathetically with certain characters and events, and cultivates a sentimental engagement with the past. However, such emotive aspects of Lee's novel and the extent to which it can be considered as a novel of sensibility have been discussed at length elsewhere.[16] Rather, my focus here remains on *The Recess* as a Gothic work and, more precisely, as a (prototypical) Female Gothic novel. Lee's novel may employ certain aspects used in the sentimental novel, but its main concern is with the cult of sensibility in her own age and the impact it had on women's lives. *The Recess* may appear to masquerade as a novel of sensibility, but, in accordance with the transgressive nature of Gothic narratives, it subverts many of the notions central to such novels. As well as encouraging emotional responses from readers, novels of sensibility tended to teach people – and particularly women – how to behave and how to express themselves. Todd notes how Richardson's didactic novels, in particular, went some way to constructing the notion that good and virtuous women were sympathetic, emotional and passive (1986, 110). In *The Recess*, certain aspects of eighteenth-century sensibility become a source of Gothic horror. Using the Gothic's focus on ancestry, the past and unwanted legacies, Lee pioneers the Female Gothic by employing the figure of the absent mother as a vehicle to critique eighteenth-century gender politics. The parallels she draws between Mary, Queen of Scots, and her daughters are also of great importance, as I will show shortly. When Mrs Marlow relates to Matilda and Ellinor the harrowing history of their mother, it emerges that spontaneous, unregulated feelings are the cause of much of her troubles: 'Fatal delusion of a prejudiced mind! Oh Mary, too tender Princess! Why were not all the past misfortunes of thy life, which had their source in love, monitors to thee?' (*R* 28). 'Why did they not teach thee to avoid this error', laments Mrs Marlow, 'which heightened every affliction, and gave new pangs to a long, long captivity' (*R* 28). Mary has a fatal flaw in the sense that she is too susceptible to the 'partial advice of her heart' (*R* 28). Unfortunately for Matilda and Ellinor, they are cursed with their mother's excessive sensibility, which proves as destructive to their own lives as it did to Mary, Queen of Scots.

One of the most notable features of *The Recess* – and one that makes it such an innovative epistolary novel – is the conflicting accounts of Leicester and Essex offered by Matilda, Ellinor and

Lady Pembroke. Matilda and Ellinor are besotted by their respective lovers and idealise them. In Matilda's memoirs, Leicester is lauded as a 'guardian angel' (*R* 106) and is described, variously, as 'amiable' (*R* 63), 'beloved' (*R* 90) and 'sainted' (*R* 124). Ellinor presents a portrait of Leicester that is 'diametrically opposite' to that of her sister's (*R* 155). She describes him as 'chilling', 'callous' and 'tyrannic in his pursuits' (*R* 155–6). Inversely, two very different representations of Ellinor's lover, Essex, emerge. Ellinor glorifies him as an 'incomparable' being 'calculated to shine in whatever light you examined him' (*R* 164). Whilst Matilda largely resists the temptation to criticise her sister's lover (*R* 271), Lady Pembroke – the person entrusted to conclude Ellinor's memoirs – presents him in a very negative light: she describes him as 'ever haughty and impetuous', 'self-deluded' (*R* 260) and 'negligent' (*R* 257). The presence of such conflicting representations of historical personages exacerbates the Gothic's (already) contentious relationship with eighteenth-century, Enlightenment historiography by undermining character analysis as a means of understanding history, and by revealing that readings of the past are not objective (as historians such as Rapin and Hume would have readers believe), but subjective and inherently discordant.[17] These broader aspects of Lee's Gothic representations of the past will be discussed later, but at this stage it is important to recognise that the twin sisters' fixation with (and idealisation of) their partners is intertwined with Lee's protracted criticism of eighteenth-century sensibility. Comparing her own impression of Leicester with that of her sister's, Matilda is confounded by the 'strange and unaccountable difference' and reflects on how 'a woman insensibly adopts the disposition of him to whom she gives her heart' (*R* 271). However, despite this observation, Matilda's conduct does not change. Like her mother, her actions continue to be dominated by her feelings and her life takes an increasingly destructive path as she remains blind to the biases of her own passions, with tragic consequences. Towards the end of the narrative, Matilda is horrified when she learns that her daughter – who, in yet another parallel to the absent mother, is named Mary – is in love with the Earl of Somerset (*R* 316). Whilst Henry, Prince of Wales, has been Matilda's 'sole object of attention' (*R* 283), she neglects to notice that her daughter has been having an affair with a married man, Somerset. Blinded by her own feelings and her attraction to Henry, Matilda fails to protect her daughter, young Mary, who is poisoned by Somerset's jealous wife (*R* 316). Having witnessed the death of her daughter, Matilda spends the rest of her days a bitter and lonely woman. Ellinor's excessive sensibility has similarly tragic consequences. Her feelings for Essex are so intense that when he dies, she lapses into total insanity (*R* 256).

Cursed with the same excessive emotionalism as their absent mother, Matilda and Ellinor are 'too tender' princesses (*R* 28). Matilda says as much when she describes herself as a 'sad inheritor of my mother's misfortunes' (*R* 144). '[M]ethinks they are all only retraced in me', she adds (*R* 144). Listening to the dictates of their hearts at the expense of reason, both girls marry morally questionable and predatory men; ruthless individuals who are arguably more attracted to the twins' links to the throne than to the girls themselves. Both girls are so blinded by passion that they fail to recognise the dangers that surround them. The target in *The Recess* is not sensibility *per se*; rather, it is excessive sensibility that disturbs Lee. *The Recess* reveals the horrific consequences of women who are encouraged to indulge their feelings and renounce reason. The eighteenth-century cult of sensibility and novels of sentiment written by authors such as Richardson compelled women to yield to their emotions and helped to construct the idea that good women were very emotional and sympathetic.[18] In the nightmare world of *The Recess*, excessive sensibility renders women more vulnerable than virtuous. In Lee's Female Gothic novel, heightened sensibility damages women because it is not accompanied by reason. Commenting more on the 1780s than the 1590s, Lee exposes how sensibility stunts women's development and prevents them from developing a strong sense of individuality and rationalism. Anticipating Mary Wollstonecraft's remarks in *A Vindication of the Rights of Woman* (1792), women in Lee's novel are kept in 'the night of sensual ignorance' (1985, 99). To adapt C. J. Barker-Benfield's words, *The Recess* presents a horrific example of the 'solipsism and mindlessness' that are just a few of the dangerous, self-destructive conditions that exaggerated sensibility can inflict on women's lives (1992, xxvii). Moreover, by using the figure of the mother and showing how the same excessive sensibility is possessed by her daughters, Lee comments on how patriarchy is maintained by the transmission of oppressive values in female behaviour. Matilda's recognition of the force and bias of her own passions, followed by her repetition of the same behaviour, shows how difficult it is for women to disentangle themselves from exaggerated sensibility's powerful hold. Focusing on female protagonists, the Female Gothic frequently reveals the frightening and incapacitating effects of an over-cultivated sensibility. Educated in the secluded and remote Recess, the girls have little else to stimulate their lives. The confined Recess functions as an allegory for eighteenth-century women trapped in domesticity and impoverished by a strict obedience to male imposed doctrines of excessive sensibility. As Ellinor's and Matilda's lives show, they are, in consequence, ill-prepared for the world. As this chapter has demonstrated, the metaphor of entombment serves to comment on multiple aspects of women's lives in *The Recess*. In this instance, Lee uses it to show how eighteenth-century women are entombed in an excessive sensibility and a slavish adherence to their passions.

'Gothicising' the epistolary: Lee and representations of the past

Having now discussed some of the gendered aspects of Lee's novel, I will move on to a broader consideration of its Gothic elements and, more precisely, the ways in which it furthers the Gothic's enthralment with the past. *The Recess* does not only comment on the sentimental novel's preoccupation with sensibility; it utilises and imitates its very form. As a previous section has shown, Lee's novel is composed of conflicting sets of letters written by multiple narrators and, in this sense, represents a rare (possibly unique) variant of the epistolary; a form that became synonymous with the novels of sentiment written by authors such as Mackenzie and, most significantly, Richardson. *The Recess* has major implications for the eighteenth-century epistolary, and it is beyond the scope of the current chapter to consider all of them here.[19] Rather, I will focus on the ways in which Lee utilises this popular eighteenth-century form to intensify and develop the Gothic's obsession with the haunting nature of history. Throughout the forthcoming discussion, the thoughts of Richardson – arguably the most popular writer of epistolary fiction in the eighteenth century – will be used to elucidate the ways in which Lee appropriates this form for the purposes of the Gothic. What makes Richardson useful for discussion here is his propensity for theorising on the nature of the epistolary. He was particularly aware of its potential for mimicry and imitation. In his correspondence, he speaks of his desire for *Clarissa* (1748–49) to maintain an '*Air* of Genuineness'; for the fictional letters of which it comprises to be '*thought* genuine' in so far as they 'should *not* prefatically be owned *not* to be genuine' (Richardson 1964, 85). He desires his epistolary novel to convey an air of authenticity and to 'avoid hurting that kind of Historical Faith which Fiction is generally read with, tho' we know it to be Fiction' (85). It is this quality of the epistolary, its ability to masquerade as a series of genuine documents and to evoke a certain suspension of disbelief, that Lee exploits.[20] Walpole's observation that 'nothing gives so just an idea of an age as genuine letters; nay, history waits for its last seal from them', is not lost on Lee (1937–83, 15: 73). She uses the epistolary to mimic historical documents and, in the process, led many eighteenth-century readers into believing that the events related were true and historically accurate.[21] Lee 'Gothicises' the epistolary by turning its attention away from contemporary events and diverting it towards humanity's uneasy and disturbing relationship with the past.

The Recess is radical in the sense that it employs the epistolary to write about the machinations of the *distant past* and not to record *recent* events. In Richardson's epistolary novels, the event has usually occurred before it is committed to narrative. *Pamela* (1740–41) serves as a good example here. Even though Pamela often 'write[s] on, as things happen' (Richardson 1985, 150), days have sometimes elapsed before she 'writes up' events either in letters or in her journal. In all epistolary fiction, there is usually a gap between witnessing an event and then writing about it. However, in contrast to Richardson's epistolary fiction, many years have often elapsed between the experience of an event and the written response in *The Recess*. Indeed, Lee's text is essentially composed of memoir-letters; the accounts the reader encounters are recollections of events that occurred quite some time ago. This is particularly the case with Matilda's memoir-letter, which dominates *The Recess*. She recounts events a number of years after they have occurred, when nearly all of the principle figures are long dead and Matilda herself is nearing the end of her life. *The Recess* is a novel very much written in retrospect. Lee 'Gothicises' the epistolary form by extending the traditional gap between the *perceiving* and *narrating* self. In contrast to Richardson's *Pamela*, for example, a significant amount of time has elapsed before the events *experienced* are translated into a *narrative form* in Lee's novel. By employing first-person narration and creating a gulf between the occurrence of a past event and its narrativisation, *The Recess* probes a theme central to future Gothic works: the presence of the past in the human psyche.

By the time Lee writes *The Recess*, the epistolary had long been identified as a literary form particularly well adapted for conveying introspection and probing human psychology. In his 1748 preface to the first edition of Volume 3 of Richardson's *Clarissa*, William Warburton (Bishop of Gloucester from 1759 and well-known English literary critic) argues that fictional collections of letters present a 'natural opportunity' of 'representing with any grace those lively and delicate impressions which *Things present* are known to make upon the minds of those affected by them' (1970, 124). The epistolary, he continues, 'leads us farther into the recesses of the Human Mind, than the colder and more general reflections suited to a continued and more contracted Narrative' (124). Lee leads us even further into the 'recesses' of the human mind; she 'Gothicises' the epistolary by focusing on the mind's disturbing, often uncanny relationship with the past. In Lee's hands, the Gothic continues to explore aspects of the past beyond historical writing and shows that our relationship with history is far more unsettling and complex than many Enlightenment historians suggest. Matilda and Ellinor not only struggle to write their histories; they have trouble *remembering* their pasts. Attempting to narrate the circumstances surrounding Leicester's death, Matilda writes, 'How, how shall I recall the scene, and preserve recollection enough to point it?' (*R* 123). As the following examples demonstrate, Matilda's memoir is pervaded by ambiguity and uncertainty, as she struggles to recollect and write the past: she says that she is 'Unable to reduce the torrent of my ideas into language' (*R* 117), 'To paint our distraction would be a vain attempt' (*R* 14) and 'I almost expire under the recollection' (*R* 311). Such protestations are not uncommon in first-person narration and epistolary works. However, *The Recess* is very much concerned with the past and the writing of history, and such remarks reveal epistemological anxieties. Utilising the psychological introspection afforded by the epistolary and adapting it to further the Gothic's obsession with history, Lee shows how the past is forever present in the human mind, and yet always out of reach and inherently incommunicable. Similarly to her twin sister, Ellinor often finds herself unable to describe the past, saying, 'Something strangely intervenes between myself and my meaning' (*R* 185), 'I am too stupefied now to explain it' (*R* 185) and 'who shall paint the feelings of Essex' (*R* 225).

In contrast to Matilda's memoirs, however, Ellinor's representations of the past are excessively disjointed and confused. Indeed, in her memoirs, the past's hold on the human mind is presented as something capable of great destruction. Gripped by madness – a theme that becomes a staple of future Gothic fiction – her 'abstracted mind' inhibits her access to the past, as 'a thousand distant ideas' engulf and confuse her writings (*R* 182). '[T]he past, the present, and the future, presented only one wild chaos to my mind', she writes elsewhere (*R* 170). Ellinor's mind becomes fixated by the past and her deceased husband, Essex: 'Good Heavens, while I relate this it appears a mere vision! – Did I really see Essex? – Were my senses really revived by that voice so long forgotten, except when fancy recalled it?' (*R* 202). Gripped by insanity, she is unable to differentiate between the past and present: 'I fear I begin again to wander, for my hand-writing appears to my own eyes that of Essex', she comments when writing her memoirs (*R* 196). Essex may be dead, but he lives on in Ellinor's mind, haunting her reality and dragging her back into the past. Utilising the epistolary for the purposes of Gothic fiction, Lee draws attention to history's enduring presence in the human mind. By extending the gap between the perceiving and narrating self and utilising the psychological insight afforded by the epistolary, Lee reveals the poisonous effects the past can have on the mind and the horrors of madness and mental decay. Continuing with one of *The Recess*'s most enduring Gothic metaphors, Ellinor effectively becomes entombed in her own history; her mind becomes imprisoned in a past so traumatic that she can neither write it, nor fully comprehend it. Overwhelmed by her history and the spectre of Essex that haunts her psyche, Ellinor, to her sister's horror, spends the rest of her days 'set in insensibility' (*R* 270). Positioning the Gothic as eighteenth-century (or Enlightenment) historiography's other, *The Recess* reveals humanity's non-linear relationship with the past and demonstrates that human experience is inherently incongruent with the order and systematisation imposed by historians.

In *The Recess*, the eighteenth-century epistolary and the Gothic's obsession with the past are fused together. Collections of letters do not only afford an insight into the power the past holds over the mind; their very presence, form and arrangements have significant implications for how the past is perceived, and representations of it. Intensifying the Gothic's preoccupation with the nature of history, Lee exposes our troubled, fragmented and enigmatic relationship with the past, challenging the historical confidence and certainty exuded by eighteenth-century historians such as Hume and Rapin. As an epistolary novel consisting of numerous letters, *The Recess* is perhaps more accurately defined as a collection of documents than as a 'manuscript'. Lee's novel significantly develops the narrative complexity of both Richardson's epistolary fiction and Reeve's Gothic novel, *The Old English Baron*. The structure of Lee's novel serves to illustrate this point and is important in terms of understanding her Gothic representation of the past. Beginning with life in the Recess and ending with her return to England, the first memoir-letter of *The Recess* is written by Matilda. Receiving Ellinor's writings from Lady Arundel, Matilda then attaches her sister's memoir (*R* 154). This account is addressed to Matilda and delivered into the hands of Lady Pembroke (*R* 219), along with the addition of two letters that are addressed from Ellinor to the latter. Lady Pembroke briefly contributes to the narrative (*R* 219–20) before the letters themselves appear. It is important to note that these particular documents differ from memoir-letters; they are actual letters that cover a much shorter span of time and are more typical of eighteenth-century epistolary novels. After these letters, Ellinor's account switches back to a memoir-letter, but this time it is written for Lady Pembroke, not Matilda. Ellinor is rendered insane by her traumatic past and Lady Pembroke concludes her memoir. Having received all of these documents from Lady Arundel, Lady Pembroke's sister, Matilda then resumes her own memoir-letter, beginning with the confounding differences in the sisters' accounts of events, to her own impending death.

The Recess is essentially an archive; it consists of multiple, interconnecting historical documents. All of the letters are (originally) collated by Matilda and addressed to Adelaide Marie De Montmorenci, the French ambassador's daughter who only features briefly towards the end of *The Recess* (*R* 325). It is because of Adelaide's tenderness towards her during the early stages of her illness, and her curiosity about her life, that Matilda decides to construct such a narrative in the first place (*R* 7). As the 'Advertisement' to *The Recess* highlights, Matilda's collection of documents are eventually discovered hundreds of years later in the eighteenth century and are then edited by Lee. In typical Gothic fashion, Lee is unable to publish the method by which she acquired the original manuscript and explains how, as an editor, she has altered the original language 'to that of the present age, since the obsolete stile of the author would be frequently unintelligible' (*R* 5). Lee wants us to believe that, throughout its turbulent history, the original, multifaceted manuscript has travelled hundreds of miles, survived several major historical events, been read by numerous personages, stored in a variety of locations, and has now, hundreds of years later in the eighteenth century, been translated and published.

Reminiscent of Richardson's thoughts on the historical suspension of disbelief afforded by the epistolary, readers of *The Recess* are encouraged to believe that underneath the neat, printed characters lay Matilda's, Ellinor's and Lady Pembroke's handwritten, time-worn manuscripts. In *The Recess*, letters serve to illuminate the 'transmittedness' of the past, its existence in the present and its propensity for resisting synthesis. To use the words of Thomas O. Beebee (1999, 15), as well as their actual content, letters are equally important as *signifiers* in *The Recess*. The sprawling, disjointed nature of Lee's epistolary novel reveals the past for what it is: a disordered mass. Letters act as foils to the sources Lee most likely consulted in writing *The Recess* (including Hume's *The History of England* and Robertson's *History of Scotland*) and negate the conceptualisation and application of 'unifying themes and plots' (Day 1966, 8). As Jayne Elizabeth Lewis highlights, *The Recess* is essentially 'paratactic', as its different elements are 'jammed together' in ways that defy readers' attempts to discover 'logical connections' amongst them (1995, 169). Lee's Gothic appropriation of the epistolary form to comment on historiography is compelling, and, at a time when a number of historians were using the epistolary format to write history, her novel reveals a profound insight into the relationship between the letter-writer and the historian.[22]

Whether it is a person writing a letter to a friend or relative, or a historian attempting to reconstruct historical events, they have one salient factor in common: they are both essentially *writing an absence*. The person who writes a letter is, firstly, writing to a correspondent who is not present at the time of writing (in terms of *The Recess*, Adelaide) and, secondly, writing about (past) events that the absent person has not witnessed (again, in *The Recess*, the events of Matilda's life). The historian (for example, Hume) is writing about events that have irretrievably passed. The writing of letters and the writing of history require acts of imagination and the translation of experience into language; both forms of writing 'bear traces of events as manifest in consciousness' (Perry 1980, 119). *The Recess* reveals that, because both letters and history write absences (events that have not been witnessed directly), they are both prone to misinformation, misrepresentation and confusion. Throughout *The Recess*, letters have a peculiar propensity for complication. Communications frequently break down, defy understanding, or are interrupted. For example, Matilda's letters to Leicester are intercepted by Williams (R 71–2), whilst, in the wake of the death of Henry (the Prince of Wales), she finds herself confused by the cryptic messages that she receives from Sir David Murray (R 293–7). After Lord Arlington's death, Essex sends a letter to Ellinor, hopeful that she will be freed from her virtual imprisonment in his house. However, Essex's letter is intercepted by watchful relations and he is sent an ambiguous note alluding to Ellinor's 'insanity and confinement' (R 211). Relating to the whole ethos of Gothic literature, *The Recess* continually undermines notions of clarity, certainty and precision. Significantly developing the Gothic's hostility towards Enlightenment historical methodologies designed to master the past, Lee uses letters to reveal how, akin to historiography, they have a penchant for obscuring, deceiving and manipulating as much as they do for 'informing, clarifying and negotiating' (Zaczek 1997, 122).

The Recess, history and the legacy of the Female Gothic

The Recess shows eighteenth-century Gothic at its most historically subversive. Indeed, Lee's novel provides an example of historiography in reverse: where a historian such as Hume takes an 'unknown' past and creates a narrative to transform what is initially strange into something familiar and understandable, Lee takes a 'known' past in *The Recess*, constructs a narrative that emphasises its unfamiliarity and incomprehensibility and, ultimately, exposes its inherent – and profoundly disturbing – 'unknowability'. Capturing humanity's paradoxical relationship with the past, we finish Lee's suspenseful Gothic novel knowing more about a historical period and yet, at the same time, less. It is a work that manages to bring the reader into closer contact with the past, and yet make that past seem further away by frustrating our access to it and illuminating the mutability of the historical record. Moreover, *The Recess* heralds the beginning of the Female Gothic. Rejecting the model of history that lauds 'Great Men' and that underpins Reeve's Loyalist Gothic agenda in *The Old English Baron*, Lee commandeers established Gothic tropes and exploits the genre's infatuation with the past in order to show that the men of history are often far from great. Establishing the Female Gothic by focusing on the terrible plight of its female protagonists, *The Recess* showed future women writers how the genre could be used to critique women's marginalisation and oppression in history and society.[23]

With its persistent images of imprisonment, tyranny and death, *The Recess* can be considered not only as one of the darkest Gothic novels discussed in this book, but as one of the bleakest novels of the eighteenth century. In Walpole's *Otranto*, an unknown, threatening past destroys the current social order (symbolised by the ruined castle), but an ancestral chain is ultimately restored (as the limb by limb re-membering of Alfonso signifies). In Reeve's Loyalist Gothic novel, she constructs a Christian past where the virtuous are ultimately saved and rewarded. In stark contrast to these previous Gothic works, patriarchy destroys nearly all of the female protagonists in Lee's Female Gothic past, and it ends on a note of despair as the ailing Matilda bequeaths a casket containing her history to a friend. There is no benevolent God to assist the virtuous in *The Recess*. In the hands of its next proponent, the Female Gothic still uses fictional pasts to probe women's oppression, but it presents a more optimistic vision. The historical specificity that had defined Gothic pasts since Reeve also disappears. If Lee pioneered the Female Gothic by hijacking staple Gothic conventions to probe women's contemporary and historical plight, it was Ann Radcliffe who continued its legacy and took it to new, hitherto unforeseen levels of influence and popularity. With the outbreak of the French Revolution in the early 1790s, existing debates surrounding the nature of the past and women's role in both history and society gathered force. As I will show in the following chapter, the past constructed in Radcliffe's Female Gothic novel, *The Romance of the Forest* (1791), engages with such contemporary anxieties and debates, as well as probing the rise of a new, unsettling sense of historical consciousness engendered by the monumental events taking place across the English Channel.

Notes

1 *The Recess* comprises three volumes. The first of these appeared in 1783 with the next two volumes following in 1785. By 1806 – twenty years after its original publication – *The Recess* had gone through five separate English editions and had been translated into French, German, Swedish, Spanish and Portuguese (Alliston 2000, xix).

2 For example, Robert D. Hume argues that *The Recess* is a sentimental-domestic novel transported to a historical setting with Gothic trimmings. 'If wearing a wool tie makes me a sheep, then *The Recess* is a Gothic novel', he remarks (1969, 283). Since its publication, Lee's novel has been variously classified. See April Alliston's introduction to Lee's text for more information (2000, ix–xliv).

3 *The Recess* exacerbates the Gothic's fraught and complex relationship with the Catholic faith. Although the main protagonists of the novel are Catholic, the conventions of this religion are presented in a very negative light. After the death of Lord Leicester, Matilda falls into the hands of Catholic servants in France and is scathing about their faith; she is outraged that they refer to her 'noble husband' as 'an heretic', 'an outcast of society' and a 'wretch not worthy of interment' (*R* 125). She accuses them of '[p]reposterous blindness' (*R* 128). Such sentiments regarding Catholicism have an added significance when considered in the context of the political unrest of Lee's own age and the recent Gordon Riots. Matilda's description of Leicester's funeral ceremony is particularly significant. She describes how nuns decorate 'his sepulchre with all the pompous insignia of Death' and questions, bitterly, other aspects of the Catholic faith: 'Can midnight tapers, suspended black, or waving plumes, relieve those eyes which seek in vain their only object? or gratify a heart writhing under the iron hand of calamity?' (*R* 128). It is these macabre and chilling ceremonial aspects of the Catholic faith that would prove to be a source of fascination for future Gothic writers, such as Matthew Lewis and Ann Radcliffe.

4 Recent books that devote considerable space to *The Recess* include E. J. Clery's *Women's Gothic: from Clara Reeve to Mary Shelley* (2004, 25–50), Sue Chaplin's *The Gothic and the Rule of Law, 1764–1820* (2007, 84–94), Anne H. Stevens's *British Historical Fiction before Scott*

(2010, 40–50), and Diana Wallace's *Female Gothic Histories: Gender, History and the Gothic* (2013, 25–66).

5 Stevens goes as far as to say that Hume's and Robertson's histories were the 'main sources for her novel' (2010, 42) whilst, in Alliston's edition of *The Recess*, she points out the similarities and differences between Lee's treatment of certain historical events and Hume's and Robertson's descriptions.

6 Early in 1567, Lord Darnley (Henry Stuart) – Mary's husband and claimant to the English throne – was killed when the house in which he was residing was blown up by gunpowder. Darnley's body was discovered at some distance from the scene of the explosion. Reports at the scene suggested that he had been strangled. Beyond the reporting of these circumstances, the historical record is sparse and Darnley's murder remains one of history's greatest murder mysteries. The Earl of Bothwell (James Hepburn) – a favourite of Mary's since the murder of Rizzio – was accused of devising the plan to kill Darnley. It was suspected that Mary herself was not wholly ignorant of the plot. Evidence substantiating this theory came to light later that year when a silver casket containing incriminating letters and sonnets allegedly written by Mary to Bothwell was unearthed. These highly contentious documents became known as the Casket Letters and debates about their authenticity raged amongst eighteenth-century historians. If authentic, they practically prove Mary was complicit in Darnley's murder. If false, however, they not only severely question the integrity of Mary's opponents, but reveal how she was unfairly represented as a murderer across Western Europe and unlawfully imprisoned in England. Debate surrounding the authenticity of the Casket Letters has raged for centuries, many arguing that they are forgeries of genuine letters that have been strategically manipulated by Mary's (predominantly male) enemies. The debate has been ignited for so long mainly because the original documents disappeared around 1584. Throughout the centuries, arguments and theories have been premised on interpretations of the copies and translations made in 1568.

7 Lee does not reveal the identity of the 'eminent historian' she refers to here. Jayne Elizabeth Lewis argues that the historian Lee alludes to is 'presumably Hume himself' (1995, 172). Following her father's death in 1781, Sophia (and her sisters Harriet and Ann Lee) opened a school in Bath for approximately seventy daughters of the gentry. By this time, Hume's multi-volume work of historiography had become the standard and definitive history of England, and, given the fact that upper- and middle-class women were encouraged to read history as part of their education (see Note 11), it is plausible that she was intimate with Hume's work.

8 Clery (2004, 41) points out that similarly to Elizabeth's attempts to defend Protestantism against the forces of Catholicism, late eighteenth-century England had recently been rocked by brutal clashes between Protestants and Catholics in the Gordon Riots. Moreover, she highlights that, in a strong parallel with the late sixteenth century, Lee's age had (as I discussed in the previous chapter) recently extended its influence abroad by unprecedented proportions, raising questions about England's role as a world power. Such contemporary colonial anxieties pervade the sixteenth-century past constructed in *The Recess*. A particularly notable example of colonial rebellion occurs during a slave revolt in the West Indies. 'Inflicted cruelty had hardened their hearts, and the sight of untested luxuries corrupted them', relates Matilda (*R* 141). Lee presents a nightmare vision of colonialism gone astray and where monstrous communities have emerged. Matilda says as much when, speaking of the mutinous slaves, she notes how their 'own wants have increased with knowledge of our enjoyments, and what they greatly desire, they have learnt to go any lengths to attain' (*R* 141). Empire has obviously been important to the Gothic since Reeve's Loyalist Gothic work, *The Old English Baron*, but it is in *The Recess* where the Gothic begins to generate terror from the nightmare possibilities of Britain's colonial expansion. For more information on Lee's novel and colonial politics, see Janina Nordius's 'A Tale of Other Places: Sophia's Lee's *The Recess* and Colonial Gothic' (2002). Empire and colonialism would become much more prominent in future Gothic fiction, particularly during the Victorian period. However, returning to the eighteenth century, Britain's expansion abroad would continue to influence Gothic narratives, particularly in William Beckford's *Vathek* (1786) – an orientalist tale recounting the exotic horrors experienced by the novel's chief protagonist, the Caliph, Vathek.

9 For a concise history of how the term has developed since Ellen Moers coined the phrase in 1976, see Diana Wallace's and Andrew Smith's introduction to *The Female Gothic: New Directions* (2009, 1–12).

10 From this point onwards in this book, the terms 'Gothic' and 'Female Gothic' will both be used. The term Gothic will be used to denote aspects that are common to the genre; it will often be used in the context of discussing how Lee adapts the conventions set out by Walpole and Reeve. The term Female Gothic will be used to highlight how Lee – and subsequent women writers – use this new strain of fiction differently to previous Gothic authors.

11 Even though eighteenth-century historiography neglects female experience and is underpinned by male paradigms, women were encouraged

to read history. For example, in 'Of the Study of History', Hume argues that 'female readers' should read history instead of romances and other 'serious compositions, which are usually to be found in their closets' on the basis that it is far more didactic, 'amuses the fancy', 'improves the understanding', and 'strengthens virtue' (Hume 1854, 528–30). The rise of modern historiography, as opposed to the history practised by the ancients, meant that a classical education was not required to read such works, thus making it particularly accessible to relatively uneducated female audiences. In accordance with Hume, many conduct manuals of the time encouraged women to read historical works as a means of widening their experience. See Looser's *British Women Writers and the Writing of History, 1670–1820* (2000) for more information on this topic.

12 There are numerous parallels with the Casket Letters throughout *The Recess*; their spectre haunts many episodes of the novel. A particularly notable incident involves Ellinor. Whilst detained by Lord Arlington, Ellinor is summoned to the bedside of a dying servant. This servant reveals how he came into possession of a casket found in the Recess which contained 'a number of papers and trifles of no value', a 'large sum in gold' and a 'few jewels' (*R* 208). Upon opening it, she finds the gold and jewels and discovers that the papers 'consisted chiefly of the correspondence between Mrs Marlow and Father Anthony' (*R* 209), these letters, in turn, containing 'ciphers, hair' and 'sonnets' (*R* 210). The similarities to the Casket Letters are unmistakeable. Whether it is the chest that Anana (the Governor's black concubine who Matilda meets in Jamaica) bequeaths to Matilda's daughter, Mary (*R* 150–1), the 'incredible and disgraceful' forged documents that Ellinor is compelled to sign (*R* 178) or the chest that Matilda leaves Adelaide at the end of the novel (the one which contains all the scripts), *The Recess* plays with the controversy and complex symbolism of the Casket Letters. For further discussion of how *The Recess* relates to the Casket Letters, see Lewis's *Mary Queen of Scots: Romance and Nation* (1998, 136–46) and Stevens's 'Forging Literary History' (2008, 223–6).

13 Richardson's epistolary novels were well known for their dramatic qualities and sense of immediacy. Furthermore, when Walpole refers to drama, he also refers to Shakespeare. The Gothic owes a huge debt to Shakespeare's plays and his dramatic techniques. This is especially the case with Lee: both of her parents (Anna Sophia and John Lee) were Shakespearean actors and the fusion of history and tragedy within such plays resonates with *The Recess*. Furthermore, it is also important to point out that *The Recess* is indebted to the French historical novel and works such as Marie de Lafayette's *La Princesse de*

Cléves (1678), Antoine François Prévost's *Cleveland* (1731–39) and Baculard d'Arnaud's *Varbeck* (1774). See Alliston's introduction to *The Recess* (2000, xv) and *Virtue's Faults* (1996, chapters 2 and 5) for more information on Lee's indebtedness to Shakespeare and the French historical novel.

14 As Janet Todd notes, even though the terms sentiment and sensibility are often used interchangeably, there is a marked difference between them. Sentiment, she argues, is a 'moral reflection, a rational opinion usually about the rights and wrongs of human conduct' and is characterised by 'generalized reflections' (1986, 7). A 'sentiment', she adds, is 'also a thought, often an elevated one, influenced by emotion, a combining of heart with head or an emotional impulse leading to an opinion or a principle' (7). In contrast to this, sensibility is more physically based and denotes an 'innate sensitiveness or susceptibility revealing itself in a variety of spontaneous activities such as crying, swooning and kneeling' (7). See Todd's *Sensibility: An Introduction* (1986) for more information on the differences between sentiment and sensibility.

15 Mothers are often absent in novels of sentiment and it is likely that Gothic authors adopted and developed this device from such works. See April Alliston's 'The Value of a Literary Legacy: Retracing the Transmission of Value through Female Lines' (1990) for a discussion of *The Recess*'s representation of the mother in comparison to novels of sentiment.

16 Citing the growing importance of sentiment to eighteenth-century historical writing, Stevens argues that Lee exploits the 'new interest in sympathetic engagements with the past' and draws on the emotional responses evoked by novels of sentiment (2010, 42).

17 In the advertisement to *The Recess*, Lee (similarly to Walpole in *Otranto*) undermines the ways in which eighteenth-century historians use character analysis as a means of reading the past. 'As painting can only preserve the most striking characteristics of the form', writes Lee, 'history perpetuates only those of the soul; while too often the best and worst actions of princes proceed from partialities and prejudices, which live in their hearts, and are buried with them' (*R* 5). As Alliston points out (2000, xvii), such a view radically undermines an assumption central to eighteenth-century historiography: that character is stable and, therefore, that the truth of character can be used to determine the truth of incident. Lee's conception of character, argues Alliston, 'emphasizes the forces of emotions like love and jealousy' and, thus, acts as a foil to eighteenth-century historians who tend to relegate such feelings 'to the realm of the private, which they exclude from history' (2000, xvii).

18 The largely male-driven culture of sensibility in the second half of the eighteenth century simultaneously enhanced and restricted women's cultural development. The attributes praised in an age of sensibility were increasingly being recognised as 'feminine': a capacity to convey feelings, compassion, modesty, self-denial, and moral goodness. As Sally Winkle notes, the literature of sensibility 'gave women a new sense of gender autonomy', but also prescribed for the female gender the 'practice of receptivity rather than creativity, feelings rather than deep reflection or analysis, and unselfishness rather than self-love' (1989, 79–80). Male writers of sentimental, epistolary fiction such as Richardson essentially function as ventriloquists for women; males assume female voices and write about female experiences, outlining examples of what they perceive as 'good' and morally prescriptive attributes of femininity throughout their works. *The Recess* represents a reaction to such attitudes.

19 In terms of narrative and structure, *The Recess* rectifies one of the main problems associated with the Richardsonian epistolary. As Henry Fielding satirically highlights in *Shamela* (1741), it is simply not feasible that Richardson's narrators can write so much so close to – or even during – events. By extending the gap between the perceiving and narrating self and drawing attention to narrators' difficulties to recall past events, Lee's novel is more believable and plausible than many of Richardson's epistolary novels.

20 *The Recess* was not Lee's only epistolary novel. Her first attempt at prose fiction was *The Life of a Lover*, a lengthy novel of letters eventually published in 1804.

21 In a similar vein to the initial reception of Walpole's *Otranto*, numerous eighteenth-century readers believed *The Recess* to be an authentic and essentially true historical manuscript. In her introduction to Lee's novel, Alliston recounts a humorous anecdote involving two ladies and their views regarding Mary, Queen of Scots. Speaking of Mary's marriage to Norfolk and the existence of her secret twin daughters, one of the ladies informs her friend that 'it's very true: I have just been reading an entertaining *novel*, which is *founded* entirely upon *that fact*' (Alliston 2000, xvii).

22 A particularly notable example of a historian who employed the epistolary to write history was Oliver Goldsmith. Published in 1764, his *History of England, in a Series of Letters from a Nobleman to his Son* closely follows Hume's *The History of England* in terms of content. Jane Austen takes aim at Goldsmith's history in her historical satire entitled 'The History of England, by a Partial, Prejudiced and Ignorant Historian' (1791).

23 *The Recess* would not be Lee's last Gothic work. She later collaborated
   with her sister Harriet to write *The Canterbury Tales* (1796 onwards): a
   critically acclaimed work that is pervaded by Gothic themes, such as
   the relationship between science and the supernatural, and features
   figures such as the Wandering Jew and the banditti. Throughout her
   writing career, Lee was a very popular and successful writer and sup-
   plemented her income with several dramas, ballads and translations,
   including *The Chapter of Accidents* (1780), *A Hermit's Tale, Recorded
   by his own Hand and Found in his Cell* (1787) and *Almeyda: Queen of
   Granada* (1796).

4

'[E]very nerve thrilled with horror': the French Revolution, the past and Ann Radcliffe's *The Romance of the Forest* (1791)

The fresh ruins of France, which shock our feelings wherever we can turn our eyes, are not the devastation of civil war; they are the sad but instructive monuments of rash and ignorant counsel in time of profound peace.

Edmund Burke, *Reflections on the Revolution in France* (1790)

Few persons but those who have lived in it can conceive or comprehend what the memory of the French Revolution was, nor what a visionary world seemed to open upon those who were just entering it. Old things seemed passing away, and nothing was dreamt of but the regeneration of the human race.

Robert Southey to Caroline Bowles (1834)

In the years between the publication of Sophia Lee's *The Recess* (1783) and Ann Radcliffe's third Gothic novel, *The Romance of the Forest* (1791), a series of events unprecedented in human history occurred; events that would alter the Gothic and the nature of history forever. 'All circumstances taken together', writes Edmund Burke in his *Reflections on the Revolution in France* (1790), 'the French revolution is the most astonishing that has hitherto happened in the world' (Burke 1986, 92). Following in the wake of the American Revolution (1775–83) and the American Declaration of Independence (1776), the French Revolution began in July 1789 with the fall of the Bastille. The Bastille symbolised social oppression and tyranny and yet, at the same time, it was an icon of historical continuity, order and stability. The storming of this Parisian prison exposed the Revolution's intention to eradicate the past and its institutions and to start anew. Events occurred at a rapid pace. In a bid to reduce the influence of the Catholic Church and return power to the state, the historic tithe – a land tax dating in France from 1585 – was abolished in August 1789. Marking the decline of the *ancien régime* and embodying Enlightenment principles such as individualism and social contract, *The Declaration of the Rights of Man and of the Citizen* was published in the same month. Amongst numerous other events and acts of rebellion, thousands of poor women reacted to harsh economic circumstances by descending on Versailles and storming the Royal Palace in October 1789. Within just a few months, the absolute monarchy that had governed for centuries had been overturned and France was transformed from a hierarchical, feudal social order to one embracing new Enlightenment principles of citizenship and inalienable rights.

Separated from events by only the short expanse of the English Channel, many individuals living in England were astonished that one of the oldest and most autocratic governments in Europe had collapsed amidst scenes of widespread violence and anarchy. This was a revolution like no other, constituting rebellion on a national scale and involving nearly all sections of society. France – England's nearest neighbour – was a nation in arms, at war with history and the historically conditioned nature of the state. The final volume of Edward Gibbon's immensely successful work of Enlightenment historiography, *The Decline and Fall of the Roman Empire*, was published in 1788 and, for many English onlookers, the revolution in France had the potential to become the new, contemporaneous fall of Rome. However, despite this comparison, the events taking place in France were so intense and occurred so rapidly that dominant, eighteenth-century Enlightenment philosophical historical theories seemed at a loss to explain them.

With its aspirations for freedom and social equality, the French Revolution promised to mark the climax of the Enlightenment's belief in progress and reason. Indeed, the early proceedings in France seemingly embodied the values that the Enlightenment and historians influenced by its principles (for example, David Hume, Paul M. Rapin de Thoyras and William Robertson) treasured: the pursuit of liberty, free-thinking, self-reliance, and the decline of historic, despotic social institutions. Nevertheless, paradoxically, the very historical theories developed by Enlightenment historians seemed powerless to explain France's radical departure from the tenets of the past. The methodological underpinnings of the histories written by Hume and the other philosophical historians of the Enlightenment were placed under severe stress; sociological histories based on the uniformity of human behaviour, stadial theories premised on gradual change and Whig interpretations of the past adhering to notions of steady progress struggled to account for such a sudden, cataclysmic event. The enormity of the French Revolution and its implications could not be explained or contained by existing Enlightenment historiographical methodologies, frameworks of understanding or rational representational strategies.

The pamphlet war, romance and historiography

Although the influence of the rationalist historians of the Enlightenment was still felt during this turbulent period – and remained essential to the Gothic's attitude towards history – it was no longer as dominant or even seemed as relevant as it had formerly been.[1] With the Revolution in its infancy in the early 1790s and its as yet unresolved 'plot' twisting and turning like that of a Gothic novel, it was proving difficult to historicise or contextualise this historical phenomenon; that task would dominate the historical agenda after the turn of the century, when the Revolution had run its (eventually bloody) course. Nevertheless, in the extraordinary outpouring of political pamphlets in this decade, pamphleteers scrutinised the past not only as a way of promoting their own political agendas, but as a means of predicting the trajectory of the French Revolution and its implications for English life. Facing such remarkable developments, it was natural that writers would attempt to draw analogies with 'known' and understood historical events. Historical debate migrated from the multi-volume tomes of Enlightenment historiographers to the domain of the political pamphlet (a 'rapid response' textual mode).

Edmund Burke's *Reflections* marks a particularly significant moment for late eighteenth-century historical writing. In this fiery political treatise, Burke responds vehemently to Richard Price's famous address to the Revolution Society in 1789 (a society formed not in honour of the recent uprisings in France and America, but of the earlier English Revolution). Capturing the mood of many dissenters and intellectuals in England in the early 1790s, Price sees the recent events in France as a blissful revolutionary dawn. He perceives the French Revolution as a culmination of Enlightenment philosophy and as the latest phase of England's as yet unfinished Glorious Revolution of 1688 (which I will discuss in more detail later). Rejecting Price's support for the Revolution in France and his hope that similar revolutions would spread throughout Europe, Burke launches a vehement defence of the unwritten English constitution and warns of the catastrophic consequences such a sudden break from the past could engender. A notable aspect of Burke's treatise is his use of 'Gothic' and sentimental language. This is particularly the case with his extraordinary description of the Jacobin assault on Marie-Antoinette, the French Queen, with whom Burke was acquainted:

> History will record, that on the morning of the 6th of October 1789, the king and queen of France, after a day of confusion, alarm, dismay, and slaughter, lay down, under the pledged security of public faith, to indulge nature in a few hours of respite, and troubled melancholy repose ... A band of cruel ruffians and assassins, reeking with blood, rushed into the chamber of the queen, and pierced with an hundred strokes of bayonets and poniards the bed, from whence this persecuted woman had but just time to fly almost naked, and through the ways unknown to the murderers had escaped to seek refuge at the feet of a king and husband, not secure of his own life for a moment.
>
> (Burke 1986, 164)

Indeed, history and romance become difficult to distinguish in Burke's *Reflections*. The queen of France (a symbol of the time-honoured social order) is idealised whilst the revolutionaries (those interested in effecting massive social change) are demonised.[2] As John Whale notes, Burke's 'appeal to chivalry and sentiment was seen by his detractors as turning history into romance, real-life politics into theatre' (2005, 541). In her rebuttal of Burke's claims, *A Vindication of the Rights of Men* (1791), Mary Wollstonecraft says as much when she argues that the *Reflections* are 'a mixture of real sensibility and fondly cherished romance' (2008, 44). In his *Rights of Man* – the first part of which was published in 1791 – Thomas Paine argues that 'Mr. Burke should recollect that he is writing history, and not *Plays*; and that his readers will expect truth, and not the spouting rant of high-toned exclamation' (1985, 49–50). In his view, the *Reflections* are 'tragic paintings', acts of 'theatrical representation'

(49–50) and not 'the sober style of history, nor the intention of it' (61). Where Hume's, Robertson's and Gibbon's histories were primarily interested in applying reason to the past in order to glean timeless lessons about statecraft and chart the growth of reason over time, history at the onset of the French Revolution is more interested in the role of feeling in historical enquiry and concerned with how the past matters to the present. As Mike Goode argues (2009, 7), with the publication of Burke's treatise, emotions and sensations evoked by the past became increasingly important to historiography. As I will discuss throughout this chapter, the Gothic refracts such resonating changes to the nature of history. Influenced by Burke, Radcliffe is fascinated with how we relate to our pasts and exploits shifting notions of history to evoke suspense and fear.

Burke's *Reflections* would have a significant impact on history and Gothic fiction in this period. Despite intellectuals such as Price, who celebrated the early events taking place in France, Burke's treatise reveals how the French Revolution remained something simultaneously awe-inspiring, dark and inscrutable for some English men and women. As the Gothic novels of Horace Walpole, Clara Reeve and Lee attest, the unknown is always a source of unease and fear. To some English onlookers, the French Revolution appeared not as a *rational* occurrence that could be explained by rationality, but as something inherently *irrational*. Before his political views on the French Revolution had hardened, Burke reveals in a letter to Lord Charlemont in August 1789 that all thoughts at home are 'suspended' by 'astonishment' at the 'wonderful Spectacle' exhibited in France (1958–78, 6: 10). England does not know whether to 'blame or applaud!' such occurrences, he writes (10). However, Burke laments that 'the old Parisian ferocity has broken out in a shocking manner' and registers his fear of something 'paradoxical and Mysterious' at the heart of the Revolution (10). France's break from history is obscure, inexplicable and deeply troubling for Burke. Despite the conservative bias of the *Reflections*, the Revolution is something almost beyond rational comprehension. 'Every thing seems out of nature in this strange chaos of levity and ferocity', writes Burke, before going on to describe the Revolution as a 'monstrous tragic-comic scene' that evokes 'alternate contempt and indignation; alternate laughter and tears; alternate scorn and horror' (1986, 92–3). The French Revolution not only transcends Enlightenment frameworks of understanding; it challenges the very limits of literary representation. In the final decade of the eighteenth century, the great question facing writers was how to represent an event without precedent in human history and one of such enormity that it resisted representation. In the gulf between the decline of Enlightenment historiography and the rise of Romantic history after the turn of the century, it was the Gothic with its fascination with the nature of history and emphasis on the irrational that proved particularly well adapted for capturing the complex experiences arising from contemplations of the French Revolution.

Revolution: the Gothic, the past and the Great Enchantress

In his insightful *Representations of Revolution*, Ronald Paulson argues that the Gothic 'did in fact serve as a metaphor with which some contemporaries in England tried to understand what was happening across the Channel in the 1790s' (1983, 217). 'When the Revolution itself came, and as it progressed', he argues, it was an 'inability to make out the events on a day-to-day basis, but with the suspicion of personal skulduggery beneath each new changing-hands of property' and power that 'made the gothic novel a roughly equivalent narrative form' (225). In his critical essay, 'Reflections on the Novel' (1800), the Marquis de Sade (a former prisoner of the Bastille) is of a similar opinion when he argues that Gothic fiction reflects the 'revolutionary upheavals experienced throughout the whole of Europe' (1989, 109). The Gothic became increasingly popular at this time. With the daily transgressions taking place across the Channel, Gothic themes such as mouldering castles, Catholicism, feudalism, fragmented documents, and unwanted, returning pasts assumed a new, terrifying significance in this period. As this chapter will highlight, the seemingly remote themes of Gothic romance suddenly had a renewed, frightening resemblance with reality. The Gothic genre may have officially commenced with the publication of *Otranto* in 1764, but, with the outbreak of the French Revolution, it received a new impetus at the beginning of the turbulent decade of the 1790s.

In the context of the present study, perhaps Paulson's most important observation regarding the complex (inter)relationship between the French Revolution, the Gothic and the past is the following: 'Behind all was a new sense of history, of what could or should happen in history, and what history was in fact about. From being about the kings, it became, in certain ways, about larger groups of subjects and their attempts to come to terms with, or create a new order from, the disorder consequent upon the overthrow of an old established order' (1983, 224–5). Driven from all sections of French society, the French Revolution highlighted that ordinary people – not just kings and queens and eminent political individuals – could effect major social change; it drew attention to the role of individual agency in major historical events. The new French government intended to give power to the people rather than the monarchy. Indeed, Paulson's observations suggest that the French Revolution triggered the demise of traditional, hierarchical Enlightenment historiographical theory and stimulated new ways of thinking about the past (as Burke's and Wollstonecraft's works suggest). In the hands of Radcliffe, the Gothic would play a major role in imaginatively exploring such emergent notions of history and a new sense of historical consciousness brought about by the events in France. Often featuring contested feudal social orders, historiographically repressed groups or individuals and entranced with the nature of historical knowledge, it is not difficult to see how the Gothic became synonymous with the French Revolution in this period. As Paulson highlights, the Gothic and the French Revolution had a number of affinities: both were informed by a zeal for reform and yet, at the same time, opened up the potential for delusions, dangerous and unforeseen contingencies, horrible consequences, and disillusionment (225). Spellbound by the collapse of one of the most enduring monarchies in Europe, uncertain what the future held for England and its own (unwritten) constitution, puzzled by the daily occurrences taking place across the Channel, and awe-struck by an elevated state of historical awareness, the English thirst for tales of terror would become insatiable during the 1790s.

It is during such resonating political and historical ruptures that Ann Radcliffe – one of the greatest proponents of Gothic fiction – would begin her illustrious writing career. Reflecting back on her achievements after the turn of the century, Sir Walter Scott lauded her as the 'first poetess of Romantic fiction' (1829, 253) whilst John Keats affectionately referred to her as 'Mother Radcliffe' (1895, 286). Despite the enigmatic nature of her life, Radcliffe's suspense-driven novels were a literary phenomenon and she became the best-selling author of the 1790s. Writing novels set in distant, wild pasts and employing Gothic tropes such as craggy mountains, orphans, fainting heroines and the (seemingly) supernatural, she became more widely known as the 'Great Enchantress' to her contemporary audience (McIntyre 1970, 49). Utilising the narrative skeleton of the Gothic from Walpole and Lee, Radcliffe's novels drop the historical 'accuracy' of *The Recess* in favour of vaguer, more ambiguous and Romantic pasts; pasts more akin to *Otranto*. Throughout her fictions, threatening, sinister pasts continually haunt the present and threaten the well-being of her female protagonists. In contrast to *The Recess*, Radcliffe's fictions are not written in the first person. However, as this chapter will show, Radcliffe develops the Female Gothic – a form of Gothic fiction pioneered by Lee in *The Recess* – by focusing on female experience. Her fictions focus on the plight of the heroine and comment on women's role in history and society.

Beginning with the publication of *The Castles of Athlin and Dunbayne* in 1789 (a work heavily influenced by Lee's *The Recess*) and *A Sicilian Romance* in 1790, her readership grew steadily.[3] However, her popularity rose sharply in 1791 with the publication of *The Romance of the Forest*, a Gothic narrative set in seventeenth-century France, but written in the immediate aftermath of the French Revolution. Despite this obvious connection between Radcliffe's text and the events unfolding in France, critics have tended to neglect the significance of the novel's location. In fact, Gothic criticism has tended to neglect *The Romance of the Forest* in its entirety. Often perceiving it merely as an early stage in the author's development, scholars have tended to marginalise it and favour readings of *The Mysteries of Udolpho* (1794) and *The Italian* (1797). However, as critics such as Rictor Norton have pointed out, it received widespread critical acclaim upon its publication and played a significant role in making the Gothic genre appealing to a middle-class readership (1999, 82–3). Arguing that the past constructed in *The Romance of the Forest* represents a complex response to the cultural context of the early 1790s, this chapter seeks to illuminate the importance of Radcliffe's third Gothic novel in its own right.

Seeking new directions for Radcliffe criticism, the first section of this chapter will examine the ways in which the seventeenth-century past presented in *The Romance of the Forest* is shaped by contemporary events in France. How important is the French location of the novel, what are the implications of such a setting for the Gothic and what is the significance of the decaying Abbey of St Clair? Following on from this discussion, I will examine the politics of historical representation in *The Romance of the Forest*. The focus here will be on two major political works published prior to Radcliffe's novel: Burke's *Reflections* and Wollstonecraft's response to it in the form of the *Rights of Men*. What is particularly significant about these fiery historico-political exchanges is their attitude towards the past, their use of 'Gothic' language and their conflicting use of the word 'Gothic'. This section will focus on such ideas and assess the extent to which they manifest themselves in the past represented in Radcliffe's novel. Concurring with David Punter, the forthcoming discussion will argue that, despite the seeming historical remoteness of eighteenth-century Gothic, the past featured in Radcliffe's Female Gothic novel engages in a 'very intense, if displaced, engagement with political and social problems' wrought by the outbreak of the French Revolution (1996, 54). Similarly to Price and Wollstonecraft, Radcliffe was a Radical Dissenter and was raised in Unitarian circles. As I will discuss, she was also familiar with some of Burke's work. The forthcoming discussion will show how Radcliffe utilises the Female Gothic and manipulates established tropes to subvert Burkean attitudes towards history by challenging the status quo and promoting the rights of women.

Contending that the French Revolution and the political debates that it triggered created a new, frightening sense of historical identity and acted as a catalyst for eighteenth-century meditations on the nature of the past, the forthcoming discussion will then move on to the various reflections on the transitory nature of history that pervade *The Romance of the Forest*. How do the recent events in France influence representations of the past in the novel? What does Radcliffe's use of certain Gothic tropes say about the nature of history and what does the novel reveal about conceptions of historical time towards the end of the eighteenth century? Developing ideas from earlier chapters, I will show how, in Radcliffe's hands, the Gothic continues to function as the dark underside of Enlightenment historiography, imaginatively exploring some of the more irrational and unsavoury aspects of the past that such historiography purposefully neglects. However, the Revolution in France coincides with a revolution in Gothic fiction; the Gothic as a genre and as an attitude towards the recapture of history also undergoes fundamental alterations during this period. Compared to Walpole and Lee,

Radcliffe is less interested in the way history becomes narrativised; she focuses more on the way we relate to the past, how we interact and experience it and how history interconnects with the present. Particular attention will be paid to the manuscript which features in *The Romance of the Forest* and Radcliffe's increasingly Romantic attitudes towards history.

It is now widely recognised that, far from being distinctive categories, the Gothic and Romanticism share a complex interrelationship and are very much 'in dialogue with each other' (McEvoy 2007, 27). In the light of this, Radcliffe's works have begun to be reassessed in both their Gothic and Romantic contexts. During her lifetime, the wild and sublime landscapes that feature in Radcliffe's novels frequently invited comparisons with the proto-Romantic paintings of Salvator Rosa and Claude Lorrain. Many canonical Romantic writers, such as Wordsworth, Coleridge, Byron, Keats, and Mary and P. B. Shelley, read and responded to Radcliffe, or were influenced by her works. As Dale Townshend and Angela Wright observe, it was the 'perceived exceptionality of Ann Radcliffe' that aligned her not so much with the 'low-cultural force of the Gothic' but rather with 'the high-cultural imperatives of Romantic aesthetics' (2014, 20).[4] Radcliffe's fictions are Romantic in the sense that they promote the power of the creative imagination, emotional directness and the freedom of individual self-expression. Indeed, Radcliffe's 'exclusion from Romanticism feels counterintuitive', as she was 'a central figure in the revolutionary tumult of new literary forms that took the 1790s by storm' (Miles 2014, 119).[5] As this chapter will reveal, *The Romance of the Forest* is fascinated with fragmentation and is suffused with Romantic impulses. Radcliffe's representation of the past draws attention to the irrational and the macabre, and places particular importance on subjectivity and spontaneous feelings. Examining the fragmented script and Adeline's reaction to reading it, a number of questions will be proposed. What is the significance of this historical artefact, what does it reveal about the nature of historical knowledge at this time and how does Radcliffe's treatment of this Gothic device differ from that of her predecessors? Discussion will encompass Romantic and aesthetic notions of literary fragmentation and will examine Radcliffe's use of the sublime in the culturally chaotic decade of the 1790s. As the forthcoming discussion will highlight, the sublime represents a point of contact between the Gothic and Romanticism and assumes a new significance in this period. At a time when the enormity of the events unfolding in France surpassed rational comprehension, the sublime proved to be particularly well suited for encapsulating emergent, late eighteenth-century (re)conceptions of history and the past. I will begin by examining the ways in which the past in *The Romance of the Forest* is shaped by the emergent French Revolution.

Seventeenth-century France, 1790s France

Set in seventeenth-century Roman Catholic France, Radcliffe's third Gothic novel follows the plight of its orphan heroine, Adeline, who is mysteriously placed under the protection of Pierre de la Motte, a Frenchman fleeing Paris with his family in order to escape his gambling debts. The newly formed family take refuge in the ruined Abbey of St Clair, which is located deep in the forest of Fontanville in France, and Adeline soon finds herself at the mercy of its proprietor, the malevolent Marquis de Montalt, whose actions eventually compel her to escape. Following Walpole's and Lee's lead – and, indeed, her own in *A Sicilian Romance* – Radcliffe attempts to lend her narrative a degree of authenticity and believability by appealing to established sources. At the beginning of the novel, she attempts to draw a distance between the seventeenth century of the novel and her own age by constructing a fallacious historical framework: 'Whoever has read Guyot de Pitaval, the most faithful of those writers who record the proceedings in the Parliamentary Courts of Paris, during the seventeenth century, must surely remember the striking story of Pierre de la Motte, and the Marquis Phillipe de Montalt' (*RF* 1). However, in typical Gothic fashion, the source pointed to is bogus. As Norton highlights, this is not an allusion to François Gayot de Pitival's *Causes célèbres et intéressants* (1734), but to the English translation of this work by Charlotte Smith, entitled *The Romance of Real Life* (1787). Smith similarly misspells de Pitaval's name as 'Guyot' (Norton 1999, 83). He goes on to note that de Pitaval's work contains neither the 'striking story' of de la Motte and de Montalt, nor any other story that even remotely resembles the narrative of *The Romance of the Forest* (83). Furthermore, as Chloe Chard points out, Radcliffe's seemingly absurd and comical historical frame also contains a much more ominous, contemporary reference. The name La Motte (as Radcliffe's character is subsequently known in the novel) was notorious in the 1780s as a result of the French trial resulting from the 'Affair of the Queen's Necklace': a historically significant event that contributed to the French populace's disenchantment with the monarchy and which (amongst other events) culminated in the French Revolution (Chard 1999, 367).[6] Even before Radcliffe's seventeenth-century set novel begins in earnest, it is haunted by her own contemporary present and recent, disturbing events in France.

This is not the only example of Radcliffe's present colouring representations of the past in *The Romance of the Forest*. Shortly after they return to Leloncourt, Arnaud La Luc (a clergyman who looks after Adeline when she falls ill) and Monsieur Verneuil (Adeline's distant kinsman) begin discoursing about 'the national characters of the French and the English' (*RF* 268). La Luc's views on this subject are of particular interest. Balancing England's refined laws, writings and manners against high suicide rates, he concludes that 'wisdom and happiness are incompatible' (*RF* 268–9). Turning his attention to England's 'neighbours, the French', La Luc sees their 'wretched policy', discourse and occupations as evidence that 'happiness and folly too often dwell together' (*RF* 269). Given that the characters featured in the novel are (supposedly) French, such reflections may seem fairly innocuous. However, it is significant that Radcliffe deems it necessary to add a footnote to La Luc's remarks concerning the French: '[i]t must be remembered that this was said in the seventeenth century', she writes (*RF* 269). Furthermore, La Luc's observation that 'happiness and folly too often dwell together' (*RF* 269) in France is very reminiscent of Burke's description of the French Revolution as a 'tragic-comic scene' that evokes 'alternate laughter and tears' (1986, 92–3). By adding a footnote designed to distance her own narrative from the policies currently being pursued in revolutionary France, Radcliffe in fact draws attention to how the seventeenth-century fictional past of which she writes is shaped by events taking place across the Channel. Indeed, the French location of the novel, the contemporary references that form an integral part of the novel's historical framework and the allusion to French policies would not have been lost on some of Radcliffe's contemporary readers. Viewing the revolutionary nation of France with a degree of awe, foreboding and incomprehension, some would have read *The Romance of the Forest* with an added degree of trepidation. Not only is Radcliffe's novel shaped by recent events in France, but some readers' perceptions of the novel would have been coloured by the French Revolution and its radical departure from the past.

The clearest parallel between Radcliffe's Gothic novel and contemporary events in France involves the abandoned abbey that features so prominently in the early parts of the story. In *The Romance of the Forest*, the Abbey of St Clair is a substitute for the Gothic trope of the mouldering castle:

> [La Motte] approached, and perceived the Gothic remains of an abbey … The greater part of the pile appeared to be sinking into ruins, and that which had withstood the ravages of time, shewed the remaining features of the fabric more awful in decay. The lofty battlements thickly enwreathed with ivy, were half demolished, and become the residence of birds of prey. Huge fragments of the eastern tower, which was almost demolished, lay scattered amid the high grass that waved slowly in the breeze … Above the vast and magnificent portal … arose a window of the same order, whose pointed arches still exhibited fragments of stained glass, once the pride of monkish devotion.
>
> (*RF* 15)

Similarly to the underground Recess featured in Lee's Gothic novel, this decaying religious edifice works on multiple symbolic levels. It has long been a staple of Gothic criticism to draw parallels between the Bastille and the mouldering castles and abbeys that are typical of 1790s Gothic fiction. However, in *The Romance of the Forest*, Radcliffe encourages such an association. Forced to move into a different section of the abbey in order to elude detection, Madame La Motte deplores the 'dismal' apartments in which she must now stay (*RF* 57). However, La Motte reminds her that 'these cells are also a palace, compared to the Bicétre, or the Bastille, and to the terrors of farther punishment, which would accompany them' (*RF* 57). Occurring just two years before the publication of *The Romance of the Forest*, the storming of the Bastille was still a fairly recent event and, as a symbol of the Revolution's might, remained strongly impressed on the English public consciousness.[7] Indeed, by November 1789, this once powerful structure was largely demolished. Although La Motte utters these words in the seventeenth century of the novel, some readers would undoubtedly have interpreted such a remark through the lens of contemporary developments in

France. Furthermore, the context of this association is very important. La Motte makes this comparison with the Bastille amidst the ruins of the mouldering abbey. Even though the Gothic has never strived for realism (historic, literary or otherwise), the Bastille would obviously not have been in ruins in the seventeenth century; it would have been at the height of its oppressive powers. By drawing a parallel between these two now ruined structures, the seventeenth century of Radcliffe's novel is once again betrayed by allusions to the present. Radcliffe exploits contemporary fears surrounding the Bastille and its fall in order to heighten the suspense and terror of her seventeenth-century narrative.

As I discussed earlier, the abbey's symbolism in *The Romance of the Forest* is multifaceted. Not only is it important in terms of its association with the Bastille, but also as a religious symbol. The past is almost always Catholic in eighteenth-century Gothic literature. The manuscript upon which *Otranto* is supposedly based is discovered in the 'library of an ancient Catholic family' and depicts a Catholic Europe gripped by fear and superstition (*O* 5). Even though Lee's novel is set predominantly in England, the major characters in *The Recess* are Catholic and the twin heroines are literally entombed in a decaying, Catholic religious edifice for much of their lives. As I have noted throughout this book, the Gothic often exploits the insecurities of its Protestant readers and presents Europe as a backward Catholic continent gripped by feudalism. Set in Catholic France, Radcliffe's *The Romance of the Forest* would appear to be no different. However, under closer scrutiny, there is something unusual about the Catholic past it presents. In Radcliffe's novels that are located in Italy – the previous *A Sicilian Romance*, the later *The Mysteries of Udolpho* (1794) and, of course, *The Italian* (1797) – Catholicism is presented at the height of its evil powers. The Catholic pasts represented are ones dominated by superstition, tyranny and persecution, and the heroines of the respective novels are frequently tyrannised by malicious religious leaders serving in corrupt, Catholic religious institutions.

However, as Chard points out, Catholicism has a rather marginal role in *The Romance of the Forest* (1999, xiii). When Adeline briefly recounts her personal history, she explains how her 'father' placed her in a Catholic convent where she is pressured to take the veil by a malevolent 'Lady Abbess' and is condemned to 'perpetual imprisonment' of the 'most dreadful kind' (*RF* 36). Although she had to spend 'several years of miserable resistance against cruelty and superstition', she eventually escapes the 'horrors of monastic life' by refusing to take the veil (*RF* 36). In contrast to the novels mentioned a moment ago, the reader does not witness her experiences at the hands of evil servants of the Catholic faith; we only learn about such experiences through this brief summation. The decaying abbey and the sense of 'monkish devotion' it inspires has obvious Catholic connotations (*RF* 15). However, this is a fading monument to a once glorious and powerful religious order; apart from creating an obscure and atmospheric setting for evoking suspense and terror, as a religious institution, this decaying edifice has no direct influence on the welfare of the protagonists. Adeline is not pursued by a tyrannical Catholic leader, but a malevolent Marquis. Readers' expectations of such corrupt religious figures are frustrated. Indeed, *The Romance of the Forest* essentially presents the reader with a paradox: in a novel that depicts a Catholic past, Catholicism appears to be history. The question we ask as readers, though, is why: why would Radcliffe forego a staple theme of Gothic fiction in *The Romance of the Forest* only to bring it back in her later novels? The key to answering this question lies in the location of Radcliffe's novel.

The French location of *The Romance of the Forest* has been rather neglected by critics. However, when it comes to understanding the representation of the past within the novel and, more specifically, the uncharacteristically marginalised role of Catholicism within this past, the setting is of great significance. The events of the 1790s in France continue to manifest themselves in the seventeenth-century past that Radcliffe represents. As I briefly discussed earlier, the French Revolution waged a war not only on the past, but on the Catholic institutions that symbolised that past. From the outset, revolutionary France was hostile towards Catholicism. As symbols of the *ancien régime* and the unfair distribution of wealth and power, it was common for the clergy to suffer mob violence directed against them. For example, on 26 June 1789, the Archbishop of Paris was viciously attacked in his carriage by an angry mob and barely escaped with his life (McManners 1969, 22). Having abolished the historic tithe in 1789, the Assembly declared that the lands of churchmen now belonged to the state. Ecclesiastical property was sold in order to ease the national debt and the secularisation of France had begun. Church properties that could not be sold were abandoned and left to decay. The passing of The Civil Constitution of the Clergy in 1790 subordinated the Roman Catholic Church in France to the French government and resulted in the destruction of monastic orders, wiping out of existence 'all priories and abbeys, whether regular or *in commendam*, likewise of either sex' (Hardman 1999, 115). Taking vows was banned, religious orders were greatly constricted and, for those concerned, there was nothing to look forward to but a bleak existence in declining institutions (McManners 1969, 34). Within just a few short years, church buildings would be taken over for military use and bells, railings and grilles would be dragged away and melted down for armaments (93). Indeed, as Burke's epigraph to this chapter intimates, France was becoming peppered with ruined buildings, defunct convents and abandoned monasteries in the early 1790s.

In the seventeenth-century past represented in *The Romance of the Forest*, the reader encounters an imaginative identification with the early events of the French Revolution. The reduced role of Catholicism within the novel echoes its marginalisation in 1790s France. The decaying, abandoned abbey – the symbol of a once powerful religious order – reflects and foreshadows the French Revolution's redistribution and abandonment of ecclesiastical properties. The fact that the abandoned abbey featured in the narrative bears traces of having been modified by more recent proprietors only strengthens such associations (*RF* 20). Indeed, there is a tension between past and present throughout *The Romance of the Forest* and this generates fear and suspense in a number of ways. The marginalisation of a malevolent Catholicism in the seventeenth-century past depicted in the novel unnerves readers by frustrating their expectations; in a Gothic novel that features a gloomy, ruined religious edifice, readers would expect evil Catholic servants to threaten the welfare of the protagonists. This would certainly have been the case for readers of Radcliffe's previous novel, *A Sicilian Romance*, where the heroine Julia is menaced by a debauched and unfeeling monastic order. With the absence of such figures and such a plot, suspense is generated by keeping readers guessing. While some readers would have drawn connections between the novel and the new French government destroying people, buildings and social frameworks, others would have been reminded of the Revolution's ruthless commitment to destroying the past and have felt a deep sense of foreboding.

Political pasts: history, romance and the pamphlet war

The seventeenth-century past depicted in *The Romance of the Forest* is not only pervaded by references to the state of contemporary France; it is heavily influenced by the political debates in England that were triggered by the French Revolution. Before I discuss this aspect of the past in Radcliffe's novel, it is necessary to outline such debates. Discussing notions of conservatism and traditionalism, Karl Manheim notes how the emergence of the French Revolution suddenly (and rather disturbingly) made people aware that they had always been living in a world of historic traditions without ever having been conscious of it; this was simply how they lived their lives and how they perceived the world. However, the Revolution in France suddenly lifted them out of this world of unreflected tradition and made them aware of these traditions for the first time (Ankersmit 2005, 326). History and tradition loomed large in the English consciousness during the 1790s, evoking a sense of the uncanny. In the unfamiliar events of the French Revolution – the overthrow of an established, monarchical social order – English men and women could see something strangely familiar: vestiges of their own revolutionary past and, more specifically, shadows of the Glorious Revolution of 1688. For example, in *A Discourse on the Love of Our Country*, Price perceives the French Revolution as a continuation of the Glorious Revolution, lauding France's desire to free itself from the 'slavish governments' of the past and calling for a similar reformation of government and 'increasing light and liberality' in England (1790, 50). As Maggie Kilgour astutely points out, even though 'the nature of the past, and its relation to the present, was debated throughout the eighteenth century, it gained new life with the French Revolution' (1995, 23). Seemingly symbolising the pinnacle of the Enlightenment, the French Revolution posed numerous uncomfortable problems, calling into question the very foundations of established systems of social order. Akin to the experience of reading a Gothic novel, France's abrupt change from the past and its implications for the English political system were both exhilarating and terrifying.

Vehemently condemning Price's argument in his *Reflections*, Burke contends that the Glorious Revolution of 1688 was a moderate and cautious settlement rather than the beginning of a revolutionary agenda. For Burke, 1688 was an end rather than a beginning, thus negating any comparisons between England and France. In contrast to France's radical departure from history, the English Revolution aimed to preserve the past, our '*antient* indisputable laws and liberties and that *antient* constitution of government which is our only security for law and liberty' (1986, 117). In Burke's view, France's abrupt break with the past is unnatural, a 'perversion of history' and will only result in catastrophe (250). By breaking so abruptly from history and creating a society based on the rights of men, Burke argues that the French have 'wrought under-ground a mine that will blow up at one grand explosion all the examples of antiquity, all precedents, charters, and acts of parliament' (148). Fearing that revolutions similar to the one taking place in France will spread throughout Europe (as Price hoped), Burke launches a vehement conservative defence of the English political system. England's government is based on evolutionary rather than revolutionary change, on organic development, thus ensuring unbroken succession and continuity of tradition. For Burke, society is 'a partnership not only between those who are living, but between those who are living, those who are dead, and those who are to be born' (46). As numerous commentators have pointed out, the *Reflections* is notable for its use of 'Gothic' language and tropes. In a particularly 'Gothic' manner, Burke depicts present-day liberties as irrevocably tied to the past and envisages an England that is bound by its ancestors:

> Besides, the people of England well know, that the idea of inheritance furnishes a sure principle of conservation, and a sure principle of transmission ... Whatever advantages are obtained by a state proceeding on these maxims are locked fast as in a sort of family settlement; grasped as in a kind of mortmain for ever. By a constitutional policy, working after the pattern of nature, we receive, we hold, we transmit our government and our privileges, in the same manner in which we enjoy and transmit our property and our lives.
>
> (119–20)

Burke lauds a society that is content to respect its past rather than embrace the future and identifies inheritance as an essential facet of the nation's stability and prosperity. For Burke, primogeniture – the 'power of perpetuating property in our families' – is 'one of the most valuable and interesting circumstances belonging to it, and that which tends the most to the perpetuation of society itself' (140). His image of England's inheritance being 'grasped as in a kind of mort-main forever' is particularly interesting. As Wright highlights, Burke views mortmain – a legal term which literally translates as a 'dead hand' and which in the eighteenth century guaranteed entailed inheritances – as a positive force (2007, 61). However, as she points out, his imagery suggests otherwise: 'mortmain' embraces England in a suffocating grasp (61).

Furthermore, as Burke's remarks on inheritance exemplify, the political and the familial are closely related in the *Reflections*. This theme runs throughout Burke's work and is particularly evident in the scene I discussed at the beginning of this chapter, the flight of Marie Antoinette. Forced out of her bed by a 'band of cruel ruffians and assassins, reeking with blood', the queen flees 'almost naked' to seek the protection of her husband, the king (Burke 1986, 164). As Eleanor Ty argues, in his 'presentation of the political act as a sexual act of violation', Burke makes an 'explicit link between the public and the domestic realms' (1993, 4). The Queen in this scene is depicted as weak and ineffectual; a powerless female (Marie Antoinette) is shown to be entirely dependent upon the active, noble and chivalrous behaviour of a male (her husband). As Tom Furniss points out, Burke contrasts the beauty of the *ancien régime*, embod-ied by Marie Antoinette, with the barbarity of the largely female revolutionary mob (2002, 61). The royal family are escorted from Versailles to Paris 'amidst the horrid yells, and shrilling screams ... and all the unutterable abominations of the furies of hell, in the abused shape of the vilest women' (Burke 1986, 165). Burke ide-alises the beautiful and (im)passive behaviour of Marie Antoinette and demonises the active, revolutionary women who seek change. Recalling Reeve's views in *The Old English Baron*, the perpetuation of a benevolent patriarchy is, for Burke, essential to the stability of the social order. Throughout the *Reflections*, Burke draws a parallel between the traditional patriarchal home and the strength of the nation. As Ty points out, in the *Reflections*, the 'family becomes a microcosmic state, a basic political unit in its own right' and rever-ence to the past, the aristocracy, primogeniture, and the patriarchal family are viewed as being essential to the longevity of the state (1993, 5).

For Burke, the willed destruction of these time-honoured social traditions in France has created a monstrous social system that will, in his eyes, only lead to catastrophe. His use of 'Gothic' language and imagery is particularly prevalent here. Throughout the *Reflections*, Burke romanticises the aristocracy and demonises the revolutionaries and lower classes, referring to them as a 'swinish multitude' at one point (1986, 173). He idealises the aristocracy in the form of Marie Antoinette and presents the Revolution as something of an anti-romance where heroes fail to save the beautiful, sexually threatened and vulnerable heroine (169–70). The French Revolution is a type of 'family drama' for Burke, emphasising the vulnerability and destruction of patriarchal rule and authority by crazed ruffians who intend to create a new society (Ty 1993, 5). Indeed, Burke laments the death of chivalry, a form of benevolent patriarchy that functions as an historic agent of social cohesion by perpetuating traditional gender oppositions (1986, 170). By willingly deviating from such social values, Burke argues that dysfunctional families have been created in France: by perpetuating such 'warped' social customs, the state literally devours its own children, he argues (194). The *Reflections* is a warning to political radicals in England who would 'subvert the aristocratic concepts of paternalism, loyalty, chivalry, and the hereditary principle' (Ty 1993, 5). As Burke argues elsewhere, the revolutionaries 'endeavour to subvert those principles of domestic trust and fidelity, which form the discipline of social life' (1893, 541). Turning away from history, rejecting primogeniture and discarding notions of chivalry, Burke perceives the French Revolution as a rupture of the historical process and views it as an example that must be avoided in England at all costs. The preservation of patriarchy – and thus gender inequality – is integral to Burke's conservative defence of the nation.

In the *Rights of Men*, Wollstonecraft reacts furiously to Burke's conservative and patriarchal defence of the state. Employing 'Gothic' language and themes, Wollstonecraft's treatise is primarily interested in replying to Burke, its aim being 'to shew you to yourself, stripped of the gorgeous drapery in which you have enwrapped your tyrannic principles' (Wollstonecraft 2008, 37). Similarly to Paine in his *Rights of Man*, she accuses him of romanticising history and idealising the historical origins of the English constitution in the *Reflections*. Refuting Burke's stance, she reaffirms the connection between the English and French Revolutions; as Steven Blakemore notes, she continually affixes the adjective 'glorious' to her descriptions of French Revolutionary events (1997, 74–5). Wollstonecraft was, like Price, a dissenter and embraced the French

Revolution's break from history, perceiving it as an opportunity to improve the lives of women throughout Europe. In her view, the new constitutional Assembly of France promises a fairer society for all, particularly for women, whereas Burke and his romantic depiction of the English constitution compels one to 'reverence the rust of antiquity, and term the unnatural customs, which ignorance and mistaken self-interest have consolidated, the sage fruit of experience' (Wollstonecraft 2008, 8). She refutes Burke's notion of the French constitution as a ruined castle (1986, 121–2), arguing that it is absurd 'to repair an ancient castle, built in barbarous ages, of Gothic materials', or to 'rebuild old walls', when a newer, more 'simple structure', such as the new constitution in France, can replace the superstition and tyranny of older, monarchic social orders (Wollstonecraft 2008, 41). The English constitution is not a sort of 'family settlement' handed down through generations, but a series of customs established by 'the lawless power of an ambitious individual', she argues (9). Whilst Burke idealises the aristocracy in the form of Marie Antoinette, Wollstonecraft exposes the 'polished vices of the rich, their insincerity' and 'want of natural affections' (59). She criticises Burke's entrenchment in the past and his defence of the unwritten English constitution, the origins of which are, contrary to what the *Reflections* infer, difficult to discern. Burke ignores the plight of the poor and the horrors that a monarchic social order forces upon them. Wollstonecraft accuses him of mourning for the 'idle tapestry that decorated a gothic pile', for the 'empty pageant of a name', whilst 'man preys on man' and 'slavery' and sickness consume the poor (60). In Burke's *Reflections*, 'Gothic' signifies anything old or time-honoured; in Wollstonecraft's rebuttal, it is anything tyrannous and defunct. As Ronald Paulson highlights, in the historico-political debates of Burke and Wollstonecraft, 'Gothic' summons up 'ideas of chivalry and courtesy but also castles, cells, locked rooms, high walls' and 'contracted marriages' (1983, 83).

Wollstonecraft is particularly infuriated by Burke's defence of primogeniture. In contrast to Burke, who believes that patrimony and its orderly transmission of property is one of the stabilising principles of the English constitution, Wollstonecraft deplores 'hereditary property' and 'hereditary honours' as forces that prohibit social progress. Inheritance has resulted in man being 'changed into an artificial monster by the station in which he was born', she writes (Wollstonecraft 2008, 8). She condemns an unwritten constitution that privileges birth and family above an individual's talent and abilities. For Wollstonecraft, primogeniture is not something that should be praised as the bedrock of the English social order, but a tyrannous social custom that has ruined countless lives throughout history and that should be viewed with contempt:

> A brutal attachment to children has appeared most conspicuous in parents who have treated them like slaves, and demanded due homage for all the property they transferred to them, during their lives. It has led them to force their children to break the most sacred ties; to do violence to a natural impulse, and run into legal prostitution to increase wealth or shun poverty; and, still worse, the dread of parental malediction has made many weak characters violate truth in the face of Heaven; and, to avoid a father's angry curse, the most sacred promises have been broken. It appears to be a natural suggestion of reason, that a man should be freed from implicit obedience to parents and private punishments, when he is of an age to be subject to the jurisdiction of the laws of his country; and that the barbarous cruelty of allowing parents to imprison their children, to prevent their contaminating their noble blood by following the dictates of nature when they chose to marry, or for any misdemeanor that does not come under the cognizance of public justice, is one of the most arbitrary violations of liberty.
>
> (21)

Countering Burke's macabre representation of revolutionary France, Wollstonecraft paints a 'Gothic' picture of England where parents imprison and tyrannise their own children; 'brutal', 'violence', 'dread', 'curse', 'barbarous' and 'contaminating' are just a few of the words that she associates with the ancient custom of primogeniture (21). Paine shares a similar view in the *Rights of Man* when he argues that the aristocracy never has more than one child: the 'rest are begotten to be devoured', he argues (1985, 82). 'Who can recount all the unnatural crimes which the *laudable, interesting* desire of perpetuating a name has produced?' questions Wollstonecraft, before castigating a time-honoured social order that has meant that 'younger children have been sacrificed to the eldest son; sent into exile, or confined in convents, that they might not encroach on what was called, with shameful falsehood, the *family estate*' (2008, 21).

Responding to Burke's depiction of women and the lower classes as a 'swinish multitude' (1986, 173), Wollstonecraft demonises the aristocracy, highlighting the cruelty and inhumanness caused by the relentless pursuit of property. The historic social custom of primogeniture has had a particularly devastating effect on women's lives: 'Girls are sacrificed to family convenience, or else marry to settle themselves in a superior rank, and coquet, without restraint' (Wollstonecraft 2008, 22). In Wollstonecraft's view, primogeniture, property and pageantry have created monstrous, dysfunctional families and, by implication, states. For Burke, it is the Revolution and its break from time-honoured social customs that has created demonic families in France. For Wollstonecraft, the horror is not abroad, where, in her eyes, beneficial social reform is taking place, but at home. Similarly to Lee's attitude in *The Recess*, Wollstonecraft suggests that it is not active, assertive women that are to be feared, but the passive slaves of sensibility that the English social order has created (24).[8] The current social order deprives women of education and property, forces them to behave in socially acceptable ways and essentially turns them into 'vain inconsiderable dolls' (24). In Wollstonecraft's view, the feudal customs perpetuated by the English constitution continue to blight the present, alienating families, inciting class disharmony and keeping women repressed.

The Romance of the Forest and the politics of the past

Although we know relatively little about Radcliffe's life and literary influences, we know for certain that she was familiar with at least one of Burke's works. In her essay, 'On the Supernatural in Poetry' (a text that I will discuss in more detail later), she speaks of his earlier work, *A Philosophical Enquiry into the Origin of Our Ideas of the Sublime and Beautiful* (1757). In *The Mistress of Udolpho*, Norton suggests that it was curiosity evoked by the vehement political debates triggered by Price's sermon and Burke's *Reflections* that led Radcliffe to read this earlier treatise (1999, 77). Taking into consideration her background as a Dissenting Unitarian, it is likely that she had knowledge of Price's sermon and had read (or was at least aware of) Burke's *Reflections*. Indeed, Radcliffe's religious and political orientation is significant.[9] As Norton points out, she emerged from a Unitarian, rather than a conventional Anglican, background and should be considered in the same context as Radical Dissenters such as Anna Laetitia Barbauld, Elizabeth Inchbald, Mary Hays, and Mary Wollstonecraft (1999, xi). Dissenters were opposed to the established Church of England and could not take the oaths necessary to secure offices under the Crown or even to take degrees at English universities.

Given their exclusion from so many civil rights, it is not surprising that dissenters such as Price and Wollstonecraft were attracted to the events taking place in France in the early 1790s. The new French constitution promised a more egalitarian society: one liberated from the social division and hierarchism of old monarchical governments. As Robert Miles notes, Radcliffe belonged to the dissenting 'middling classes': a respectable, non-conformist social group that were hostile to the upper classes, felt themselves to be self-reliant and did not identify their interests with the 'Establishment' (1995, 3–4). She was not a complacent member of the suburban middle classes and, as the forthcoming discussion will reveal, her words 'conceal a hard edge, one sharpened by the robust, liberal, critical energies of the dissenting "middling classes" to which she belonged' (4).[10] As a dissenter, Radcliffe was a supporter of the Glorious Revolution and her husband, William, had links with a journal that celebrated the anniversary of the French Revolution.[11] The forthcoming discussion argues that *The Romance of the Forest* can be read as a complex engagement with Burke's and Wollstonecraft's 'Gothic' political debates and, in agreement with Norton (1999) and Miles (1995), posits that Radcliffe's Gothic pasts are more subversive than many critics have traditionally given her credit for.

As the political debates I discussed previously demonstrate, the French Revolution prompted a profound questioning of the status and role of women in society. With the boundary between history and romance more indistinguishable than ever at the end of the eighteenth century, Radcliffe utilises the woman-centrism of the Female Gothic and its emphasis on inheritance to critique Burke's conservative, patriarchal defence of the state.[12] Focusing on Adeline's traumatic experiences at the hands of men, the past that Radcliffe writes in *The Romance of the Forest* engages with Wollstonecraft's notion of the 'Gothic' as anything barbaric and backward. As I will show, at a time when history was particularly relevant to the present, the border between history and reality, the foreign and the domestic, the past and the present is particularly faint in Radcliffe's Female Gothic novel. Indeed, the past presented in *The Romance of the Forest* is a manifestation of the historico-political debates trig-gered by the outbreak of the French Revolution.

Subverting Burke's *Reflections*, Radcliffe demonises the aristoc-racy in the form of the malevolent Marquis de Montalt. Driven by 'ambition', 'the love of pleasure' and 'voluptuous inclinations' (*RF* 342–3), he terrorises Adeline throughout the novel. He tries to force Adeline to marry him, kidnaps her in an attempt to seduce her, ruthlessly pursues her when she escapes and, at one point, has her imprisoned in the Abbey of St Clair. His sexual advances frustrated, the Marquis later hatches a plan to have Adeline murdered. His jus-tification for this murder is particularly chilling: 'self-preservation is the great law of nature; when a reptile hurts us, or an animal of prey threatens us, we think no farther, but endeavour to annihilate it', he remarks (*RF* 222). As Nicola Trott argues, the Marquis may readily be seen as a 'corrupt aristocrat of the *ancien régime*' and as a Gothic villain whose intellectual 'sophistry' shows the deplorable uses to which 'philosophy' may be put (2005, 494). The Marquis also terrorises La Motte. Threatening to hand him into the author-ities in Paris, the Marquis intimidates La Motte and makes him complicit in his various diabolical schemes. Furthermore, at the end of the novel, it is revealed that the Marquis is a murderer. This 'atro-city' is 'heightened' by the fact that he kills one 'connected with him by the ties of blood, and by the habits of early association': his own brother and Adeline's father, the late Henry Montalt (*RF* 342–3). The actions of the malevolent Marquis and his 'passion for mag-nificence and dissipation' (*RF* 343) compel readers to reconsider the Burkean ideal of the benevolent patriarch by revealing how such authority figures can in fact become tyrants and abuse their positions.

Influenced by the historico-political debates of the 1790s, the seventeenth-century past depicted in *The Romance of the Forest* is dominated by an evil aristocrat who has abused his inheritance. Indeed, male abuse of inheritance and the unfair distribution of property is the root of all evil in Radcliffe's Female Gothic novel. At the end of the novel, we learn that the late Henry Montalt received from his ancestors a 'patrimony very inadequate to sup-port the splendour of his rank; but he had married the heiress of an illustrious family, whose fortune amply supplied the deficiency of his own' (*RF* 343). Although Phillipe (who eventually becomes the malevolent Marquis) married 'a lady, who, by the death of her brother, inherited considerable estates, of which the Abbey of St. Clair, and the villa on the borders of the forest of Fontangville, were the chief', he soon finds himself in financial 'difficulties' (*RF* 343). Reminiscent of Walter in *The Old English Baron*, it is the Marquis's financial plight and desire for the 'title of his brother' that compels him to form the 'diabolical design of destroying his brother' (*RF* 342–3). By chance, Adeline escapes the same fate as her father. Once he realises that Adeline is in fact Henry's daughter and that, if she should 'ever obtain knowledge of her birth', he would lose his property, his title and, indeed, his life, we learn that 'he did not hesitate to repeat the crime, and would again have stained his soul with human blood' (*RF* 344). Writing of a seventeenth-century past dominated by the terrible exploits of an evil aristocrat, Radcliffe's Female Gothic novel negates the idea that primogeniture is a good thing and problematises the late-eighteenth-century Burkean belief in patriarchal authority (Ty 1993, 21).

Echoing the views of Wollstonecraft (a fellow dissenter), Radcliffe reveals how men are often turned into 'artificial monster[s]' by their station and the property they inherit (Wollstonecraft 2008, 8). In a similar vein to Wollstonecraft (and Lee in *The Recess*), Radcliffe reveals that, far from functioning as a time-honoured social custom that ensures the stability and longevity of the state, inheritance is frequently abused by men, often devastating the lives of women in the process. Until the end of the narrative, Adeline is suffocated in the grasp of her usurped, male-dominated inheritance. Akin to Matilda's and Ellinor's trials in *The Recess*, the dead hand of the past continually arrests Adeline's fight for freedom in the present. Reminiscent of Wollstonecraft's Gothic vision of England, Adeline experiences the 'unnatural crimes' that the male 'desire of perpetuating a name' produces (Wollstonecraft 2008, 21). At various points in her history, she is sent into exile, confined in a convent and imprisoned in an abbey, all so that she is prevented from encroaching on the '*family* estate' (Wollstonecraft 2008, 21). Furthermore, in another parallel with Wollstonecraft's *Rights of Men*, inheritance and primogeniture are shown to create alienated, dysfunctional families in *The Romance of the Forest*. The Marquis uses the property he inherited in marriage to aid his sexual advances towards Adeline when his own wife, the Marchioness, is still alive (*RF* 146). La Motte marries his wife on the grounds that her 'birth was equal, her fortune superior to his' and drags her into exile with himself as a result of gambling debts accumulated in Paris. We also learn that he 'seldom consulted his wife till he had determined how to act' (*RF* 23). However, it is Adeline's family that suffers the most as a result of male abuse of inheritance. The ancestral crimes committed by the Marquis's desire to assume his brother's title and property force her to live as an 'orphan, subsisting on the bounty of others, without family, with few friends, and pursued by a cruel and powerful enemy' (*RF* 346). Adeline's family is destroyed by aristocratic greed and she is left to depend on the chivalry of others or, rather, her own powers of self-reliance, to survive.

This brings me to another important aspect of the past in *The Romance of the Forest*: chivalry. For Burke, chivalry is a time-honoured European tradition that has, throughout history, safeguarded the state. He identifies chivalry as the glory and security of the English nation and argues that, by exalting the 'weaker' sex, the nation grows stronger. Burke's conception of chivalry is not dissimilar to the one that Reeve presents in *The Old English Baron*; both writers present it as an old, idealised code of civilised behaviour that combines prowess, loyalty and honour.[13] Although there is little historical evidence of the existence or implementation of such a code of behaviour, Burke and Reeve argue that the values it embodies – for example, valour, generosity and gallantry – must be perpetuated in the present in order to ensure national stability. As I discussed in Chapter 2, Reeve draws upon notions of chivalry and romantic images of armed conflict in order to create a strong and unified sense of national identity at a difficult historical moment. Citing the failure of ordinary men to rescue Marie Antoinette, Burke argues that the 'age of chivalry is gone' in France; 'sophisters, oeconomists, and calculators' have 'extinguished' this ancient institution which, Burke argues, will have devastating consequences for French society (1986, 170). Indeed, Burke and Reeve invoke the mythical concept of chivalry as an ancient form of courtly protectionism that maintains national stability by providing valorous codes of male behaviour which, in turn, protects so-called 'weak' women. In the past presented in *The Romance of the Forest*, a somewhat darker view of chivalry is revealed; a view closer to that shared by Wollstonecraft.

Subverting Burke's conservative defence of the state, a warped sense of chivalry pervades the past in Radcliffe's Female Gothic novel. Compelled to escape the sexual advances of the malevolent

Marquis, Adeline arranges for Peter (La Motte's servant) to assist her. However, whilst escaping on horseback, she realises that the rider is not Peter, but one of the Marquis's servants (*RF* 155). She is consequently taken to a secluded villa where the malevolent Marquis attempts to seduce her (*RF* 156–8). She is compelled to make her own escape before Theodore (her lover) eventually appears to aid her flight (*RF* 164–7). However, they are pursued and, accused of violating the king's orders, Theodore is wounded and Adeline is once again compelled to save herself (*RF* 176). Recovering from his wound, Theodore is held prisoner and Adeline finds herself once again imprisoned in the ruinous abbey (*RF* 199). Acts of chivalry are frequently undermined or frustrated in the seventeenth-century past of *The Romance of the Forest* and the heroine is often compelled to save herself. La Motte's actions often appear chivalrous, but frequently harm Adeline. Even though he is terrorised by the Marquis, his 'weak' and 'sometimes vicious' character flaws result in her oppression (*RF* 2). For example, having inadvertently rescued Adeline from the banditti at the beginning of the narrative, he threatens her with the return of her 'father', encourages her to marry the Marquis, is complicit in her abduction and, for a time, agrees to imprison her in the decaying abbey. Described as someone whose conscience has not been 'entirely darkened' by vice, La Motte functions variously as Adeline's saviour and oppressor (*RF* 211). Using the past to comment on the present and the political debates triggered by the French Revolution, Radcliffe demonstrates how seemingly chivalrous acts often ensure the domination and oppression of women by men. Chivalry may have flourished in medieval literature, Arthurian legends and romances such as *The Old English Baron*, but it was notably absent from much medieval warfare. Subverting Burke's and Reeve's conception of chivalry, Radcliffe exposes it as a myth that enslaves and harms women. In the past presented in *The Romance of the Forest*, chivalry is portrayed as an anachronistic social mechanism that fails to accord with the increasingly self-reliant and mobile heroine.

The past presented in Radcliffe's Female Gothic novel is 'Gothic' in the Wollstonecraftian sense: it is feudal, backward and oppressive. Far from experiencing a time-honoured and noble political system, Adeline is subject to the horrors of a patriarchal social order where male abuse of inheritance has ruined her family and chivalry is presented as something totally outdated and obsolete.

Radcliffe suggests that it is positively harmful for the heroine of the novel to rely on such a 'system' to save her and exposes the falsity of Burke's notion of chivalry as an idealised (and probably non-existent) version of the past that is invoked to criticise the present. The past in *The Romance of the Forest* challenges and subverts Burke's – and Reeve's – notion of benevolent patriarchy. Just as it was for Wollstonecraft, the past is a scene of ignorance, superstition and oppression in Radcliffe's Female Gothic novel. She demonises the time-honoured social customs treasured by Burke (and Reeve in *The Old English Baron*) and rejects the notion that the historic tried and tested English political system cannot be improved upon. As I will discuss in a moment, by the end of the novel, an old, male-dominated and tyrannical social order has given way to a new one that accommodates women's rights. Miles has examined the social change evident in Radcliffe's novels and has noted how many of them tend to be set on 'the "Gothic cusp", the mid-seventeenth century, where the medieval is on the wane, and the Enlightenment begins to wax' (1995, 114). *The Romance of the Forest* is no exception. Set in seventeenth-century France, the historical change effected in *The Romance of the Forest* is analogous with the outbreak of the French Revolution at the end of the eighteenth century and Radcliffe's own, dissenting inclination towards social and gender reform in England. Featuring the exploits of a dynamic woman, Radcliffe's Female Gothic novel subverts a notion that Burke's *Reflections* tried to sustain: the eighteenth-century ideological construction of the passive and docile eighteenth-century woman.

To recall Paulson's thoughts from earlier, the French Revolution inculcated a new sense of history: one which demoted the roles of kings and noblemen and drew attention to the exploits of lesser known individuals and groups. Events such as the march on Versailles demonstrated that women were playing an active and prevalent role in the French Revolution. Despite their marginalisation in traditional historiography and demonisation in Burke's *Reflections*, ordinary women were suddenly at the centre of history and effecting major historical change. The French Revolution presented new possibilities for women; changes embraced by Wollstonecraft and reflected in Radcliffe's fictional pasts. Reminiscent of *The Old English Baron*, the personal is political and vice versa in *The Romance of the Forest* as Radcliffe uses fictional characters and situations to comment on politics and society in her own time. Rejecting Burke's idealisation of the passive, docile eighteenth-century woman who depends on acts of male chivalry to survive, Adeline covers a geographically large area, escapes the clutches of male tyranny on numerous occasions and demonstrates great self-reliance. Whilst *The Romance of the Forest* does feature terrifying pasts dominated by male oppression, the heroine is not constrained by excessive sensibility and largely escapes patriarchal tyranny. As a result, Radcliffe's Female Gothic novel is far more optimistic about women's lives than *The Recess*. Influenced by the dissenting zeal for reform of the 1790s and the events taking place across the Channel, Radcliffe places an active and resourceful woman at the centre of her fictional history and records her journey from male oppression and manipulation to self-control. Indeed, at the end of the novel, Adeline is 'transformed to the daughter of an illustrious house, and the heiress of immense wealth' (*RF* 346): her 'rich estates' are 'returned to her' and she is in control of her own financial affairs (*RF* 353). After the death of the Marquis, she remains 'some time at Paris to settle her affairs' and instructs for 'the remains of her parent' to be 'removed from the Abbey of St. Clair, and deposited in the vault of his ancestors' (*RF* 353–4). We learn that Adeline rejects 'several suitors which her goodness, beauty, and wealth' had 'already attracted' (*RF* 356) in favour of Theodore: the 'lover who deserved, and possessed, her tenderest affection' (*RF* 355).

The extent to which Radcliffe's Gothic pasts can be considered conservative or radical has been fiercely debated over the decades. Some critics point to the fact that Radcliffe's novels generally end in marriage as proof that she is a conservative writer who supports notions of gradual, Burkean change. In this view, it is argued that Radcliffe criticises patriarchy without seriously challenging it.[14] However, as Miles (1995) and Norton (1999) argue, such a view does not accord with Radcliffe's dissenting views or, as this chapter has shown, her subversion of traditional gender politics. Indeed, Radcliffe may not be as radical as Wollstonecraft, but she is certainly not as conservative as Burke. Akin to most of Radcliffe's Female Gothic novels, *The Romance of the Forest* does end in marriage, but it is not one where the man dominates. Nor is it a forced or contracted marriage. In this sense, Radcliffe's novel differs from Walpole's, Reeve's and Lee's fictional Gothic pasts, where men control their wives and their affairs. Wollstonecraft may point out the dangers of marriage and the devastating consequences it can have on women's lives, but she is not totally against it. In her later *A Vindication of the Rights of Woman* (1792), she admits that she 'respect[s] marriage' as the 'the foundation of every social virtue' and believes that marriage should be an equal partnership between two individuals (1985, 165). Radcliffe's Female Gothic novel reveals a similar view by showcasing a marriage based on equality. Adeline marries the man she loves, remains in control of her affairs and enjoys with her husband 'the pure and rational delights of a love refined into the most tender friendship' (*RF* 362). In comparison to the patriarchal tyranny Adeline suffers in her previous life, a significant alteration in relations between the sexes has occurred by the end of the novel and there is much greater equality between sexes. As Carol Margaret Davison suggests, Radcliffe 'boldly imagines an ideal, Wollstonecraftian world where women and men are equal citizens under the law and women handle their own financial affairs' (2009, 99). The seventeenth-century past of *The Romance of the Forest* is a product of the dissenting historico-political debates sparked by the outbreak of the French Revolution: a series of events which triggered a wider eighteenth-century awareness of the sweep of history.

The Romance of the Forest, the Gothic and historical consciousness

Now that I have examined the ways in which the past in *The Romance of the Forest* engages politically with contemporary events in France, I will turn my attention to how the text encapsulates changing, increasingly Romantic notions of history. *The Romance of the Forest* exploits the diverse emotions evoked by the recent events in France; from excitement and hope, to fear and trepidation. The decaying Abbey of St Clair discussed earlier is important here. Walking through the ruinous abbey – a structure that is associated with the Bastille – La Motte makes a 'comparison between himself and the gradation of decay' (*RF* 16). 'A few years', he comments, 'and I shall become like the mortals on whose relics I now gaze, and like them too, I may be the subject of meditation to a succeeding generation, which shall totter but a little while over the object they contemplate, ere they also sink into the dust' (*RF* 16). La Motte contemplates how he may 'be standing over the ashes of the dead' and we learn that his fancy and imagination 'bore him back to past ages' (*RF* 15). There are numerous instances of such historical reflections in *The Romance of the Forest*. During one of her walks with La Luc (after her escape from the abbey), Adeline spots the remains of an old castle, describing it as a 'monument of faded glory' (*RF* 264). Viewing its broken turrets and 'picturesque beauty', Adeline discloses to La Motte that it 'seems … as if we were walking over the ruins of the world, and were the only persons who had survived the wreck' (*RF* 265).

Such reflections may not seem that uncommon in the context of Gothic fiction or, indeed, eighteenth-century literature in general. Throughout the eighteenth century, the picturesque, sublime and beautiful nature of ruins and landscapes were a source of fervent debate. The ruin, in particular, was a means of meditating on history and the transitory nature of humanity. Influenced by Burke's work on the sublime (which I will discuss a little later), Gothic writers such as Lee wrote of vast, gloomy, decaying edifices in order to induce suspense and terror and to emphasise the brevity of human life. However, it is Radcliffe who dwells on mouldering architecture and the nature of history perhaps more than any other eighteenth-century Gothic novelist. The cultural context in which she is writing goes some way to explaining this. With the outbreak of the French Revolution and the fall of the Bastille, the nature of history and ruined edifices assumed a new, disturbing significance. William Hazlitt captures the late eighteenth-century *zeitgeist* when he speaks of 'the supposed tottering state of all old structures at the time' (1845, 145). Set in France and revealing a seventeenth-century past permeated by contemporary references to the French Revolution, *The Romance of the Forest* reflects a wider cultural awareness of the passage of time and the force of history at the end of the eighteenth century.

As Georg Lukács argues, it was the French Revolution 'which for the first time made history a *mass experience*' and forcibly compelled eighteenth-century English men and women to 'comprehend their own existence as something historically conditioned' (1969, 20–2). To an age already fascinated with history and antiquity, the French Revolution acted as a catalyst for further scrutiny of not only significant historical events (such as the Glorious Revolution of 1688), but the very nature of history and the past. Major, world-changing historical events were no longer something remote that (educated) readers read about in tomes written by historians such as Hume, Robertson and Gibbon; eighteenth-century men and women were now very much part of the historical process. Historiography no longer seemed the bedrock of knowledge and, with their beliefs in the longevity of historical institutions shaken, some members of the educated classes in England viewed the past, the present and the future with a deep sense of unease and foreboding. In *The Romance of the Forest*, Adeline's meditations on the mouldering castle and the 'ruins of the world' illuminate a renewed recognition of the force of history whilst La Motte's remarks on the decaying abbey reveal a heightened awareness of historical change. Influenced by the tumultuous context of the French Revolution, its war on the past and the shifting notions of history that it engendered, Radcliffe's Gothic novel reveals a heightened sense of historical consciousness. La Motte's remarks, in particular, underscore a renewed and frightening sense of historical identity and reveal a wider, disturbing cultural realisation: that history no longer belonged to the eighteenth-century people. Rather, they belonged to it. With its emphasis on dark, repressed histories, problematised historical transmission, the unrepresentable, and fascination with the foreign, the Gothic became a perfect means for scaring people by exploiting and exploring this new, frightening sense of historical awareness. In *The Romance of the Forest*, Radcliffe exploits the ruined castle and, perhaps more importantly, the gloomy, decaying abbey in order to illuminate the dark and violent forces (physical and spiritual) that drive human history.

It is important to note at this juncture that, whilst Radcliffe's novel displays distinctive, Romantic attitudes towards the past and an elevated state of historical consciousness, it also conducts a number of its more traditional functions. In *The Romance of the Forest*, the Gothic continues to prey on Enlightenment histories' omissions in order to evoke suspense and terror. The Abbey of St Clair, in which Adeline, La Motte and his family take refuge, and where many of the key sequences of action and suspense take place, is surrounded by sinister conjectures and rumours. We learn that 'strange appearances' and 'uncommon noises' have long been connected with the abbey and that, one night in the past, a stranger was brought to the abbey and confined in one of its apartments (*RF* 30). Gripped by superstitious fears, residents ceased visiting the spot and the abbey has remained 'abandoned to decay' ever since (*RF* 31). The Gothic remains concerned with marginalised, sinister pasts that return to haunt the present. Indeed, it is in this abandoned, decaying abbey that such rumours gather force. In a secret apartment in the Abbey of St Clair, Adeline discovers an 'old dagger' which is 'spotted and stained with rust' and a fragile, decaying manuscript: 'It was a small roll of paper, tied with a string, and covered with dust. Adeline took it up, and on opening it perceived an handwriting. She attempted to read it, but the part of the manuscript she looked at was so much obliterated, that she found this difficult' (*RF* 116). Earlier in the narrative, La Motte discovers the 'remains of a human skeleton' in a 'large chest' located in one of the rooms of the abbey (*RF* 54–5). In order to avoid scaring Adeline and his wife, he keeps the discovery to himself. Gothic tropes – a mouldering skeleton, a rusty dagger and a fragmented manuscript – symbolise the irrational and violent aspects of the past. The fact that such historical artefacts are discovered in a French abbey only serves to heighten fear and trepidation. However, it is the discovered manuscript that plays a key role in tying these historical artefacts together and recovering the repressed history of which it writes.

Whereas Walpole and Lee use the Gothic device of the discovered script to frame their narratives, Radcliffe integrates it into the main body of her narrative. By doing so, the manuscript becomes a focal point and comments on the nature of the past. Having initially browsed it, Adeline waits until she is alone to read it in full.[15] Echoing the rumours circulated by the local community, the script reveals the harrowing experiences of a man who was imprisoned in the abbey and met his death there. However, the reader is only granted access to the manuscript when Adeline finds enough time and seclusion to read it. Throughout the narrative, the reader is granted access to splinters of this repressed history, as in the following example:

> [Adeline] was preparing for rest, when she recollected the MS., and was unable to conclude the night without reading it. The first words she could distinguish were the following:
> 'Again I return to this poor consolation – again I have been permitted to see another day. It is now midnight! My solitary lamp

burns beside me; the time is awful, but to me the silence of noon is
as the silence of midnight: a deeper gloom is all in which they differ.
The still unvarying hours are numbered only by my sufferings! Great
God! when shall I be released!

*   *   *   *   *   *   *   *   *

*   *   *   *   *   *   *   *   *

'But whence this strange confinement? I have never injured him. If
death is designed me, why this delay; and for what but death am
I brought hither? This abbey – alas!' – Here the MS. was again illegible, and for several pages Adeline could only make out disjointed
sentences.

(RF 139)

In Radcliffe's hands, the Gothic continues to highlight the textuality of the past and our frustrated access to it in the present.
However, Radcliffe employs the decaying manuscript in *The
Romance of the Forest* for an additional purpose. The French
setting of the novel and the fact that Adeline discovers this fragmented manuscript in a ruinous French abbey (a structure which
La Motte likens to the Bastille) are important factors here. As
a Gothic novel that is as much about Radcliffe's present as it is
about the seventeenth century it represents, the splintered manuscript that features in the novel symbolises the chaotic reality and
shattered sense of history engendered by the French Revolution.
Written by a Frenchman and discovered in a ruined French abbey,
the fractured history that the manuscript represents attests to the
revolutionary destruction of the past in France. With the demoli-
tion of the Bastille and the abolition of historic legislation (such
as the tithe), the splintered and fractured manuscript featured in
The Romance of the Forest reflects not only the broken nature of
the past in 1790s France, but the broken sense of history at the
end of the eighteenth century. The Gothic continues to react to
shifting notions of eighteenth-century historiography. The decaying script illuminates the frightening fragility of history and the
force and rapidity of historical change. With Enlightenment philosophical histories losing their explanatory power and appeals to
prior historical events proving inconclusive, the past at the end of
the eighteenth century had actually become what the Gothic had
always suggested it was: a formless, chaotic mass often driven by

irrational forces. Asking questions rather than providing answers, the fractured manuscript that features in *The Romance of the Forest* reveals a past that challenges rational understanding.

Utilising and adapting the trope of the discovered manuscript, Radcliffe's Gothic novel continues to exhibit a heightened sense of historical consciousness. This brings me to another important point. Gothic manuscripts are typically centuries old. For example, *Otranto* is (supposedly) translated from an 'ancient' document (*O* 5), *The Old English Baron* claims to be based on a 'manuscript in the old English language' (*OEB* 139) and *The Recess* is (allegedly) transcribed from sixteenth-century documents (*R* 5). Similarly to these examples, the decaying manuscript that features in *The Romance of the Forest* certainly has the appearance of an ancient historical artefact. As the above quotations illustrate, discovered along with a rusty dagger in a mouldering, cobwebbed room, the fragile, decaying and 'almost obliterated' script would seem to pre-date the seventeenth-century action by multiple decades, if not centuries (*RF* 127). However, Radcliffe makes it possible to date the fragmented manuscript with surprising accuracy. Frightened that his whereabouts have been discovered and that he is about to be arrested and taken back to Paris to account for his gambling debts, La Motte hastily (if somewhat wordily) inscribes the following message over the door of the abbey's tower in order to elude detection: 'P – L– M – a wretched exile, sought within these walls a refuge from persecution, on the 27th of April 1658, and quitted them on the 12th of July in the same year, in search of a more convenient asylum' (*RF* 56). When Adeline discovers the manuscript and begins reading it, we learn that the events of which it relates began on 'the twelfth of October, in the year 1642' (*RF* 128).

If we are to assume that La Motte inscribes a fairly accurate date, then the apparently 'ancient', decaying manuscript is in fact only approximately sixteen years old. Traditionally, Gothic manuscripts have decayed over centuries, but, in Radcliffe's novel, the script that Adeline discovers has become almost indecipherable in less than two decades. Indeed, the manuscript featured within *The Romance of the Forest* reflects the accelerated sense of historical time engendered by the French Revolution. As Eelco Runia points out, with the rapid pace of events – the storming of the Bastille, the eradication of thousand-year-old traditions in a moment, the desecration of the Church, the attempt to start history anew – the

Revolution threw one into a breathtaking 'rollercoaster of terrifying events' and challenged Enlightenment, philosophical histories premised on slow, incremental historical change (1999, 144). The mutilated manuscript featured in Radcliffe's novel underscores the frightening force and rapidity of history and reflects a wider cultural realisation that historical time had gained speed towards the end of the eighteenth century. Preying on readers' contemporary unease about France's radical and rapid departure from the past, *The Romance of the Forest* reveals how the present can become the past in a frighteningly short space of time.

Romantic impulses: the Gothic manuscript, the past and the sublime

The French Revolution triggered new ways of thinking and writing about history and drew attention to the nature of the past in an unprecedented way. Notions of fragmentation and Romantic attitudes towards the past remain important here. As I discussed in the introduction to this chapter, Burke's *Reflections* heralds a significant moment for eighteenth-century historical writing by attaching greater importance to feelings and emotions. This marks an important development from Enlightenment historical attitudes, where historians such as Hume, Rapin and Robertson enforced an emotional distance between themselves and their subjects. With the publication of the *Reflections*, feeling in history and how one reacts emotionally to historical stimuli became increasingly significant. An integral part of such increasingly Romantic attitudes towards the past involves the sublime. As critics such as Paulson (1983, 59) and Kilgour (1995, 32) have pointed out, Burke reworks a number of his aesthetic ideas from his earlier *Enquiry* in the *Reflections*. Furthermore, elements of England's history are identified as sources of the sublime in his political treatise. For example, as Philip Shaw points out (2006, 66), the time-honoured and inherited English constitution is sublime for Burke because it inspires awe, reverence and respect in its subjects. Indeed, the sublime gained a new significance towards the end of the eighteenth century. The *Reflections* attest to numerous speculations on France at this time, which were accompanied by a sense of the sublime. Hearing about the Revolution from the safety of English shores and unsure of the implications of such events for their own society, many men and women living in England experienced a sense of 'tranquillity tinged with terror' (Burke 2004, 165). France's break with history seemed to be shrouded in mystery and obscurity. As a point of contact between the Gothic and Romanticism, Radcliffe was attracted to the sublime and its potential for representing the past. The forthcoming discussion will show how, in *The Romance of the Forest*, Radcliffe utilises and develops the classic Gothic convention of the discovered manuscript to examine this new, developing Romantic sense of history inculcated by the outbreak of the French Revolution. Before I examine the impact of such ideas on the past constructed in *The Romance of the Forest*, I will outline Burke's notions of the sublime.

In Burke's influential *Enquiry*, he draws a distinction between the sublime and the beautiful. Their effects are unalike and opposite. Beauty is associated with pleasure, society and the aim of reproduction. The sublime is associated with mingled pain and delight instead of pleasure and is linked to notions of terror, danger and self-preservation: 'Whatever is fitted in any sort to excite the ideas of pain, and danger, that is to say, whatever is in any sort terrible, or is conversant about terrible objects, or operates in a manner analogous to terror, is a source of the sublime; that is, it is productive of the strongest emotion which the mind is capable of feeling' (Burke 2004, 86). It is this concentration on the negative aspect of the sublime that marks a critical difference between Burke and his predecessors and which made his ideas so appealing to writers of Gothic fiction. Perhaps the most influential aspect of the *Enquiry*, however, is Burke's aesthetic of obscurity. 'To make any thing very terrible', he writes, 'obscurity seems in general to be necessary' (102). When something is clear, the full extent of any danger can be assessed; when it is obscure, a sense of dread and danger are evoked. As Nicola Trott highlights (2003, 80), Burke's obscurity 'stems from a rejection of (Enlightenment) clarity' for a darkness that is, to use his own words, 'more productive of sublime ideas than light' (Burke 2004, 121). Burke is firm in his conviction that nothing 'can strike the mind with its greatness … whilst we are able to perceive its bounds' and shows a preference for suggestion over definition, limitlessness instead of lucidity (106). For Burke, darkness, uncertainty and confusion are 'sublime to the last degree' (103).

In her essay, 'On the Supernatural in Poetry' (1826), Radcliffe makes numerous remarks on Burke's notion of the sublime as 'a sort of tranquillity tinged with terror' and speaks of the 'thrill of horror and surprise' (2000, 168).[16] Interpreting Burkean aesthetics for her own art, she draws a distinction between terror and horror: they are 'so far opposite', she argues, that 'the first expands the soul, and awakens the faculties to a high degree of life; the other contracts, freezes and nearly annihilates them' (168). The 'great difference between horror and terror', she continues, lies in 'the uncertainty and obscurity' that 'accompany the first' (168). Radcliffe also responds to Burke's critics by defending his addition of the obscure to discussions of the sublime. She argues that those who believe 'certainty is more terrible than surmise' must have 'very cold imaginations' (168) and, in agreement with Burke, she argues that things seen 'in glimpses through obscure shades, the great outlines only appearing' are far more conducive of terror and the sublime than objects 'distinctly pictured forth' (169). Obscurity and indistinctness 'excite the imagination to complete the rest' and leave something for the mind to 'exaggerate' (169). Such remarks throw an interesting light on Radcliffe's fictional techniques and the representation of the past in *The Romance of the Forest*.

Burke's thoughts on the sublime tend to focus on architecture, poetry, nature, landscape, colours, sounds, and smells. As many Gothic scholars have highlighted, Radcliffe's novels certainly focus on the sublime nature of wild landscapes and vast, mouldering architectural edifices. With the obscure, ruined French abbey and the feelings of awe and terror that it evokes in La Motte featuring so prominently within the narrative, *The Romance of the Forest* certainly utilises such notions of the Burkean sublime. However, my attention here remains fixed on the Gothic figure of the fragmented manuscript. Indeed, Radcliffe's third Gothic novel is unique in this sense: it is the only time she elects to splinter a discovered script throughout key sequences of action.[17] By employing this device, she demonstrates that it is not just historic ruins that function as a source of the sublime; the textual nature of the past can evoke sublime sensations too. *The Romance of the Forest* draws attention to the sublimity of the past.

In a decade rocked by the French Revolution's destruction of the past and where history was heavily scrutinised, the mutilated manuscript is a cogent reminder that the past is sublime in the Burkean sense that it is obscure, formless, remote, and potentially limitless. Radcliffe firmly positions this textual, historical artefact as a source of the sublime. We are told that the ink is 'almost obliterated in places' (*RF* 127), that numerous pages are 'discoloured' and that large sections are 'decayed with damp and totally illegible' (*RF* 131). The obscure and disjointed fragments of the script that are interspersed throughout *The Romance of the Forest* play upon readers' imaginations by promising or suggesting more than what they are and symbolise the Gothic's obsession with the haunting and chilling nature of history. To adapt Sophie Thomas's remarks on the literary fragment, the disjointed sections of script that pervade *The Romance of the Forest* function as 'disturbing entities' (2005, 502). Not only are they figures of disruption and discontinuity, but they serve to remind the reader that the glimpses of the macabre history that they disclose are precisely that: vestiges of a past that can never be recovered or fully experienced. Concurring with Burke, Radcliffe highlights absence as a source of the sublime. The past is sublime because it forces us to contemplate our transience and insignificance in the wider sweep of human history. Such thoughts gained force with the outbreak of the French Revolution. The splintered, historic script compels the reader to reflect on the disturbing relation of 'the part to the whole, presence to absence, and present to past' (Thomas 2005, 504). Acting in a similar way to the novel's decaying abbey, Radcliffe's fragmented Gothic manuscript is a manifestation of the past locked into the present and provides a rather Romantic and 'uncanny suspension of time and history' (502). Influenced by the tumultuous cultural context of the emergent French Revolution, the challenge posed to Enlightenment historical understanding and the increasing importance of emotion in historical enquiry, Radcliffe utilises the Gothic in *The Romance of the Forest* to highlight humankind's essentially 'Gothic' relationship with the past: despite its seeming tangibility in the present, it frequently remains elusive, frustrating our access to it and resisting rationality. To use Burke's words, the decaying script excites ideas of pain and danger, it is conversant about terrible objects and experiences, and evokes terror. Utilising Burkean notions of the sublime, Radcliffe adds a new impetus and dimension to the Gothic's fascination with horrible and repressed histories. Obscure, formless, remote, and potentially limitless, it is no surprise that so many eighteenth-century Gothic writers chose not only to set their narratives in obscure pasts, but to use narrative devices and structures that draw attention to the nature of the past; it is the perfect place and subject to evoke terror.

Terror: history, Adeline and the sublime

Not only is the past positioned as a source of the sublime in *The Romance of the Forest*; Adeline is revealed to experience a number of sublime sensations. As I mentioned previously, she experiences a type of delightful terror whilst reading the macabre history related by the manuscript. On her first, scant perusal of the script, we are told that the 'few words' that are legible 'impressed her with curiosity and terror' and that numerous circumstances 'crowded upon her mind' (*RF* 116). When she is once again alone in her gloomy apartment, her light slowly 'expiring in the socket', we are informed that what Adeline has managed to read has 'awakened a dreadful interest in the fate of the writer, and called up terrific images to her mind' (*RF* 129). She frequently shudders and even sheds tears during her late night readings of this unfortunate man's plight (*RF* 132). The full horror of the gruesome history begins to dawn on Adeline. Macabre, fragmented and disjointed, Adeline's imagination is 'strongly impressed' by the events recounted; 'strange images of fantastic thought' (*RF* 134) cross her mind and 'to her distempered sense the suggestions of a bewildered mind appeared with the force of reality' (*RF* 132). Conforming to Burkean notions of astonishment and terror, we are told that 'her imagination had filled up the void in the sentences, so as to suggest the evil apprehended' (*RF* 12). Obscure, formless and offering splintered glimpses of a horrific past, the manuscript leaves Adeline to 'imagine horrors more terrible than any, perhaps, which certainty could give' (*RF* 131). We are told that her 'fancy' now 'wandered in the regions of terror', subduing her 'reason' and raising 'other dreadful ideas' (*RF* 134).

Adeline's reaction to the horrific past represented by the manuscript relates closely to another important aspect of the Burkean sublime; one that is essential to Radcliffe's wider attitude towards the past. Indeed, most commentators agree that the Burkean sublime involves a suspension of reason. 'Hence arises the great power of the sublime', proposes Burke, that 'far from being produced by them, it anticipates our reasonings, and hurries us on by an irresistible force' (2004, 101). Akin to reading a Gothic novel, the sublime pre-empts rational analysis and presumes an aesthetic of non-representability. Interpreting Burke's concept of the sublime, F. R. Ankersmit argues that the sublime is encountered when 'the epistemological instruments we ordinarily use for making sense of the world suddenly prove themselves to be no longer equal to the task' (2005, 174).[18]

Similarly to Burke's thoughts on recent events in France in the *Reflections*, Adeline finds herself unable to rationalise or contextualise the enormity of the events related by the manuscript. Adeline's experience of the manuscript is so horrifying and shattering that 'normal' patterns of experience are disrupted; she experiences sensations associated with the sublime because she is confronted with contradictions, oppositions and paradoxes that are utterly unthinkable in terms of prior experiences. Gripped by terror and deprived of reason, she can only speculate that some 'supernatural power' lurks behind the manuscript and the macabre history it relates (*RF* 141). Developing the psychological introspection that formed such an important part of Lee's *The Recess*, Radcliffe's *The Romance of the Forest* focuses increasingly on how the past imprints itself on the mind and illuminates the creative capacity of the human imagination when it comes to conceiving history. Radcliffe's attitude towards the past is Romantic in the sense that she places an emphasis on the irrational, wild and uncontrollable nature of history and a focus on the terrifying sensory impressions that can be evoked by the past. In contrast to Enlightenment historiography, Radcliffe's novel focuses precisely on the areas where memories, expectations and certainties do not fit into neat patterns and defy intuitions about what the past is like. It is in these gaps, these menacing, unsettling experiences where the past itself is encountered as uncompromisingly strange, or, in other words, sublime.

Focusing on a violent and irrational past and utilising the Burkean sublime, Radcliffe's work frequently examines experiences of history beyond language and explores the spontaneous sensations that the past is capable of evoking. At a time when the French Revolution was destabilising England's knowledge of its own past, *The Romance of the Forest* suggests that our relationship with the past is far more fluid and uncertain than the historical writing informed by Enlightenment doctrines suggests. With its emphasis on repressed, fractured histories, the Gothic probes the experience of the past that underlies the language of the historian. In this light, perhaps one of the most important elements of Adeline's experience of reading the manuscript is her sense that the events described occurred in the very place she is staying:

> 'In these very apartments', said she, 'this poor sufferer was confined – here he' – Adeline started, and thought she heard a sound; but the stillness of night was undisturbed. 'In these very chambers', said she,

'these lines were written – these lines from which he then derived a comfort in believing that they would hereafter be read by some pitying eye: this time is now come. Your miseries, O injured being! are lamented, where they were endured. *Here*, where you suffered, I weep for your sufferings!'

(RF 132)

It is important to note that, during this scene, Adeline's fear is exacerbated by the nightmares she experiences before the discovery of the script (*RF* 108–10) and two new sources of terror: strange whisperings and the presence of a ghostly figure (*RF* 133–4). These factors aside, however, it is Adeline's reading of the manuscript that triggers a type of sublime historical experience. The 'wretched writer' appeals 'directly to her heart' and, for a moment, past and present seem to merge: it 'seemed as if his past sufferings were at this moment present' (*RF* 132), writes Adeline. Revealing an increasingly Romantic interest in history, the past is located as a site of trauma in Radcliffe's Gothic novel, producing a combination of pleasure and pain. At this moment where history seems closer and more tangible than ever before for Adeline, the past is still in fact as irrecoverable and out of reach as it has ever been. Reading this macabre history in the very room where the horrific events recounted took place, the manuscript creates a disturbing illusion of closeness in distance. The decaying script evokes an aura of a past that can never be fully recovered or experienced. In *The Romance of the Forest*, the past (as embodied by the manuscript) evokes sublime sensations by producing the paradoxical union of feelings of loss and love, pleasure and pain. Radcliffe's work is especially interested in the emotional and psychological reactions that historical artefacts can elicit.

Although the script evokes such sublime sensations and has a prominent role in *The Romance of the Forest*, the document itself does not solve the novel's mysteries. As Miles highlights, Radcliffe's novel is unusual in the sense that the Gothic device of the discovered manuscript is essentially incidental to the resolution of the plot; in the court scene that features towards the end of the novel, everything that needs to be known about the grim history emerges independently of Adeline and the fragmented script (1995, 115). In that court scene, we learn not only that the person who wrote the manuscript was murdered in the Abbey of St Clair, but that this man was in fact Adeline's father (*RF* 341). As a result of the trial, Adeline discovers her true ancestry and obtains the rights of her birth. She gives the skeleton of her deceased father a proper burial and preserves the 'MS. that recorded his sufferings' with the 'pious enthusiasm so sacred a relique deserved' (*RF* 355). However, the script remains important in its own right and is significant in terms of Radcliffe's wider attitudes towards the past. In the midst of the court scene, Adeline suddenly remembers the manuscript and the sublime sensations that she experienced whilst reading it in the decaying abbey. During the various testimonies, she vividly recalls the 'MS. she had found, together with the extraordinary circumstances that had attended the discovery' (*RF* 341). She grows 'faint' and, mirroring her experience in the abbey whilst reading the manuscript, her nerves are once again 'thrilled with horror' (*RF* 341). The manuscript may not resolve the plot, but it haunts these legal proceedings and evokes chilling memories for Adeline. After the trial, we learn that the 'sufferings of her dead father, such as she had read them recorded by his *own hand*, pressed most forcibly to her thoughts' (*RF* 346–7). Indeed, even though Adeline's history and identity have been discovered, she is traumatised by the past recounted in the manuscript. 'The narrative had formerly so much affected her heart, and interested her imagination', we are told, 'that her memory now faithfully reflected each particular circumstance there disclosed' (*RF* 347). Such is the power of the fragmented script that, whenever she reflects on having 'been in the very chamber where her parent had suffered', the 'anguish and horror of her mind defied all control' (*RF* 347).

Reminiscent of Burke's configuration of history in the *Reflections*, there is a tension between feelings about the past and knowledge of it in *The Romance of the Forest*. As I discussed in the Introduction, evoking irrationality and mysticism and yet obsessed with legitimacy and the status quo, the Gothic is a manifestation of pro- and anti-Enlightenment impulses. This is particularly the case with Radcliffe. Even though reason triumphs in *The Romance of the Forest* by dispelling many of the novel's mysteries and accounting for the identity and fate of the manuscript's author, Radcliffe continues to probe aspects of the past (and our relationship with it) that are beyond the scope of logic and reason. Whether it is La Motte's thoughts on the mouldering abbey, Adeline's reflections on the ruined castle or her reaction to historical artefacts, *The Romance of the Forest* values moods and feelings as much as truth and knowledge. In the late eighteenth century, the former qualities (moods and feelings) were often gendered feminine, and so Radcliffe's Female Gothic novel can be read as an attempt to inscribe women's perspectives and experiences into history. The fact that Adeline is shown to experience sensations associated with the sublime is significant in itself.[19] Drawing attention to the role of the individual and emotions in historical enquiry, Radcliffe's Gothic novel conducts a Romantic reconfiguration of history by asserting that how we *feel* about the past is no less important than what we *know* about it. Conveying Romantic attitudes towards history, *The Romance of the Forest* is interested in spontaneous rather than receptive experiences of the past and focuses on what is peculiar and disturbing about history rather than what is common. Writing in an age captivated by the past and a culture experiencing a heightened sense of historical awareness engendered by the French Revolution, *The Romance of the Forest* is more concerned with how the historical past comes into being, how we relate to the past and how it persists in our hearts and minds. Focusing on the more chilling aspects of human history, Radcliffe's Gothic novel probes the very nature of historical consciousness.

Conclusions: the Enlightenment and providence

The past constructed in *The Romance of the Forest* represents the most complex reaction to Enlightenment historiographical methods discussed in this book. Radcliffe's vision of social advancement from a tyrannous and feudal social order to a more egalitarian one echoes the work of Enlightenment historians and their theories of social progress.[20] However, whereas Enlightenment historians such as Hume (and, to a certain extent, Rapin) attempted to purge the past of the unknown by explaining everything with reason and rigorous methods, Radcliffe aims to restore a sense of mystery and awe to contemplations of the past. Radcliffe does not only position the past as a source of the sublime; her novel suggests that the past is also shaped by divine forces that challenge rational comprehension. In a similar vein to Reeve's *The Old English Baron*, the notion of a 'Great Author' rewarding virtue, punishing vice and shaping important events pervades the past presented in *The Romance of the Forest* (RF 265). Adeline often confides in the 'benevolence of God', suggests that the 'uncommon' circumstances that she has endured are not 'accidental' and speculates that she is a divine instrument for the 'retribution of the guilty' (*RF* 141). The ending of the novel is reminiscent of Reeve's didacticism. Radcliffe argues that Adeline's and Theodore's 'former lives afforded an example of trials well endured – and their present, of virtues greatly rewarded' (*RF* 363). Such a conclusion offers a sharp contrast to the sense of despair that characterises *The Recess*. Radcliffe follows Reeve's lead in *The Old English Baron* by constructing a past that is ultimately shaped by a benevolent providence and the mysterious ways of God.

It is also important to note that, in contrast to her future novels, Radcliffe had not yet fully developed her technique of the 'explained supernatural' and not all the strange occurrences described in the narrative are explained rationally. For example, we never find out who (or what) makes the mysterious noises in Adeline's chamber (*RF* 134) or what her horrific dreams signify or mean (*RF* 41, 108). Indeed, it is telling that Radcliffe chooses to leave such events unexplained in a novel set in France; a romantic country of seemingly impossible inversions and opposites to late eighteenth-century English eyes. As I will show in Chapter 5, the French Revolution continues to have a large impact on Gothic fiction. Placing heroines at the centre of her works, Radcliffe's Female Gothic novels continue to engage with events in France and the debates triggered by them at home. *The Romance of the Forest* greatly enhanced Radcliffe's reputation, but the peak of her success – and, moreover, the climax of the Gothic's popularity – coincided with the increasingly chaotic and violent events of the French Revolution. As I argue in the following chapter, the fact that the Gothic becomes so popular in England at this time is no coincidence. The increasingly macabre French Revolution, the debates triggered by it in England and the response of the English government would have a profound effect on Gothic pasts and locations of terror.

Notes

1 Despite Enlightenment historical methodology coming under pressure with the outbreak of the French Revolution and the pamphlet war becoming the primary form of historical discussion in England, such philosophical histories remained popular across Europe. Interestingly, Hume's Stuart volume of *The History of England* enjoyed spectacular

success in France during the revolutionary years. As Laurence L. Bongie notes (1965, 77–9), the seemingly close parallel between the French Revolution and English Revolution caught hold of the conservative imagination in France between 1789 and 1800. The seventeenth-century English Revolution provided the only really significant modern European precedent to the French Revolution and counter-revolutionists in France paid particular attention to Hume's description of the restoration of the monarchy in England. Indeed, Bongie also suggests that Hume's conservatism influenced Burke's politics (171). See Bongie's *David Hume: Prophet of the Counter-Revolution* (1965) for more information.

2 Walpole admired Burke's *Reflections*. 'Every page', he argues, 'shows how sincerely he is in earnest – a wondrous merit in a political pamphlet – All other party writers *act* zeal for the public, but it never seems to flow from the heart' (1937–83, 34: 98). He praises Burke's representation of Marie Antoinette and recalls the first time he set eyes on the Queen of France. Burke 'paints her exactly as she appeared to me the first time I saw her', he argues. 'She was going after the late king to chapel', continues Walpole, 'and shot through the room like an aërial being, all brightness and grace and without seeming to touch earth ... Had I had Mr Burke's powers, I would have described her in his words' (97–8).

3 With its emphasis on female subjectivity, mouldering ruins, secret passages, strange occurrences and fragmented manuscripts, it is now widely acknowledged that Lee's *The Recess* had a powerful influence on Radcliffe's Gothic fiction. As Norton points out, there is evidence to suggest not only that Radcliffe had read *The Recess*, but that it was one of her favourite novels (1999, 46). Furthermore, despite a degree of uncertainty, it is often assumed that Radcliffe attended the school run by Sophia, Harriet and Ann Lee at Bath and that, as a result, she personally knew the Lee sisters (Norton 1999, 46–7).

4 Examining Radcliffe's reception in the Romantic period, Townshend and Wright conclude that she was ultimately viewed as an exceptional figure and 'deemed worthy of a place in the Romantics' construction of a national canon and literary history' (2014, 31).

5 As Miles points out, Radcliffe's use of the 'explained supernatural' (rational explanations for seemingly supernatural occurrences) has often resulted in her being relegated to 'a pre-, and very much non-, Romantic status' (2014, 118). However, he suggests that there is little basis for this exclusion, as the tensions between reason and emotion, religion and superstition, and the rational and the irrational that typify her works also characterise Romanticism. Indeed, Radcliffe's Romanticism resides in the 'popular expression' she gives to 'deeply embedded attitudes in which past and present, modern and pre-modern' continually 'overlap

and destabilise each other' (134). Restrictive definitions of Romanticism, which privilege poetry and cultural elitism over prose and the popular, have, traditionally, prevented Radcliffe from being discussed in Romantic contexts. Miles contends that, in order to fully appreciate Radcliffe's work, we 'need to adjust our concept of Romanticism, from a set of ideas and styles associated with irony, nationalism and the organic, worked out through high-cultural forms such as lyric poetry, to an expanded notion of the popular' (120). See Miles, 'Popular Romanticism and the problem of belief: *The Mysteries of Udolpho*' (2014), and Gamer, *Romanticism and the Gothic* (2000), for detailed explorations of the relationship between an emerging Romanticism and the already popular Gothic.

6　The 'Diamond Necklace Affair' or the 'Affair of the Queen's Necklace' rocked both the foundation of the French monarchy and triggered defiance of royal authority. In 1785, Cardinal Louis René Édouard de Rohan, who was out of favour at the French court, was convinced by his mistress, an adventuress known as the countess de la Motte, that he could regain his position if he acted as an intermediary in securing a valuable diamond necklace for the queen, Marie Antoinette. Rohan ordered the necklace from a Parisian jeweller, who gave it to him and the countess, believing they were the queen's agents. The necklace was never seen again. It is believed that the countess's husband took it to London, where it was broken up and sold. When the jeweller failed to receive payment, Rohan and the countess were arrested and charged with fraud. He was exiled to a monastery; she was whipped, branded and sentenced to life imprisonment but later escaped. Popular revulsion at the scandal, especially the queen's supposed involvement, helped discredit the monarchy on the eve of the French Revolution. The story and the name La Motte gained notoriety throughout Europe. See Frances Mossiker's *The Queen's Necklace* (1961) for a comprehensive account of the scandal.

7　As the previous chapter noted, the Gordon Riots were still a fairly recent event and evoked memories of religious conflict and social rebellion.

8　Even though Wollstonecraft's venom targets Burke's *Reflections*, she also takes aim at his earlier work, *A Philosophical Enquiry into the Origin of Our Ideas of the Sublime and Beautiful* (1757). She argues that Burke reworks such ideas in his political treatise and criticises his gendered aesthetics. She deplores his association of littleness and weakness with beauty and women, and strength, awe and terror with the sublime and men (Wollstonecraft 2008, 45–6). Wollstonecraft's critique has interesting implications for Radcliffe's *The Romance of the Forest*, which places an assertive and active female heroine at the centre of the novel's action.

9　Miles records in his entry for Ann Radcliffe in the *Oxford Dictionary of National Biography* that she was the only child of William Ward and Ann Oates. In 1772 the family moved to Bath, where her father managed a showroom for the firm of Wedgwood and Bentley in the Westgate buildings before moving to the more fashionable Milsom Street in 1774. Thomas Bentley was Radcliffe's uncle, having married Ann Oates's sister Hannah in 1754, and played a significant role in her upbringing. After her father's haberdashery business collapsed at the beginning of the 1770s, Radcliffe appears to have spent long periods with the Bentleys. Bentley was one of the country's most prominent dissenters, who, as a founder and trustee of the dissenting academy at Warrington, included among his friends and acquaintances Joseph Priestley, Dr John Aikin, and his sister Anna Laetitia (later Mrs Barbauld). As well as being subject to the views of these eminent dissenters, Radcliffe may also have been influenced by Dr John Jebb, the radical Unitarian and distinguished theologian, who, for much of Ann Radcliffe's childhood, lived nearby in London. For more information on Radcliffe's childhood and her connections with dissenters, see Miles (2005) and Norton (1999, 26–53).

10 Prior to *The Romance of the Forest*, perhaps the clearest parallel between Radcliffe's Gothic pasts and the cultural context of the French Revolution is contained in her previous novel, *A Sicilian Romance* (1790). In an often quoted passage, Radcliffe describes the period in which her novel is set as a time when the 'dark clouds of prejudice break away before the sun of science' (1998, 116–17). Such a passage heralds the Enlightenment dawning over feudal, Gothic institutions and echoes the dissenting rhetoric of emancipation surrounding the outbreak of the French Revolution.

11 In 1795, when the French Revolution had turned violent and, due to abrasive government policy to stamp out foreign radicalism, it was dangerous to talk about such subjects, Radcliffe continues to praise the Glorious Revolution of 1688. She argues that it is 'impossible to omit any act of veneration to the blessings of this event' (1795, 389). Her husband, William Radcliffe, shared these beliefs and had a certain zeal for reform; he wrote for the *Gazetteer*, a journal with strong republican sympathies.

12 Although Burke is primarily responding to Price's *Discourse*, the *Reflections* is hostile towards dissenters in general. Indeed, Burke argues that religion and politics should never mix. 'Wholly unacquainted with the world in which they are so fond of meddling, and inexperienced in all its affairs, on which they pronounce with so much confidence', dissenters such as Price 'have nothing of politics but the passions they excite', he argues (1986, 94). In his view, 'politics and the pulpit are terms that have little agreement' and no 'sound ought to be heard in the church but the healing voice of Christian charity' (94). Such comments throw an interesting light on Radcliffe's political Gothic pasts.

Inverting numerous ideas from the *Reflections*, the past presented in *The Romance of the Forest* can be read as a reaction to Burke's hostility towards dissenters and their involvement in the political debates triggered by the French Revolution.

13 In contrast to Burke's negative reaction to the French Revolution, Reeve supported it in its early stages. Writing to Joseph Cooper Walker in April 1791, she reveals that she had 'been reading nothing but Politics for some time past', including Burke's *Reflections* and 'all the answers to it' (Reeve 1791b). As Kelly notes (2003, 117), at first she welcomed it as 'a realization of old Whig principles of constitutional monarchy'. In the same letter to Cooper, Reeve reveals her early political views on the French Revolution: 'I am a friend to liberty, and the security of property, and the rights of man. I wish well to them & all those who defend them' (Reeve 1791b). As the French Revolution grew increasingly violent, Reeve's views changed considerably (see Note 4 on Reeve in Chapter 5).

14 For example, Janet Todd argues that Radcliffe is a staunchly conservative writer who endorses slow change (1989, 255). Jane Spencer plays down the political aspects of Radcliffe's works: '[h]ers are novels of escape, criticizing the status quo of male authority but not ultimately challenging it', she argues (1986, 207). However, Radcliffe's fictions reveal fundamental changes in the situations of her heroines (a movement from oppression to a greater degree of freedom in marriage) and it is important to underscore that gender equality *is* a radical concept at the close of the eighteenth century.

15 Adeline's encounter with the manuscript comments on the process of reading and offers clues about how to read a Gothic novel (for example, alone and by candlelight). Miles draws on this metafictional aspect of the novel when he argues that the manuscript's significance is 'metonymic: it stands for "romance", for writing by women, for the secretive process whereby women romancers produce their ambiguous, multivalent texts' (1995, 115).

16 This essay originally formed part of Radcliffe's final work of fiction, *Gaston de Blondeville*, a historical novel that was published posthumously in 1826. Functioning as a framing prologue, it features two contemporary travellers on their way by horseback to Kenilworth who reveal diverse views on literature and imagination. It was first published separately by the *New Monthly Magazine* as an independent essay in aesthetic theory in January 1926.

17 Radcliffe would not choose to splinter large sections of a decaying manuscript through any of her future novels. Perhaps the closest she comes to reusing such a device is in *The Mysteries of Udolpho* (1794) where, after her father's death, Emily is instructed to burn his secret letters.

However, Emily accidentally and illicitly catches a glimpse of one of these manuscripts and, similarly to Adeline, is led to speculate wildly about the past (Radcliffe 2001, 99–100). Akin to the manuscript in *The Romance of the Forest*, the absent letter in *The Mysteries of Udolpho* seeks to highlight the sublimity of the past and reveals Romantic attitudes towards the recapture of history.

18 Immanuel Kant would develop this aspect of the Burkean sublime. He was particularly interested in how unbounded objects evoke sublime sensations and how they transcend the limits of reason. See Philip Shaw's *The Sublime* for further discussion of such notions (2006, 72–90). Kant's ideas were becoming increasingly influential in England towards the end of the eighteenth century. However, knowing so little about Radcliffe's life and literary influences, it is difficult to assess the extent to which Kantian philosophy shaped her art.

19 As Shaw notes, by associating the beautiful with women and the sublime with men, Burke's *Enquiry* suggests that women are unfit subjects for the trials of the sublime; it implies they are too 'sensual to overcome the bonds of nature, too weak to sustain visionary flight' (2006, 106). At various points in *The Romance of the Forest*, Adeline engages in the sustained visionary flight associated with the sublime (*RF* 132–3) and, in this sense, Radcliffe's novel can be read as a complex reaction to Burke's gendered aesthetics.

20 Robert Mighall explores such aspects of Radcliffe's pasts in his *A Geography of Victorian Gothic Fiction* (1999). He draws parallels between eighteenth-century Whig interpretations of history and the conflicts between reactionaries and progressives in a number of Radcliffe's works (6–7). Mighall also examines the impact of travel writing on Radcliffe's Gothic pasts (21–6).

5

'Things as they are': William Godwin, Mary Wollstonecraft and the perils of the present

'Thank God', exclaims the Englishman, 'we have no Bastille! Thank God, with us no man can be punished without a crime!' Unthinking wretch! … Go, go ignorant fool! and visit the scenes of our prisons! Witness their unwholesomeness, their filth, the tyranny of their governors, the misery of their inmates! After that, show me the man shameless enough to triumph, and say, England has no Bastille!

William Godwin, Caleb Williams (1794)

Marriage had bastilled me for life.

Mary Wollstonecraft, Maria, or The Wrongs of Woman (1798)

In his *Reflections on the Revolution in France* (1790), Edmund Burke argued that France's sudden break with the past could only lead to catastrophe and bloodshed. As the Revolution became increasingly violent, his conjectures turned out to be prophetic. In 1792, the September Massacres left more than a thousand dead and in January 1793, Louis XVI – the King of France and living embodiment of one of the most enduring monarchies in Europe – was executed. The Queen of France, Marie-Antoinette, was guillotined in October of the same year. Symbolising the French Revolution's desire to erase the past, a new calendar beginning with Year One – the creation of the Republic – was established in 1793. By the end of 1793, France was at war with England and most of Europe, Robespierre was in charge of the revolutionary government, and the 'Reign of Terror' was firmly under way. In a savage period of French politics, estimates suggest that at least 16,000 people perished between 1793 and 1794. In 1790, writers such as Richard Price and Thomas Paine had heralded the Revolution as a triumphant new dawn; by 1795, it had descended into chaos, violence and bloodshed. During this period, the Gothic continued to exhibit a heightened sense of historical consciousness and respond to the events occurring in France. As this chapter explains, the worsening situation in France and the subsequent debates and sense of alarm it triggered in England had significant implications for Gothic representations of the past. As one would expect, Gothic responses to such events were very diverse. However, despite its variety, the demand for Gothic novels surged as the French Revolution became more violent. The enormous success of Ann Radcliffe's next novel played a major role in the genre's increasing popularity.

Published three years after *The Romance of the Forest*, Radcliffe's *The Mysteries of Udolpho* (1794) became the most popular novel of her time and secured her lasting fame. Similarly to her previous work, the past constructed in Radcliffe's next Female Gothic novel is intertwined with its own historical context. As Ronald Paulson argues, even though the Gothic genre originates from 1764, by 'the time *The Mysteries of Udolpho* appeared (1794), the castle, prison, tyrant, and sensitive young girl could no longer be presented naively; they had all been familiarised and sophisticated by events in France' (1983, 221). Reminiscent of Marie Antoinette's flight from persecution, Emily (the novel's heroine) is menaced by the malevolent Montoni (the novel's villain) and compelled to escape from his tyrannical rule. Preserving the spirit of the Female Gothic, Radcliffe constructs a fictional past to draw attention to the plight of women in the eighteenth century: a subject that was brought into focus in England by the French Revolution. In a similar vein to her previous novels, *The Mysteries of Udolpho* is set on 'the Gothic cusp': a seventeenth-century transitional historical setting that draws inevitable parallels with the French Revolution by featuring the overlap of old and new social orders. Furthermore, the description of the castle of Udolpho bears resemblances to the Bastille. Emily describes the 'terrific images' awakened in her mind at the sight of its 'gothic greatness' and 'mouldering walls'. Shortly after this, she likens it to a 'prison' (Radcliffe 2001, 216–17). Indeed, for some readers, Radcliffe's Female Gothic novel would have been influenced by recent events in France.

The phenomenal success of *The Mysteries of Udolpho* triggered a wave of imitations. The literary marketplace became flooded with Gothic tales and stories.[1] Furthermore, Radcliffe's novel gave rise to one of the most notorious works of Gothic fiction: Matthew Lewis's *The Monk* (1796).[2] As the French Revolution became increasingly gruesome, there was a notion during the 1790s that Gothic writers tried to compete with the horror conjured by such events. For example, the Marquis de Sade suggests that Gothic writers of the day had to 'call upon the aid of hell itself' (1989, 109) in order to rival the terror and horror of such macabre events, while Horace Walpole argues that, with France choosing to 'avow atheism, profess assassination, and practise massacres on massacres for four years', it 'remained for the Enlightened eighteenth century to baffle language and invent horrors that can be found in no vocabulary' (1937–83, 34: 177). This is certainly the case with Lewis's novel. Influenced by the German school of horror and the *Schauerroman*, Lewis was a resident in Paris in 1791 and witnessed numerous revolutionary events.[3] *The Monk* may be set in a vague historical period and located in Roman Catholic Spain, but it bears numerous parallels to the social and political turmoil that engulfed France and Europe in the 1790s. The destruction of the tyrannical Prioress of St Clare and her convent by a mob has been frequently discussed as a clear parallel to the events of the French Revolution. Lewis tells us that the 'rioters heeded nothing but the gratification of their barbarous vengeance'. The mob murders the prioress and then 'exercised their impotent rage upon her lifeless body': they 'beat it, trod upon it, and ill-used it, till it became no more than a mass of flesh, unsightly, shapeless, and disgusting', writes Lewis. The rioters later attack the convent of St Clare and resolve to 'sacrifice all the nuns of that order to their rage, and not leave one stone of the building upon another' (Lewis 1998, 306–7). This scene has been compared to the storming of the Bastille and described as 'an echo of the French September Massacres' of 1792 (Parreaux 1960, 132). Allied to a host of other obscene and horrific images presented in *The Monk*, such scenes raised fears of foreign disorder and anarchy to anxious English readers, while at the same time being titillating and safely distanced.

While Radcliffe's and Lewis's Gothic pasts were influenced (either deliberately or by association) by the French Revolution, a very different Gothic response to such events was occurring. The

Gothic continued to be a diverse and conflicted genre in the 1790s. In Chapter 2, I discussed Watt's notion that Clara Reeve's *The Old English Baron* could be read as a prototype of the Loyalist Gothic. This strain of Gothic fiction, which favours English medieval settings and which interprets the 'Gothic' as indicative of anything time-honoured and to be treasured rather than barbaric and defunct, became very popular during the French Revolution, particularly once France had declared war on England. Notable examples of such works include Richard Warner's *Netley Abbey: A Gothic Story* (1795), John Bird's *The Castle of Haradyne, A Romance* (1795), T. J. Horsley Curties's *Ethelwina, or the House of Fitz-Auburne. A Romance of Former Times* (1799), and two works penned by anonymous authors: *Mort Castle* (1798) and 'Kilverstone Castle, or the Heir Restored, A Gothic Story' (1799). Even though it is not a Gothic novel, Watt also discusses Reeve's *Memoirs of Sir Roger de Clarendon* in the context of the Loyalist Gothic and the French Revolution.[4] As Watt notes, during the conflict with France, such tales refashioned the self-image of England and 'led to the "historical" category of Gothic being purged of its associations with either democracy or frivolity and defined increasingly in terms of a proud military heritage' (1999, 44). Castles are central to many of these works and, rather than conjuring up terrific images of the Bastille, are 'viewed as symbols of the immemorial, if embattled, authority of Fortress Britain' (55). Such works are particularly interesting when considered alongside Burke's conservative historical attitudes in the *Reflections* (especially in terms of his association of castles with ancient constitutions) and the increasingly nationalistic nature of historical writing in this period.[5] Indeed, castles in these narratives serve to remind the English of what holds them together historically and, in general, the Loyalist Gothic calls for unity at a time of national crisis.

Gothic pasts not only continued to be shaped by the menacing events taking place across the Channel; they became increasingly influenced by the situation at home. In order to prevent a similar revolution taking place in England, the Prime Minister, William Pitt the Younger, swiftly implemented a number of repressive and abrasive policies to silence reformers and those whose political agitation was, in his view, counter to the national interest. Habeas corpus was suspended on 12 May 1794. This was the same day that saw the arrest of Thomas Hardy, a leading radical of the London Corresponding Society (LCS): an organisation perceived by government to be encouraging political 'revolution' along French lines. Ten other London radicals were arrested shortly after this and, in September, the notorious Treason Trials got under way. The Treasonable Practices Act and Seditious Meetings Act of 1795 (often referred to as the 'Two Acts') broadened definitions of treason and aimed to limit anti-government activities by prohibiting political meetings of more than fifty people taking place. Pitt established spy networks, 'believing, or professing to believe, that the radical societies threatened a "whole system of insurrection … laid in the modern doctrine of the rights of man"' (Porter 2000, 450). Fearing invasion and the spread of dangerous foreign radicalism, England was gripped by fear and paranoia. This had significant implications for the historical settings of Gothic narratives.

In terms of the historical locations of Gothic novels discussed in this book, the Gothic can be seen to move forward in time periods: the events described in *Otranto* took place somewhere between the eleventh and thirteenth centuries, Reeve chose the fifteenth century for *The Old English Baron*, *The Recess* is set in the sixteenth century, while Radcliffe elected for a seventeenth century past in *The Romance of the Forest*. Furthermore, in *The Italian* (1797) – the novel that followed *The Mysteries of Udolpho* – Radcliffe deviates from her previous works by electing not to set the action on the Gothic cusp; instead, she chooses to set her novel in the very recent past, the late 1750s. Even though it is still a Female Gothic novel and features the plight of its heroine, Ellena, *The Italian* represents a contrast to her previous works. As Robert Miles points out, this is a Gothic novel of spies, informers, false witnesses, and forged plots in a way 'quite unlike any of Radcliffe's previous romances' (2004, xxiii). Discussions of *The Italian* frequently argue that Radcliffe was (at least in part) reacting to Lewis's *The Monk*: a novel that also features spying, subplots and conspiracies. Radcliffe's and Lewis's novels both feature the Inquisition, the mysterious workings of which, among other things, preyed on its readers' fears by offering parallels to the spy networks that Pitt set up to monitor the spread of radicalism. *The Italian* and *The Monk* are preoccupied with the theme of surveillance and, in this sense, respond to the politics and mood of the moment. Geographical remoteness is still an important facet of these novels, but there is less emphasis on historical displacement. Indeed, the crisis in England triggered by the French Revolution accelerated the Gothic's movement through historical time.

The Gothic 1790s: Godwin, Wollstonecraft and the prisonhouse of history

Godwin and Wollstonecraft were revolutionary figures living in a revolutionary time. They were well established in the radical circles of the 1790s and supported the French Revolution (until it turned violent).[6] Both writers were dissenters and engaged in reform efforts at home in England. As well as this shared radicalism, Godwin and Wollstonecraft became lovers in 1796 and married on 29 March 1797. Before their relationship began, they were both accomplished political writers and contributed to debates about the French Revolution in the 1790s. In 1792, Wollstonecraft followed up *A Vindication of the Rights of Men* (1790) with *A Vindication of the Rights of Woman*. In this latter political treatise, Wollstonecraft argued that the revolutionary principles of liberty and equality were applicable to women as much as to men, and outlined a vision of a future egalitarian society. The *Rights of Woman* tackled some of the most controversial issues of the day and asked profound questions about gender, sex, marriage, reason, and sensibility. Wollstonecraft's political treatise was generally well received when it was published but, after the declaration of war between France and England, it became associated with dangerous foreign radicalism and levelling principles.[7] Wollstonecraft herself was increasingly vilified, with Horace Walpole famously calling her a 'hyena in petticoats' (1937–83, 31: 397). Godwin also had a penchant for inspiring controversy.[8] In 1793, shortly after the execution of Louis XVI and the outbreak of war between England and France, he published *An Enquiry Concerning Political Justice*, which was a rebuttal of Burke's *Reflections*. In this influential work of political philosophy, he targets the corruption of government, arguing that it threatens individuality and uses the law as a tool of oppression. He believes that rational creatures can live in harmony without laws and institutions and envisions a better society that is founded on the basis of the moral perfectibility of humankind. *Political Justice* brought Godwin immediate renown and, due to his philosophical anarchism and atheism, no small degree of notoriety.[9] As the British government became increasingly intransigent towards reformers in the

1790s, Godwin and Wollstonecraft became interested in fiction as a way of disseminating (and further exploring) their political ideas.

They were particularly attracted to the Gothic novel, its popularity across the social scale and its conventions. Godwin had read a number of Radcliffe's novels and may have been personally acquainted with her.[10] He had also met Sophia Lee and her sister, Harriet.[11] Godwin published *Things as they Are; or, the Adventures of Caleb Williams* in 1794 as a way of communicating his ideas in *Political Justice* to 'persons whom books of philosophy and science are never likely to reach' (*CW* 312). Wollstonecraft followed a similar path and, like her husband, she had a good knowledge of the Gothic genre. In her capacity as a reviewer for Joseph Johnson's progressive journal, the *Analytical Review* (launched in 1788), she reviewed a number of Gothic works, including Radcliffe's *The Italian*, and Loyalist Gothic texts such as James White's *Earl of Strongbow* (1789).[12] Wollstonecraft also published a translation of Christian Gotthilf Salzmann's *Elements of Morality for the Use of Children* (1790), which, as Matthew O. Grenby has recently pointed out (2014, 248), incorporates Gothic elements. Wollstonecraft started working on *The Wrongs of Woman: or, Maria* in 1796 as a means of dramatising her arguments about gender inequality in the *Rights of Woman*. Because of Gothic literature's popularity among young eighteenth-century women, Wollstonecraft deliberately invokes some of its conventions in her novel in order to connect with a wider female readership. However, *Maria* was only two-thirds complete when she died after giving birth to her second daughter, named Mary Wollstonecraft Godwin (later Shelley), on 30 August 1797. In 1798, Godwin published the corrected and uncorrected portions of the manuscript of the novel – along with Wollstonecraft's conflicting outlines and notes from the novel's conclusion – in his first two volumes of her posthumous works. As the rest of this chapter will show, *Caleb Williams* and *Maria* are in dialogue with each other and both novels show close affinities in terms of politics and narrative style. They also explore similar themes, such as the horrors of the present, the tyranny of the past, the ideological power of history, female persecution, and the horrors of injustice. Both novels are also notorious for defying genre categorisations.[13] However, despite such debates, what remains clear is that Godwin and Wollstonecraft were heavily influenced by the eighteenth-century Gothic novel and that they invoke the genre explicitly in their fictions. Both writers made significant contributions to the development of the Gothic novel, particularly in terms of opening up new territories, such as the present, for tales of terror.

With the implementation of draconian legislation designed to restrict the spread of radicalism, 1790s England had become a frightening place. Godwin captures the national mood when he writes that 'Terror was the order of the day' (*CW* 311). In *Caleb Williams*, he abandons the Gothic practice of presenting a veiled critique of contemporary events and chooses to focus on the very real socio-political terrors associated with late eighteenth-century England. For Godwin, tyranny is not supernatural, but material and political. As the title of his novel, *Things as They Are*, suggests, he makes the present a site of terror and takes aim at 'the modes of domestic and unrecorded despotism by which man becomes the destroyer of man' (*CW* 312). Featuring the relentless pursuit and surveillance of Caleb Williams by Ferdinando Falkland and his malevolent agent, Jones, Godwin's novel reflects the anxiety and paranoia of late eighteenth-century England.[14] For example, Caleb feels that his every move is watched by Falkland and comes to regard 'the whole human species as so many hangmen and torturers ... confederated to tear me to pieces' (*CW* 177). As numerous commentators have pointed out, *Caleb Williams* bears immediate and obvious resemblances to Pitt's spy networks and the 'surveillance society' of the 1790s.[15] Godwin domesticates the Gothic by revealing that real everyday horrors exist on his readers' doorsteps. As Godwin's epigraph to this chapter demonstrates, tyranny is not exclusive to revolutionary France; it is firmly embedded at home in barbaric social institutions, such as the English criminal justice system. The prison that features in *Caleb Williams* is likened not only to the Bastille, but also to the Inquisition. Caleb makes this analogy explicit when, after enduring prolonged 'agony and despair' (*CW* 175), he says, 'I envied the victim of the inquisition in the midst of his torture' (*CW* 141). When his friend, Thomas, visits him, he cannot comprehend that Caleb is treated so badly in a 'Christian country' and believes that his 'usage is too bad for a dog' (*CW* 195). Caleb's experience in prison exposes the 'engines' of 'tyranny' (*CW* 175) that lie beneath the façade of seemingly civilised and liberal eighteenth-century England. Godwin manipulates Gothic conventions, and the genre's emphasis on suffering and persecution, to attack English national identity and severely undermine any sense of cultural supremacy and complacency felt by eighteenth-century English men and women.

Wollstonecraft was studying *Caleb Williams* when she was writing *Maria* (Kelly 1996, 39) and, in a similar vein to her husband, she brings Gothic conventions to bear on the eighteenth century and relocates terrors from revolutionary France to England. She reconfigures the Female Gothic in *Maria* by dispensing with its reliance on both metaphor and the past; she chooses, instead, to focus on the horrors that many women face every day in contemporary society and launches an assault on society's patriarchal institutions. Maria, the protagonist of Wollstonecraft's novel, has her four-month old child taken away from her by her tyrannical husband, George Venables, who condemns her to a mental asylum. Wollstonecraft deliberately invokes the Gothic genre when she describes this institution as a 'mouldering' and 'gloomy pile' that is 'half in ruins' (*M* 118). In *Maria*, the mental asylum is a reincarnation of the Gothic castle and symbolises women's suffering, persecution and entrapment in the present. Wollstonecraft's reconfiguration of the Gothic castle also involves a reassessment of the spectacle of the ruin. For her, the real ruins associated with Gothic architecture are not the 'fallen column, the mouldering arch' or 'the crumbling marble', but the 'terrific ruins' of the 'human soul' (*M* 16). Aesthetic contemplations of Gothic ruins mask the tyranny of barbaric social institutions that have oppressed (and, in many cases, destroyed) vulnerable and disenfranchised women throughout history. The horrors that Maria experiences in the asylum are 'far more terrific than all that dreaming superstition ever drew' (*M* 25): she finds herself in 'a tomb of living death' where '[h]orror still reigned in the darkened cells, suspicion lurked in the passage, and whispered along the walls' (*M* 35). As Wollstonecraft points out, Gothic novels have frequently described '[a]bodes of horror' and 'castles, filled with spectres and chimeras'. However, these are merely 'formed on such stuff as dreams are made of' when compared to the 'mansion of despair' that Maria – and, by implication, many eighteenth-century women – find themselves in (*M* 7). Wollstonecraft does not locate Gothic terrors in the imagination, European or historical locations; she shows that Gothic horrors are very much 'social realities for women' (Mellor 2007, 242). Employing Gothic language and themes, she launches a savage attack on the 'partial laws and customs of society' that ensure the 'misery and oppression' of women (*M* 5) and render the world a 'vast prison' for them (*M* 11).

Godwin and Wollstonecraft are both concerned with how the present is enslaved by the feudal past and believe that contemporary society – and everyone living in it – is trapped in the prisonhouse of history. In *Political Justice*, Godwin suggests that the present is yet to emerge from the tyranny of the past and launches a bitter critique of the current social order, which, he argues, is founded on 'the records and charters of a barbarous age' (1985, 167).[16] Godwin shatters the (Burkean) notion that the present social order represents the pinnacle of progress, human development and justice. He is particularly critical of the tendency of the law and contemporary society to 'look back to the folly of their ancestors, rather than forward' (167). For Godwin, the law embodies many of the worst aspects of history, and, while it is enshrined in contemporary society as 'the wisdom of our ancestors' (690), it is, in 'reality', a 'cloak for oppression' (693). He suggests that Pitt's recent authoritarian policies have made already antiquated and tyrannical social institutions such as the law even more oppressive. As a result of this, the past, through its legal precepts, has effectively increased its stranglehold over the present. Godwin dramatises these ideas in *Caleb Williams*, where he attacks the antiquity of the law and the way that it is manipulated by the wealthy to oppress the poor and disenfranchised. When Caleb is (wrongfully) accused of stealing from his master, he is denied a fair trial. He is instructed to leave out of his defence 'whatever tells to the disadvantage of Mr Falkland' and told that 'begging pardon' of his master is his best course of action (*CW* 167). Caleb reacts to this advice with 'extreme shock' (*CW* 167) and opts, instead, to defend his innocence and expose his master's villainy. However, Falkland has incriminating evidence planted on his employee and, when this is presented to the assembled jury, he is charged with theft (*CW* 162). Caleb is denied the opportunity to contest the charge, or to explain how this evidence came to be found in his possession. The jury rejects his notion that the items were placed in his belongings by 'Mr Falkland's contrivance' (*CW* 165) and he is consequently condemned as a 'serpent' and a 'monster of ingratitude', who 'first robs his benefactor, and then reviles him' (*CW* 168). For the first time in his life, Caleb is exposed to the old, arbitrary and, ultimately, 'gore-dripping fangs of the law' (*CW* 262). He is branded as a 'felon' and 'monster of depravity' largely because he is a 'poor country lad' and 'Mr Falkland is a man of rank and fortune' (*CW* 165). Foiled by Falkland's villainy and denied a fair trial, Caleb comes to learn that the 'law was better adapted for a weapon of tyranny in the hands of the rich, than for a shield to protect the humbler part of the community against their usurpations' (*CW* 42).

Whereas Godwin concentrates on the class bias of the law in *Caleb Williams*, Wollstonecraft focuses on the legal structures of patriarchy in *Maria*.[17] For her, society is in the 'deadly grasp' of the feudal past and this has devastating consequences for women's lives (Wollstonecraft 1985, 99). In the *Rights of Woman*, Wollstonecraft deplores the 'mysterious sanctity' that surrounds 'arbitrary' principles (267) and is critical of 'moss-covered opinions' which 'assume the disproportioned form of prejudices' (216). Her views here are applicable to the laws that govern England; some of them 'are indolently adopted only because age has given them a venerable aspect, though the reason on which they were built ceases to be a reason, or cannot be traced' (216). Wollstonecraft is particularly critical of the 'laws respecting women' and how marital laws 'make an absurd unit of man and his wife', reducing the latter to 'a mere cypher' (257). These ideas receive expression in *Maria*. Soon after marrying Venables, Maria realises, to her horror, that she is 'united to a heartless, unprincipled wretch' (*M* 73): he gambles, womanises, drinks, squanders her fortune, and even attempts to sell her into prostitution. When Maria explains the terrible deeds that her husband has committed to a judge, he informs her that it is 'her duty to love and obey the man chosen by her parents and relations, who were qualified by their experience to judge better for her, than she could for herself' (*M* 133). Using the 'woman-centrism' of the Female Gothic, Wollstonecraft shows how the antiquated and arbitrary laws of England afford women 'no protection or redress' from their male 'oppressor[s]' (*M* 92). Bound by the laws of marriage, Maria is compelled to stand by her husband and endure his cruelty. Wollstonecraft uses a particularly Gothic analogy to describe the plight of women in Maria's situation. She points out that, historically, 'despots' have been stigmatised for commanding 'dead bodies' to be 'chained' to 'even the most atrocious criminals' (*M* 98). However, she suggests that marital laws are 'much more inhuman' than even this grim custom, as they 'forge adamantine fetters to bind minds together, that never can mingle in social communion!'

(*M* 98). Maria comes to the shocking realisation that a wife is 'as much a man's property as his horse, or his ass, she has nothing she can call her own' (*M* 91). The feudal and patriarchal laws that govern marriage in the eighteenth century make women frighteningly vulnerable to the dictates of men and essentially render them the 'property of their husbands' (*M* 78). *Maria* presents a horrifying vision of eighteenth-century society, where marriage is often a form of legalised prostitution and men have full control over the lives of their wives. While Godwin shows how the law is employed so that 'man becomes the destroyer of man' (*CW* 312), Wollstonecraft concentrates on marital law and how it 'enable[s] men to tyrannize over women' (*M* 97).

The ideological legacy of the past: Godwin and ventriloquism

In contrast to previous Gothic novelists, Godwin and Wollstonecraft are not only concerned with the antiquity of the law and the survival of barbaric customs in the present, but also with how the thoughts of individuals in the present are shaped by the past. As I will discuss in this section, both writers have a keen interest in developmental psychology and how cultural influences shape individuals. They draw attention to how exposure to dominant (and long-standing) social ideas and conventions from a young age often has a determinate effect on individuals in later life, influencing both their conscious ideals and unconscious character traits. *Caleb Williams* and *Maria* explore the disturbing ideological power of the past and the pernicious and insidious effect that it has on individuals living in the present. As Handwerk and Markley astutely point out, Godwin's and Wollstonecraft's 'real innovation in regard to Gothic is to make explicit the ideological implications lying beneath the surface of its literary forms' (2000, 33). Both writers manipulate the Gothic's preoccupation with the past, brooding atmospheres and coercive environments in order to reveal the ideological aspects of history and to show how the Gothic (feudal and backward) past endures in the minds of those living in contemporary society. As this chapter has demonstrated so far, the notion of 'things as they are' – the material conditions of the present – is of central importance to *Caleb Williams* and *Maria*. However, at this juncture, it is requisite to draw attention to the politically charged nature of this phrase.[18] Eric Lindstrom contends that 'things as they are' needs to be understood as 'a potentially dynamic locus of attention' (2010, 481), rather than as shorthand for the status quo. 'Things' dwell in a 'constant, contested kind of present' and definitions of the expression, 'things as they are', must 'always shake free of this attempt to fix it, to take it for granted as the inertia of old times' (482). Godwin and Wollstonecraft are very interested in this notion of a 'contested present' and how individuals are coerced into thinking that the conditions of the existing, hierarchical social order are natural, or just 'the way things are'. Both writers expose the ways in which consciousness is socially constructed and how anachronistic social customs, such as chivalry and sensibility, are internalised by men and women living in the present.

In *Political Justice*, Godwin argues that all forms of government are 'an evil, an usurpation upon the private judgement and individual conscience of mankind' (1985, 408). He contends that 'Man is in reality a passive, and not an active being' (354) and draws attention to how early influences shape character and consciousness. In Godwin's view, the 'actions and dispositions of mankind are the offspring of circumstances and events, and not of any original determination that they bring into the world' (97). Government is the 'perpetual enemy of change'; it teaches individuals to seek 'the public welfare, not in alteration and improvement, but in a timid reverence for the decisions of our ancestors, as if it were the nature of the human mind always to degenerate, and never to advance' (252). Due to the dissemination and internalisation of ideology, men and women are 'perpetually under the influence of sinister and unacknowledged motives' (313). They are 'enslaved by shame, superstition or deceit' and are 'perpetually exposed to an internal war of opinions' (2013, 26). This is particularly the case in relation to the class structure of society and relationships with social superiors. Ordinary individuals are 'kept in perpetual vibration'; sometimes they 'suppose their governors to be the messengers and favourites of heaven, a supernatural order of beings' and, at other times, they 'suspect them to be a combination of usurpers to rob and oppress them' (1985, 503–4). For Godwin, government (and the class structure of society) conditions the way that people think and thus destroys personal identity. A person growing up in eighteenth-century society 'cannot become a real individual', as he or she will be 'fettered by the prejudices, the humours, the weakness and the vice of those with whom they act' (558). Society inhibits the enquiring mind and, instead, encourages people to 'adhere to certain fixed principles' (615). When this happens, argues Godwin, it is the 'instant of intellectual decease' and the moment when a person becomes a 'ghost' rather than an autonomous individual (615). 'To dragoon men into the adoption of what we think right', argues Godwin, 'is an intolerable tyranny' (262).

Godwin is very concerned about the persistence of feudal ideology in the present and how it has the power to shape private beliefs, values and judgements. He is particularly anxious about the ideology of chivalry. For Godwin, the 'feudal system', which he describes as 'a ferocious monster, devouring, wherever it came, all that the friend of humanity regards with attachment and love' (476), is 'the direct parent of the ideas of chivalry' (1804, 47). He challenges Burke's conception of chivalry as a benevolent social custom in the *Reflections* by representing it as a force of division and social alienation: it denies personal merit and enables members of the aristocracy (who inherited their privileged social status) to hold their dependents 'in the most barbarous slavery' (2013, 327). For Godwin, ' "the age of chivalry is" not "gone"!', as the 'feudal spirit still survives that reduced the great mass of mankind to the rank of slaves and cattle for the service of a few' (1985, 726). Godwin dramatises these ideas in *Caleb Williams*, where he is particularly interested in how early social influences shape consciousness.

Caleb is an impressionable young man when he is first exposed to Falkland's authority and social views. He soon learns that his master has 'imbibed the love of chivalry' (*CW* 9) and that he has made 'reputation' the 'idol, the jewel' (*CW* 99) of his life. After 'about three months' in the service of Falkland, Caleb becomes convinced that his master is hiding a terrible secret. When he hears a 'deep groan expressive of intolerable anguish' (*CW* 6) coming from the library, he enters to discover his master hastily locking the lid of a chest. Falkland is furious with him: 'Villain, cried he, what has brought you here? … Wretch, interrupted Mr Falkland with uncontrollable impatience, you want to ruin me' (*CW* 7). Caleb vividly recalls how Falkland's voice 'seemed supernaturally tremendous' and how the 'sound of it thrilled' his 'very vitals' (*CW* 7). Falkland is the major figure of authority in Caleb's life and has a significant impact on his early development. He becomes increasingly incensed by Caleb's insinuations and continual questions regarding his involvement in the murder of Barnabas Tyrrel (a rival squire), and the deaths of Benjamin Hawkins and his son, Leonard (two local tenant farmers). He is very quick to remind his servant of his lowly social status and that he should show his master more respect: 'Who gave you a right to be my confident? Base, artful wretch that you are! learn to be more respectful! Are my passions to be wound and unwound by an insolent domestic? (*CW* 114). After Falkland confesses to be 'the murderer of Tyrrel' and the 'assassin of the Hawkinses' (*CW* 131), Caleb attempts to quit his master's service, but Falkland discovers his employee's intentions and reacts with 'fury' (*CW* 150). He calls Caleb a 'miserable wretch', declares that he has 'sworn to preserve' his 'reputation at whatever expense' (*CW* 159) and warns him that there is no escape from his power: 'You might as well think of escaping from the reach of the omnipresent God, as from mine!' (*CW* 140). From a young age, Caleb is subjected to the full force of Falkland's feudal and aristocratic values. As numerous commentators have pointed out, Godwin uses Falkland's obsession with chivalry to challenge Burke's *Reflections*.[19] In *Caleb Williams*, chivalry is founded on brute force; it is manipulated by members of the aristocracy to preserve their status at the top of the social class hierarchy and to dominate over others. Falkland has been deeply influenced by the feudal ideology of chivalry and, in turn, he imposes his views on his young servant, Caleb. As Maggie Kilgour notes, the social values that Caleb's master promotes are reminiscent of 'the old feudal system', in which lines of authority were clearly demarcated, the social hierarchy was maintained and 'loyalty and love' bound servants to their superiors (1995, 62). Young Caleb is governed by Falkland and, in accordance with his master's feudal values, is conditioned to revere his social superior. When he fails to respect his master, he is exposed to a tirade of verbal abuse from Falkland, whose favourite derogatory term to describe Caleb is 'wretch'. Indeed, Falkland's language is notable for its ferocity and portentousness. As Pamela Clemit notes, his speech is reminiscent of 'a Burkean rhetoric of Old Testament authority' and 'charged with the ideological notions that man is inherently sinful and in need of legislative restraints' (1993, 60). Moreover, it is important to note that Falkland employs feudal language; his use of pejorative and degrading words (such as 'villain' and 'wretch') lowers Caleb's social position, thus protecting his own status and maintaining the class hierarchy. Fictionalising his ideas from *Political Justice*, Godwin explores the effects that Caleb's early social environment has on his psyche.

In *Caleb Williams*, Godwin examines how anachronistic social customs are perpetuated in the present through the dissemination and internalisation of feudal ideology. A useful way of approaching ideological concerns in both *Caleb Williams* and *Maria* is through two related concepts: ventriloquism and possession. It is necessary to pause, briefly, to discuss these concepts before analysing Godwin's novel. Ventriloquism is defined as the 'art or practice of speaking or producing sounds in such a manner that the voice appears to proceed from some person or object other than the speaker' (*Oxford English Dictionary*). More specifically, it 'relates to the voice, the origin and destination of that voice as well as its appearance in surprising places or through other mouths, as is the case with the ventriloquist's dummy' (Cooke 2008, 86). It is of ancient origin (traces of it are found in Egyptian and Hebrew archaeology) and, in contrast to impersonation, it can occur when we least expect it (and even without our awareness). Ventriloquism is one of the darker arts and is linked to the 'throwing' of the voice, puppets, doubling, transgression, the uncanny, and to demonic possession. The notion of possession is inherently Gothic and, etymologically, it means the domination or control of a person by a demon or spirit (and to a change in mental disposition or a substitution of personality). It also refers to the domination of a person by an idea, thought or feeling. As I will now demonstrate, in *Caleb Williams* and *Maria*, Godwin and Wollstonecraft exploit these related (Gothic) notions of ventriloquism and possession in order to explore the workings of ideology in the present, and how it enslaves individuals by conditioning how they think and 'naturalising' the current oppressive social order (which is really a manifestation of the unenlightened past). These concepts are particularly useful for examining the ideological influences that act on Caleb's mind.

Godwin employs first-person narration in *Caleb Williams* in order to give the reader an insight into Caleb's mind and thought processes. At times, Caleb seems to be largely unaffected by Falkland and the feudal principles that he has been exposed to from a young age. He often comes across as an independent and spirited young man and, despite his persecution, he frequently undermines his master's attempts to oppress him and strikes a defiant note: 'What concern have I with danger and alarm! I feel that I am free; I feel that I will continue so' (*CW* 152). Caleb also diminishes the extent of Falkland's influence when he questions whether there is in fact any 'power' that is 'able to hold in chains a mind ardent and determined?' (*CW* 152). This leads him on to a broader contemplation of the nature of society. For example, he reflects on how 'every man is fated to be more or less the tyrant or the slave' and is 'astonished' that his 'species' does not 'rise up as one man, and shake off chains so ignominious and misery so insupportable' (*CW* 152). Caleb resolves to hold himself 'disengaged from the odious scene, and never fill the part either of the oppressor or the sufferer' (*CW* 152). In these instances he appears a resolute young man and also an outspoken social critic. For example, he is angry with his master, deplores the upper-class bias of the legal system and is outraged that he is denied the opportunity to defend his innocence: 'Six thousand a year shall protect a man from accusation; and the validity of an impeachment shall be superseded, because the author of it is a servant!' (*CW* 265). Indeed, Caleb's social and political views can be classed as radical, particularly when considered in the wider context of the French Revolution and Pitt's attempts to stop the spread of levelling principles.

However, Caleb is characterised by contradiction. He may question the class system and have radical impulses, but he is also revealed to be quite a conservative figure. Despite all of the many injustices that Falkland has inflicted on him, Caleb continues 'to pity, rather than hate' his 'persecutor' (*CW* 218) and hold him in 'the most ardent admiration' (*CW* 298). Caleb admits that he has 'long cherished a reverence for him, which not even animosity and persecution on his part could readily destroy' (*CW* 263). Falkland's early influence over Caleb is evident here. However, there is a moment when, struggling under his master's tyranny, Caleb temporarily loses 'all regard' for his master's 'intellectual greatness' (*CW* 263). He manages to convince a magistrate to summon Falkland to court so that he can make his accusations public and expose Falkland's guilt. After years of subterfuge and lies, Falkland finally confesses, in public, that he is responsible for the deaths of Tyrrel and the Hawkinses. Falkland dies shortly after this and, as a result, Caleb's persecution is over. The reader expects that this will be a source of relief (or even joy) for Caleb. However, strangely, Caleb is overcome by guilt and feels that he has betrayed his master:

> I have been his murderer ... It would have been merciful in compari-
> son, if I had planted a dagger in his heart. He would have thanked me
> for my kindness. But, atrocious, execrable wretch that I have been!
> I wantonly inflicted on him an anguish a thousand times worse than
> death. Meanwhile I endure the penalty of my crime. His figure is ever
> in imagination before me.
>
> (*CW* 302)

Considering the severity and longevity of Caleb's suffering and his master's cruelty, his reaction to Falkland's demise is extraordinary. He proclaims that Falkland is a man 'worthy of affection and kindness' and views himself as 'the worst of villains' (*CW* 300). Caleb eulogises Falkland: a 'nobler spirit lived not among the sons of men', his 'intellectual powers were truly sublime' and his 'bosom burned with a godlike ambition' (*CW* 303). By bringing Falkland to justice, Caleb sees himself as a 'cool, deliberate, unfeeling murderer' and suggests that '[d]eath would be a kindness' compared to what he currently feels (*CW* 301). In this episode, there is a disparity between the suffering that Caleb has endured and his veneration of Falkland. Caleb's use of language in this scene is particularly reveal-ing, as his speech replicates the feudal language used by his master. For example, he uses the same words – 'wretch' and 'villain' – that Falkland used to remind Caleb of his lowly class position and to assert his own superior social status. Caleb's language is portentous and he speaks with the same inflections, stresses and intonations as his master. Falkland may be dead, but it is as if he is speaking 'through' Caleb here. Indeed, Caleb is ventriloquised by his master's voice and anachronistic social values. Godwin makes Caleb vocal-ise the opinions of his master in order to reveal how vulnerable individuals are to the opinions of those who have power over them (especially when they are exposed to such authority figures from a young age). By employing this ventriloquistic technique, Godwin shows that Caleb's thinking and speech have been infiltrated by the restrictive, feudal ideological conventions of his social environment and the major authority figure in his life, Falkland.

Godwin's fears about ideology, individuality and the persistence of feudal values in *Political Justice* are therefore fully realised in *Caleb Williams*. Caleb's consciousness and private judgement have been usurped by Falkland's thoughts. Using a first-person narra-tor to give the reader an insight into the psyche and the process of ideological indoctrination, Godwin shows how Caleb is perpetually under the influence of 'sinister and unacknowledged motives' (1985, 313). At the end of the novel, he believes that he is the disobedient feudal servant that Falkland always claimed that he was, and he has been coerced into a reverence for his master and social superior (whom he views as a deity).[20] Caleb's more radical views on society and (in)justice have been replaced by Falkland's conservative values, and he is possessed by the feudal notions of chivalry, class hierarchy and loyalty to one's master. He has internalised the feudal values of his master to such an extent that he is unaware that his own thinking in the present ventriloquises a feudal past which upholds class division, injustice and deference to the wealthy.[21] At one point, Caleb comes close to recognising the feudal ideology that possesses him, stating that: 'I have been hurried along I do not know how. I have always tried to stop myself, but the devil that possessed me was too strong for me' (*CW* 116). However, as his reaction to Falkland's death demonstrates, he does not fully understand the feudal ideology that governs him and which stifles his more radical impulses and prevents him from acting independently, because it has destroyed his sense of self and individuality. Caleb says as much in the final paragraph of his account: 'I began these memoirs with the idea of vindicating my own character. I have now no character that I wish to vindicate' (*CW* 303). The illusion of the present as merely 'the way things are', rather than as a manifestation of the feudal past, is maintained through ideological dissemination and the destruction of individuality. This, suggests Godwin, is how the past has become naturalised as the present: the values of the feudal past live on in the speech, behaviour and minds of individuals living in contemporary society, thus diverting the true course of history by inhibiting the enquiring mind and preventing change and progress.

Possession: Wollstonecraft and 'gothic manners'

Where Godwin focuses on how feudal values continue to shape the thoughts of men in the present, Wollstonecraft examines how anachronistic social mores promoted by social institutions influence the thinking and behaviour of eighteenth-century women. In the *Rights of Woman*, Wollstonecraft argues that early social influences and education have a 'determinate effect' on later character and that the associations that are built up in childhood (and adolescence) can 'seldom be disentangled by reason' later in life

(1985, 219–20). Furthermore, it is not only men and women's conscious ideals that are established in early life, but also their unconscious character traits and habits. She is particularly concerned with how women are exposed to the eighteenth-century cult of sensibility from a young age, and the impact that this has on their psychological development and later lives. For Wollstonecraft, sensibility is comparable to gallantry, in the sense that it is a 'vestige of gothic manners' (197) that is perpetuated in the present and ensures that women 'become the prey of their senses … and are blown about by every momentary gust of feeling' (152). As with Lee in *The Recess*, Wollstonecraft is not against sensibility *per se*; she is opposed to excessive sensibility, or, as she calls it in the *Rights of Woman*, 'overstretched sensibility' (152).[22] A young woman growing up in the eighteenth-century patriarchal social order is coerced into becoming 'the slave of her own feelings' and, as a result, is 'easily subjugated by those of others' (202). In Wollstonecraft's view, women are denied the opportunity to develop their own identities. By promoting 'overstretched sensibility' as a social virtue and something to be commended, men ensure that women's thoughts are 'constantly directed to the most insignificant parts of themselves' (131). Exposed to the ideology of 'overstretched sensibility' from such a young age, women are 'made to assume an artificial character' (131) – and are 'thus formed in the mould of folly' (152) – before 'their faculties have acquired any strength' (131). A woman is 'only taught to look for happiness in love' (306) and becomes the victim of 'romantic, wavering feelings' (169). 'Thus degraded', continues Wollstonecraft, a woman's 'reason, her misty reason! is employed rather to burnish than to snap her chains' (202). Society encourages women to indulge their feelings almost entirely at the expense of reason and, thus, they become 'slave[s] of sensibility' (232). Wollstonecraft fictionalises these arguments in *Maria*. She also intensifies Lee's earlier (Gothic) critique of sensibility in *The Recess* by focusing on the destructive consequences of excessive emotions. However, Wollstonecraft concentrates exclusively on women in the present and is more interested in how the Gothic (anachronistic) ideology of excessive sensibility survives in the minds of eighteenth-century women. The interlinked notions of ventriloquism and possession remain important here. In *Maria*, Wollstonecraft employs free indirect discourse in order to give the reader not only an insight into what Maria is thinking, but how she thinks.

We learn that Maria has a 'romantic mind' (*M* 83) and that she is vulnerable to male attention and the strength of her own passions. It is this 'overstretched sensibility' that leads to her disastrous marriage to Venables. When she first met him, Maria enjoyed the 'particular attention' that he paid her and found his 'attainments and manners superior to those of the young men of the village' (*M* 63). He appeals to the 'romantic turn' of her 'thoughts' and she falls in love with him when he contributes a guinea to Maria's charitable work on behalf of a lady: 'In short, I fancied myself in love – in love with the disinterestedness, fortitude, generosity, dignity, and humanity, with which I had invested the hero I dubbed' (*M* 64). However, she discovers that Venables has 'acquired the habits of libertinism' and that his seemingly superior social manners are really a 'mask' he wears to cover his 'real visage' (*M* 64). He is addicted to gambling and has severe financial problems. As I mentioned earlier in this chapter, Maria's marriage to Venables turns out to be a living hell: he imprisons her in her own home, has an affair with a servant, attempts to sell her into prostitution, and has her incarcerated in a madhouse. Even though Maria ends up imprisoned in an asylum, she rejoices that her 'mind is freed' from the 'fetters' of marriage and she vows not to be 'so eager to open my heart to new affections' (*M* 63). Indeed, Maria seems to have some recognition of her vulnerability to strong feelings, as she tells the reader that it is 'necessary to elucidate some peculiarities in my character, which by the world are indefinitely termed romantic' (*M* 62). In the wake of her terrible experience at the hands of Venables, the reader (as well as Maria herself) is inclined to think that she will not be misled by her feelings again and that she has control over her 'overstretched sensibility'. Her exposure to other tragic stories of women being misled by men would also, the reader is inclined to think, further prevent her from surrendering to the dictates of her heart.

As well as her own experiences of patriarchy, Maria also learns of the plight of other women and, in this sense, the embedded narratives so characteristic of the Gothic novel allow for political case studies. For example, she learns about the history of Jemima, her jail-keeper and caretaker in the asylum. Jemima explains to Maria (and the reader) how she was 'born a slave, and chained by infamy to slavery during the whole of my existence' (*M* 40). Jemima's father 'seduced' her 'mother, a pretty girl, with whom he lived fellow-servant' (*M* 36). Despite becoming 'estranged' from her, he is compelled to marry her to 'screen her from reproach' and, as a result, he 'began to hate' Jemima before she 'was born' (*M* 36). Jemima's mother dies when she is an infant and, from then on, she is subjected to a life of poverty, pain and brutal exploitation by men. For example, she is beaten and raped by her master when she is sixteen, and the resulting pregnancy forces her onto the streets. Unable to support herself, she aborts her child and becomes a prostitute. After the death of the gentleman keeping her, she is left destitute and is forced to be a washerwoman, thief and pauper before she becomes employed in the asylum where Maria is incarcerated. After considering 'Jemima's peculiar fate and her own', Maria's thoughts 'take a wider range' and she is 'led to consider the oppressed state of women, and to lament that she had given birth to a daughter' (*M* 54). As Mary Poovey points out, Jemima's harrowing history of patriarchal oppression has the potential to call into question the 'organizational principles of bourgeois society and the sentimentalism that perpetuates romantic idealism' (1984, 104). Similarly to Caleb, Maria comes across as an outspoken social critic at times. For example, she execrates the 'institutions of society, which thus enable men to tyrannize over women' (*M* 97). However, Maria's reflections on Jemima's history are very brief. In fact, it is notable that she does '*not* develop the revolutionary implications of Jemima's narrative' and, instead, the story is 'quickly, ostentatiously, suppressed' (Poovey 1984, 104). It is almost as if Maria is resistant to Jemima's 'anti-romantic' history (Ty 1993, 38). Indeed, Maria is more preoccupied with the feelings of her 'heart' and with her 'affection' – an 'affection … she wished to inspire' (*M* 54) – for a fellow inmate in the asylum, Henry Darnford.

Maria does not seem to learn either from Jemima's account or her own experiences of exploitation by men. Despite her own self-professed intention not to be so eager to open her heart to 'new affections' (*M* 63), she quickly becomes attracted to Darnford. Maria idealises him before she meets him. She first becomes aware of Darnford when she reads the marginal notes that he has written in a copy of Jean-Jacques Rousseau's *Julie ou la Nouvelle Heloise* (1761), a novel that Wollstonecraft criticises in her *Rights of Woman*. She reads his notes 'over and over again' (*M* 18). She is able to 'think of nothing else' (*M* 23) and 'fancy, treacherous fancy, began to sketch a character, congenial with her own, from these shadowy outlines' (*M* 18). Maria is impatient to meet her 'fellow-sufferer' (*M* 26). We learn that she has been '[a]ccustomed to submit to every impulse of passion' and, thus, 'every desire became a torrent that bore down all opposition' (*M* 26). When she does eventually meet Darnford, he tells her that he used to be a 'thoughtless, extravagant young man' (*M* 27) and that, not 'being adept in gallantry', he could only enjoy the company of women by 'making downright love to them' (*M* 29). Darnford has been something of a libertine in the past, but he claims that he has now matured and outgrown the 'egotism' of his youth (*M* 27). In many ways, Darnford is reminiscent of Maria's first husband, Venables. However, Maria fails to see these disturbing similarities and the possible dangers that may arise from them. As soon as she has heard Darnford's history, we learn that the 'enchanting graces of love sported on her cheeks, and languished in her eyes' (*M* 34). She combines 'all the qualities of a hero's mind' and projects them on to him (*M* 33). Just as Caleb's respect for his master seems quite extraordinary after the suffering that he has endured, the intensity of Maria's passion for Darnford so soon after her disastrous relationship with Venables is surprising. Even though she has 'had to struggle incessantly with the vices of mankind' (*M* 33) and has listened to Jemima's terrible plight, she is still frighteningly vulnerable to the force of her own romantic sensibilities. In her mind, Darnford is a romantic hero who will do anything for her: 'With Darnford she did not taste uninterrupted felicity; there was a volatility in his manner which often distressed her; but love gladdened the scene; besides, he was the most tender, sympathizing creature in the world ... Darnford appeared ever willing to avail himself of her taste and acquirements' (*M* 127). This particular insight into Maria's thoughts is very significant. In this instance, the narrator effectively provides a vocalisation of Maria's internal voice, rather than simply informing the reader of what Maria is thinking.[23] There is a sense that we are hearing Maria's inner voice when she describes Darnford as the 'most tender, sympathizing creature in the world'. This ostensibly external yet internal voice essentially 'ventriloquises' Maria, who is presented in such a way that the reader can hear the voices that are speaking through her. This also occurs at other times in the novel. For example, before she meets Darnford, she overhears him and reflects on his 'accents': 'They were manly, and characteristic of a noble mind; nay, even sweet' (*M* 23). In these instances, the narrator is essentially speaking with Maria's voice and, as a result, the patriarchal ideology that is at work within Maria's thinking is exposed to the reader. Indeed, we can hear the language of sensibility – exemplified by the words 'love', 'tender', 'sympathizing' and 'sweet' – speaking through Maria. This is a deliberate political manoeuvre by Wollstonecraft.[24] She demonstrates how Maria's thinking and language is influenced by patriarchal ideology to the extent that she has become a 'puppet' of sensibility. The reader can detect the Gothic past – in this case, the vestiges of 'overstretched sensibility' – operating in Maria's mind, even though she is often unaware that her thinking ventriloquises a patriarchal social convention that compromises her safety, autonomy and identity.

Maria is possessed by the ideology of sensibility. She may believe that she is in control of her romantic excesses, but her thoughts and actions reveal that they are very much in control of her. Maria has been socialised in a patriarchal society that coerces women into becoming 'slave[s]' of their 'own feelings' and, as a result, she has not only been influenced by 'overstretched sensibility', she has internalised it (Wollstonecraft 1985, 202). '[R]omantic notions' have 'taken root in her mind' (*M* 127). This is why she largely fails to see the relevance of Jemima's narrative and why she dismisses it so quickly. Jemima's story is devoid of romance and heightened emotional experiences and, as a result, Maria's overly romantic mind is effectively resistant to it (and too preoccupied with fantasising about Darnford). Maria has been indoctrinated with the anachronistic ideology of 'overstretched sensibility' and, as a result, she, 'like a large proportion of her sex', is 'only born to feel' (*M* 32). This susceptibility to the power of her passions explains Maria's attraction to (and idealisation of) Darnford. Maria cannot see the disturbing similarities between Venables and Darnford; in her mind, Darnford is a hero of romance who she can depend upon and who will protect her. Even though Maria has only known Darnford a very short time, she becomes very dependent on him. She craves his affection and, at one point, even calls him 'by the sacred name of "husband"' (*M* 124). Although the novel is unfinished, there is evidence that Maria's perception is faulty and that Darnford is no saviour. In one of the proposed endings to the novel, Wollstonecraft suggests that he will betray Maria. Her plan reads, 'Divorced by her husband – Her lover [Darnford] unfaithful – Pregnancy – Miscarriage – Suicide'

(*M* 136). Indeed, Maria is an embodiment of Wollstonecraft's worst fears regarding sensibility; she is romantic instead of realistic and more emotional than rational. Wollstonecraft focuses on Maria's psyche in order to reveal how 'overstretched sensibility' effectively 'shackles the mind, and prepares it for a slavish submission to any power but reason' (1985, 268), and to show the devastating consequences that this has on women's lives. Maria finds herself unable to 'live without love', indulges her feelings at the expense of reason and forms an 'attachment to rakes', which is an 'inevitable consequence' of her limited 'education' (223–4).

Wollstonecraft laments that Maria is 'systemically degraded' by 'overstretched sensibility', a patriarchal custom which men such as Venables and Darnford manipulate, 'insultingly', to support 'their own superiority' (147). The past – in the form of 'overstretched sensibility' – exercises a firm grip on the present through ideological dissemination and Maria's internalisation of age-old patriarchal social customs. Women such as Maria are even more vulnerable to the effects of excessive sensibility because of their lack of opportunities in society. It is 'difficult' for Maria to 'avoid growing romantic' when she has 'no active duties or pursuits' (*M* 20). Maria, like Caleb, does not have any sense of independent identity. Wollstonecraft attacks the fact that many women have no identity of their own; they are products of patriarchal ideology. In *Maria*, Wollstonecraft delivers a damning critique of the ideology of 'overstretched sensibility', which she believes is a 'specious slavery which chains the very soul of woman, keeping her for ever under the bondage of ignorance' (1985, 256). Unaware that she has internalised the patriarchal social custom of 'overstretched sensibility', Maria unknowingly participates in her own oppression. The link between this anachronistic social custom and contemporary society endures – and is so difficult to break – largely because women like Maria are unaware that they are effectively 'possessed' by it.

Godwin, (Gothic) romance and reform

In their political works, Godwin and Wollstonecraft often strike an optimistic note. For example, in the *Rights of Woman*, Wollstonecraft reveals that her ideas concerning reform 'may be termed Utopian dreams' (121). Godwin draws attention to the injustices of the present in *Political Justice*, but he still believes that '[m]an is in a state of perpetual progress' (2013, 104) and that all 'human intellects are at sea upon the great ocean of infinite truth, and their voyage though attended with hourly advantage will never be at an end' (123). The optimism that suffuses Godwin's and Wollstonecraft's political works is notably absent in *Maria* and *Caleb Williams*, which are very pessimistic about the past and present. This is particularly the case in Godwin's novel. By the end of the novel, Caleb has lost his identity and has effectively become a mouthpiece for the feudal ideology of his deceased master. The ending of *Caleb Williams* is exceptionally bleak; the past has effectively claimed Caleb's individuality and there is very little hope that he will escape from the 'deadly grasp' of history, or recover from Falkland's death. However, Godwin makes his novel even bleaker by intertwining Caleb's plight within larger historical cycles of suffering and persecution. As Marilyn Butler points out (1987, 73), *Caleb Williams* has more 'historical range and depth' than it may initially appear. For example, during his early residence with Falkland, Caleb discusses Alexander the Great with his master. Caleb argues that Alexander is a 'Great Cut-throat' who 'spread destruction and ruin' wherever he went (*CW* 107–8).[25] Falkland disagrees with Caleb and defends the conqueror as 'gallant, generous and free' (*CW* 107). For Falkland, Alexander set out to 'civilise mankind' and is a 'model of honour, generosity and disinterestedness' (*CW* 107–8). At different points in the novel, Falkland is not only associated with Alexander, but with the 'bloody rulers' and 'unrelenting tyrant[s]' of the Roman Empire, such as 'Nero' and 'Caligula' (*CW* 291). Furthermore, Tyrrel – Emily's oppressor and Falkland's nemesis – is associated with several disreputable historical figures. For example, his name links him to Sir James Tyrrell (the alleged murderer of the princes in the Tower), Anthony Tyrrell (a traitor and spy during Elizabeth's reign) and Walter Tyrrell, or Tirel (the murderer of William Rufus). Indeed, Caleb is not only trapped in the prisonhouse of history; he is also ensnared in a historical 'pattern of class struggle, oppression, and attempted self-assertion unbroken from Alexander's times to Louis XVI's' (Butler 1987, 73). For Godwin, terrible deeds perpetrated in the present are 'no better than old incidents under new names' (2000, 457). Godwin makes it clear that Caleb's persecution and loss of identity has been repeated throughout history and, unless contemporary society frees itself from the despotism of the past, such tyranny will be inflicted on countless generations to come.

For Godwin, it is not only history, but also the way that history is interpreted and written in the present, that is part of the problem. In his important essay, 'Of History and Romance' (1797), he argues that eighteenth-century historiography is 'dry and repulsive' (2000, 454). He suggests that the 'modern' mode of writing history, which consists of 'logical deduction and calculation of probabilities', answers 'none of the legitimate purposes of history' (462).[26] In Godwin's view, historiography should not 'rest contented with considering society in a mass, but must analyse the materials of which it is composed' (457). General histories poison society by suggesting that the individual cannot make an impact on, or change, history. Godwin counters the grand narratives of modern Enlightenment historiography and proposes a new way of writing history:

> It will be necessary for us to scrutinise the nature of man, before we can pronounce what it is of which social man is capable. Laying aside the generalities of historical abstraction, we must mark the operation of human passions; must observe the empire of motives whether grovelling or elevated; and must note the influence that one human being exercises over another, and the ascendancy of the daring and the wise over the vulgar multitude ... He that would prove the liberal and spirited benefactor of his species, must ... regard the knowledge of the individual, as that which can alone give energy and utility to the records of our social existence.
>
> (457)

In this new model for historiography, Godwin favours individual narratives that are capable of capturing the complex psychological motives that drive the historical agent. It is only by focusing on the individual instead of general abstractions that we will be able to 'understand events as they arise' and 'add, to the knowledge of the past, a sagacity that can penetrate into the depths of futurity' (457). For Godwin, it is romance, rather than history, that will facilitate this focus on the individual and help to deliver society from the past. Indeed, Godwin contends that history is 'little better than romance under a graver name' (463) and that the 'writer of romance' is to be considered 'as the writer of real history' (466). In contrast to the historian, the writer of romance can utilise the 'ardour, the enthusiasm, and the sublime licence of the imagination' to write 'true history', which 'consists in a delineation of consistent, human character' (466). This 'nobler species' of history would exhibit the 'manner in which such a character acts under successive circumstances, in showing how character increases and assimilates new substances to its own, and how it decays, together with the catastrophe into which by its own gravity it naturally declines' (466). This alternative type of history would reveal how individuals are influenced by their social environment, and how consciousness becomes shaped by social institutions and dominant ideologies. By focusing on the individual and revealing how individuals become coerced into certain ways of thinking, Godwin suggests that this reconfigured mode of historical writing will have the power to break oppressive cycles of history and free people from their 'mind-forg'd manacles' (Blake 2005). For Godwin, romance has the potential to inspire reform. 'Make men wise', he argues in *Political Justice*, 'and by that very operation you make them free' (Godwin 1985, 263).

Caleb Williams was published before 'Of History and Romance' but, in several respects, the former work can be considered as a practical example (or even a prototype) of the new 'species' of history outlined in the latter. Gothic romance, with its focus on persecuted protagonists and how they react to oppression, provides Godwin with the ideal means to experiment with this alternative form of historical enquiry. *Caleb Williams* may not initially strike the reader as a form of historiography, but, as Gary Kelly points out, it is ultimately a 'historical' work that is 'set, paradoxically, in the present, but dealing nevertheless with the moral history of man' (1976, 208). Godwin talks about *Caleb Williams* in historical terms. For example, he explains that, when he started writing the novel, he actually began his 'narrative, as is the more usual way, in the third person' (*CW* 350). However, he 'speedily became dissatisfied' with this approach and 'assumed the first person', making Caleb 'his own historian' (*CW* 350). It is important to point out that Caleb writes his narrative in retrospect; he begins with events in the very recent past and moves forward to the immediate present. Godwin's novel is effectively a history of the present or, as David Punter suggests, '*a present account of the past*' (1996, 1: 121). In accordance with his views in 'Of History and Romance', Godwin substitutes history's concern with generalities and mass society for (Gothic) romance's focus on the specific and the individual in *Caleb Williams*. He places an individual at the centre of his narrative and, by having Caleb relate his account in the first person, the reader can observe the operation of his passions, examine his motives, assess how he acts under different circumstances, and consider how his character 'increases and assimilates new substances to its own' (Godwin 2000, 466). As Godwin reveals, he focuses on Caleb and employs first-person narration – which he refers to as his 'metaphysical dissecting knife' – so that he can trace and lay 'bare the involutions of motive', and record 'the gradually accumulating impulses' which lead him to 'the particular way of proceeding in which' he 'afterwards embarked' (*CW* 448). This is one of Godwin's primary aims in *Caleb Williams*: to show, in detail, how an individual is shaped by society, its social institutions and social interactions. By recording Caleb's internalisation of Falkland's feudal ideology and eventual loss of self, *Caleb Williams* shows readers how vulnerable people are to the pernicious and anachronistic ideologies disseminated by social institutions and powerful members of the aristocracy. In this sense, Godwin's Gothic romance answers more to the 'genuine purpose of history' than eighteenth-century historiography: its focus on the individual enables the reader to 'understand the machine of society' (2000, 456). It is only by showing how individuals are influenced by their social environment – and how the past controls the present – that history's stranglehold over the present can be loosened.

In contrast to previous Gothic novelists, Godwin does not use Gothic romance to simply critique contemporary society: the aim is to change it. He wants his readers to query not only *why* things are the way that they are, but to question, fundamentally, the nature and origin of their own beliefs. This is why the optimism that pervades *Political Justice* is missing from Godwin's novel: Caleb's history is meant to serve as a stark warning to the reader. The usurpation of Caleb's personal identity by Falkland's feudal views is designed to prompt the reader to question commonplace beliefs that they may formerly have taken for granted. Godwin admits that this was his aim when he was planning the novel: 'I said to myself a thousand times, "I will write a tale, that shall constitute an epoch in the mind of the reader, that no one, after he has read it, shall ever be exactly the same man that he was before"' (*CW* 349–50). Godwin's Gothic romance aims to make readers realise that they inhabit the same nightmare world as Caleb, where individuals are strangers to themselves and are influenced by the past in more ways than they may (consciously) realise. Indeed, Godwin aims to shock his readers and make them contemplate whether they, similarly to Caleb, are prisoners of the past and ventriloquise feudal values. Even though

Caleb does not escape from history, Godwin wants his readers to learn from his example and realise that they do not have to share his disturbing fate.

In *Caleb Williams*, Godwin uses Gothic romance as a vehicle for promoting social reform and, by doing so, pursues his radical agenda in *Political Justice*. For Godwin, the true principles of social and political improvement are knowledge and 'correcting public opinion' (2013, 122). Furthermore, 'truth' needs to be 'incessantly studied, illustrated and propagated' (1985, 565). A 'universal illumination' is required to promote change: individuals will 'feel their situation, and the restraints, that shackled them before, [will] vanish like a mere deception' (2013, 123). For Godwin, it is knowledge, individual autonomy and self-scrutiny that can release society from the iron grip of history. As Kilgour points out, while external systems monitor and oppress individuals, Godwin believes that 'internal self-awareness liberates us from the powerful force of custom and habit, and makes involuntary actions subject to volition' (1995, 51). Godwin says that he wrote the novel not only to 'expose the evils which arise out of the present system of civilized society', but 'to lead the enquiring reader to examine whether they are, or are not, as has commonly been supposed, irremediable' (1795, 94). In *Caleb Williams*, Godwin uses Gothic romance, reconfigures historical writing and focuses on an individual's disturbing transformation in order to make readers analyse themselves and stimulate the self-scrutiny that is necessary for social change. Gothic horrors and Caleb's mental disintegration are designed to shock the reader and stimulate the enquiring mind. Godwin uses Caleb's plight in an attempt to 'disengage the minds' of his readers 'from prepossession, and launch them upon the sea of moral and political enquiry' (94). He does not endorse sudden or violent revolutions, but believes in gradual change through the dissemination of knowledge, the cultivation of the enquiring mind and the empowerment of the individual.[27] *Caleb Williams* is part of Godwin's scheme to stimulate gradual change. Contrary to the impression conveyed by the grand narratives of 'modern' eighteenth-century historiography, Godwin wants the reader to realise that, by gaining greater self-awareness, they can change history and break the oppressive cycles of the past that continue to blight the present. The individual still has the power to change the present and the course of history, but they have to recognise this.

It is only by gaining this knowledge that individuals can begin to 'direct' society to its 'best purposes' (Godwin 2000, 456).

Wollstonecraft: Gothic didacticism and patriarchal emancipation

As with Godwin's *Political Justice*, Wollstonecraft's *Rights of Woman* is pervaded by optimism. Wollstonecraft suggests that, despite the horrors of the present, 'as sound politics diffuse liberty, mankind, including woman, will become more wise and virtuous' (1985, 121–2). However, this positivity is missing from *Maria*. In a similar vein to Godwin's *Caleb Williams*, Wollstonecraft's novel also contains a number of disturbing historical allusions. As Kelly notes (1996, 39), the name of the novel's heroine, Maria, is closely associated with 'the notorious and celebrated woman of feeling from the past, Mary Queen of Scots (another actual prisoner of sex)'. The name of Maria's lover, Darnford, is similar to Darnley, the second husband of Mary, Queen of Scots. Wollstonecraft associates Maria with Mary, Queen of Scots, in order to draw attention to the persistence of patriarchy throughout history and how women in the present continue to be victims of the excessive emotions that society encourages them to cultivate. In this sense, there are compelling links between *Maria* and the *The Recess*, particularly in terms of the internalisation of the culture of sensibility. Moreover, Kelly suggests that there is a parallel between Wollstonecraft and Marie Roland, a leading woman of the early French Revolution (39). Madame Roland (as she was more widely known), was arrested for harbouring royalist sympathies, imprisoned and conveyed to the guillotine in 1793. Similarly to Wollstonecraft's Maria, Madame Roland wrote her memoirs while she was imprisoned, criticised the exploitation of women throughout society and addressed her memoirs to her absent daughter as a legacy and a warning. In *Maria*, Wollstonecraft sets the trials of her protagonist against larger historical patterns of patriarchy and female oppression. Although Wollstonecraft's novel is set in the present, it 'echoes two centuries of the lives of women as prisoners of sex, on both the domestic and the national scale' (Kelly 1996, 39–40). *Maria* reveals how very little has changed for women over the centuries: socially, emotionally and psychologically, they are still prisoners of patriarchy.

Wollstonecraft focuses on Maria's internalisation of excessive sensibility and alludes to other historical examples of female oppression and affliction in order to draw attention to 'how few women have emancipated themselves from the galling yoke of sovereign man' (1985, 119). By focusing on the operation of the past in the present, *Maria* reveals how, in the entire 'history of woman … she has always been either a slave or a despot' (144). Each of these situations, she argues, 'equally retards the progress of reason' (144). Wollstonecraft is particularly outraged by the fact that 'the power of reflecting on the past, and darting the keen eye of contemplation into futurity' is the 'grand privilege of man' (265). A lot of men 'enjoy this prerogative in a very limited degree' and, as a result, '[e]verything new appears to them wrong; and not able to distinguish the possible from the monstrous, they fear where no fear should find a place, running from the light of reason as if it were a firebrand' (265). Indeed, the problem for Wollstonecraft is not only the fact that history repeats itself in the present by oppressing women and preventing change, but that many women do not recognise the persistence of patriarchy due to being excluded from serious historical debate and enquiry. As the present is really the past in disguise, Wollstonecraft believes that it is important for women to have some historical knowledge in order to better understand the persistence of patriarchy in contemporary society.

In contrast to her husband, Wollstonecraft endorses 'modern', eighteenth-century philosophical history and believes that, if read in detail, it could stimulate women's minds and, by doing so, help them begin to see the patriarchal ties that bind their thinking and behaviour.[28] As Mark Salber Phillips notes, 'in Wollstonecraft's campaign against the gendering of reading, philosophical history evidently stands for a wide understanding of politics and history that should be open to all rational observers, male and female alike' (2000, 115). However, denied historical and political knowledge by the patriarchal system of women's education, she fears that, for many women, the 'reading of history will scarcely be more useful than the perusal of romances, if read as mere biography; if the character of the times, the political improvements, arts, etc. be not observed' (Wollstonecraft 1985, 261). Because the vast majority of women are 'denied all political privileges' (306), Wollstonecraft fears that they read history merely as a record of manners and eminent personages. For her, reading historiography without due diligence reinforces patriarchal stereotypes by suggesting that women do not have the rational or intellectual capacity to understand politics and history (and thus the present). Wollstonecraft fears that, due to the limited educational opportunities that women are afforded, many are simply unable to understand history at all. Taught to indulge their feelings at the expense of reason and 'confined to trifling employments', many women are '[u]nable to grasp anything great' (306). In consequence, such women 'find the reading of history a very dry task, and disquisitions addressed to the understanding intolerably tedious, and almost unintelligible' (306). Conscious that a historical work would have little impact on a female readership – and that many women were not educated enough to understand her earlier *Rights of Woman* – Wollstonecraft turns to an unlikely form to popularise her political views: the (Gothic) novel.

Wollstonecraft's decision to write a novel – especially a novel with Female Gothic elements – is surprising, considering, first, her views on the utility of historical writing for women's education and, second, her condemnation of fiction in the *Rights of Woman*. Wollstonecraft is very critical of novels, arguing that they 'corrupt the taste', 'draw the heart aside from its daily duties' (306) and help to 'make women the creatures of sensation' (152). However, it is important to point out that Wollstonecraft is not against all fiction. 'When I exclaim against novels', she writes, 'I mean when contrasted with those works which exercise the understanding and regulate the imagination' (306). For Wollstonecraft, 'any kind of reading' is 'better than leaving a blank still a blank, because the mind must receive a degree of enlargement, and obtain a little strength by a slight exertion of its thinking powers' (306–7). Ideally, Wollstonecraft would prefer women to 'read something superior' to novels (308), but she acknowledges that even the 'productions that are only addressed to the imagination, raise the reader a little above the gross gratification of appetites, to which the mind has not given a shade of delicacy' (307). In the *Rights of Woman*, she gives an account of a man who was left in charge of two young women. This 'sagacious man' encouraged his niece, who 'had considerable abilities', to read history and essays. However, his daughter, whom a 'fond weak mother had indulged', was 'averse to everything like application'. Instead, he 'allowed her to read novels ... saying that if she ever attained a relish for reading them, he would have some foundation to work upon' (308). Indeed, for Wollstonecraft, fiction can play an important role in the improvement of women's understanding and the fight against patriarchy. Following Godwin's design in *Caleb Williams*, Wollstonecraft turns to fiction in order to activate women's minds and get them thinking about the inequities of the patriarchal social order. For Wollstonecraft, awareness of the injustices of patriarchy, the role of history in supporting the gender hierarchy and self-knowledge are prerequisites for social reform. She chooses a popular form – the novel – in order to reach as many women readers as possible.

It is important to emphasise that *Maria* is not a Gothic romance *per se*: it is a realistic novel with identifiable Female Gothic elements. The conventions of the Gothic – and, more precisely, the Female Gothic – provide her not only with a way of popularising her political beliefs in the *Rights of Woman*, but a means of educating women about patriarchy. In some respects, Wollstonecraft's attitude towards fiction is similar to Clara Reeve's in *The Progress of Romance* (1785): all romances – including the Gothic – must have a strong social purpose and promote virtue, morality and reason. Wollstonecraft fears that many romances carry women's 'imaginations still further from nature and reason' and, similarly to Reeve, she believes that fiction should have a didactic function (Wollstonecraft 1788). However, while both writers recognise the utility of Gothic romance, they manipulate it for very different ends. In *The Old English Baron*, Reeve uses the Loyalist Gothic to teach readers about the importance of preserving the past and ancient English institutions. In sharp contrast to this, Wollstonecraft manipulates Female Gothic conventions in *Maria* in order to expose the horrors of patriarchy in the present and to encourage reform. She aims to shock women and, at the same time, educate them about the pernicious influence of the past on the present. In Wollstonecraft's novel, Female Gothic tropes such as women's persecution, domestic violence, imprisonment, and possession are not used to evoke sublime sensations or for romantic purposes: they are used as a means of conveying the reality of women's lives and rendering the terrors that 'literally exist within the average domestic household in England' (Mellor 1994, xvi). Wollstonecraft uses the Gothic to enable her readers to see the 'world stripped of all its false delusive charms'; she challenges women's '*false* views of life' and encourages them to 'see everything in its true colours' (1985, 212). As Godwin points out in his preface to *Maria*, the novel has a 'great moral purpose': it places in a 'striking point of view, evils that are too frequently overlooked' and 'drag[s] into light those details of oppression, of which the grosser and more insensible part of mankind make little account' (*M* 138).

Wollstonecraft uses the form of the novel and appropriates Female Gothic conventions not only to criticise the horrors of 'things as they are', but to stimulate reform. For her, education is of critical importance for forming rational individuals who can, in turn, help to cultivate more progressive social institutions and engineer social change.[29] Women's education is essential for defeating patriarchy and ending the past's domination of the present. Reminiscent of Godwin's *Caleb Williams*, *Maria* essentially provides a history of the present and is designed not only to educate, but to encourage self-scrutiny. However, Wollstonecraft's novel is more explicitly didactic than Godwin's work. In the latter part of the novel, Maria writes a memoir that is intended to instruct her daughter: 'From my narrative, my dear girl, you may gather the instruction, the counsel, which is meant rather to exercise than influence your mind' (*M* 58). Maria writes a circumstantial narrative of her own life in order to give her daughter 'an education' and to 'prepare her body and mind to encounter the ills which await her sex' (*M* 55). She wants her daughter to be 'warned' by her 'example' (*M* 59). Maria's account, of course, reveals more than she (consciously) realises: it shows that she is possessed by the ideology of sensibility, which controls her thinking and behaviour. Maria's memoirs function not only as a means of educating her daughter about the horrors of patriarchy, but as a warning to young women readers. The personal is both public and political in *Maria*. As Wollstonecraft writes in the preface to the novel, the 'history' that it contains 'ought rather to be considered, as of woman, than of an individual' (*M* 5).

By exhibiting Maria's susceptibility to her own emotions and her tendency to repeat the same mistakes, Wollstonecraft's novel is designed to encourage women to question if they, too, have internalised the 'Gothic' ideology of 'overstretched sensibility' and are vulnerable to the strength of their own passions. As Godwin notes, the 'province' of Wollstonecraft's 'true genius' is to 'give reality' to events and make them 'take a hold upon the mind of a reader of taste, from which they can never be loosened' (*M* 138). *Maria* presents its readers with a nightmare vision of contemporary society where that past – in the guise of internalised sensibility – distorts women's view of the present and controls their behaviour in insidious ways. Wollstonecraft's aim in *Maria* is to frighten her female readership by showing them that real horrors lie in the patriarchal construction of the female psyche. Where Godwin uses Gothic romance in order to help his readers understand the 'machine of society' (2000, 456), Wollstonecraft uses the novel and adopts Female Gothic conventions in a bid to make women see the workings of the machine of patriarchy. Exploiting the didactic potential of the Gothic novel, she aims to 'exercise', rather than merely 'influence', the minds of her female readers (*M* 58). By observing Maria's example, she wants women to 'learn to despise the sensibility' that has 'been excited and hackneyed in the ways of women' (1985, 223). For Wollstonecraft, the 'grand source of female folly and vice' arises from a lack of education and 'narrowness of mind' (144). In order to escape the same fate as Maria, women need to not only recognise the pernicious effects of sensibility on women's behaviour in the present, but seek wider social, economic and intellectual 'independence', as this is the 'basis of every virtue' (85). *Maria* is very much part of Wollstonecraft's ambition to 'effect a revolution in female manners', and to 'restore' women to their 'lost dignity, and make them, as a part of the human species, labour by reforming themselves to reform the world' (132). For Wollstonecraft, self-knowledge and independence are the first steps towards reform. *Maria* is designed to evoke this sort of self-scrutiny and thus to stop women participating in their own oppression by perpetuating patriarchal and Gothic (backward and anachronistic) values in the present. With independence and equal rights, women will be able to 'emulate the virtues of man' (319) and emancipate themselves from destructive cycles of history and the patriarchal prisonhouse of the past.

Gothic imaginations: the Romantic period and beyond

Wollstonecraft's and Godwin's new option for Gothic fiction – dark and brooding narratives set in contemporary society – had far-reaching implications for Gothic literature and the historical novel.[30] However, the present did not completely displace the past as the Gothic's location of choice. Later manifestations of the Gothic would utilise both historical and contemporary settings. This is exemplified by Godwin's later works. For example, in 1799, he published *St Leon: A Tale of the Sixteenth Century*, which incorporates numerous Gothic conventions, including the supernatural, the Inquisition and a subterranean vault. As Kelly observes, *St Leon* reveals that Godwin's 'interest in applying historical-analogy to the present had already become less fervent and pointed than in *Things As They Are*': he moves 'away from Enlightenment critical history of contemporary life toward a sociology of the origins of the present in the past' (1996, 37). Whether they were set in the present or the past, subsequent Gothic works were heavily influenced by Godwin and Wollstonecraft. By opening up new territories for tales of terror, both writers left an indelible mark on the development of the Gothic novel. Indeed, it was not just their geographical relocation and domestication of the Gothic that influenced future Gothic writers. Perhaps their most significant Gothic legacy was their emphasis on the complex inner lives and the psychology of their protagonists. The ability of the past to live on in the minds of those living in the present – and the unwanted ideological legacy of the past – became prominent Gothic themes in later works. The natural scenery of the early Gothic increasingly gives way to landscapes of the human mind. Godwin and Wollstonecraft fortified the Gothic's abilities as a vehicle for social, cultural and political critique. Furthermore, they pushed the boundaries of Gothic fiction and extended its capabilities by showing how it could be used to effect reform and social change. Their fusion of the political and psychological changed the nature of Gothic literature forever.

Wollstonecraft's and Godwin's Gothic novels had an immediate impact on literature across the Atlantic. Charles Brockden Brown is often referred to as America's first professional writer and Gothic novelist. His first work, *Alcuin: A Dialogue* (1798), explicitly supported Wollstonecraft's *Rights of Woman*. Brown was also heavily influenced by Godwin's political and literary works and was, in fact, known as the American Godwin. Similarly to Godwin and Wollstonecraft (and Sophia Lee), Brown had a keen interest in history and, early in his life, he 'confessed' his 'attachment to factitious history' (Brown 2013, 732). He saw romance – and particularly Gothic romance – as a means of exposing the motivations of human behaviour and as a way of understanding the past. He wrote six Gothic romances, which were inspired by both Godwin and Radcliffe, and the London editions of his novels were published by the Minerva Press. In terms of the Gothic, Brown's most interesting novel is *Wieland, or, The Transformation* (1798), which is set in the contemporary world and recounts the story of a melancholy young man, Theodore Wieland, who is compelled to commit terrible deeds (including the murder of his own family) by 'voices'. These voices (and the events they trigger) are explained in conflicting and contradictory ways. In one sense, the voices are created by a rationalist friend of Theodore's named Carwin, who is a mischievous ventriloquist (or biloquist, as he is referred to in the novel). He claims that he is using his ventriloqual skills in order to test (and expose) Theodore's religious credulity. However, Brown's novel also suggests that, if it were not for Theodore's already credulous nature and religious self-deception, he would not have been duped by these voices to begin with. *Wieland* functions simultaneously as both a warning against religious extremism and the dangers of the cold rationality that Carwin endorses and uses against Theodore. Indeed, it is telling that Brown draws on the theme (and technique) of ventriloquism, which, as this chapter has shown, is such an important aspect of *Caleb Williams* and *Maria*. Godwin's and Wollstonecraft's ventriloqual legacy endures and voices (internal and external) assume increasing prominence in the Gothic imaginary. Whereas ventriloquism is implicit in *Caleb Williams* and *Maria*, Brown makes it much more explicit in his Gothic novel. However, similarly to Godwin and Wollstonecraft, ventriloquism is intertwined with ideology in *Wieland*. Brown focuses on ventriloquism and (inner) voices in order to show how frighteningly vulnerable individuals are to powerful ideologies, and the destructive consequences that can result from religious enthusiasm and the internalisation of religious dogma. Theodore does not question the voice in his head, and this is one of the main targets of Brown's Gothic novel: the disturbing ease with which individuals accept, unquestioningly, evidence that appears to match their own preconceptions (religious, philosophical or otherwise). *Wieland* shares the didacticism of Godwin's and Wollstonecraft's Gothic novels; it is designed to challenge its readers and make them consider how (religious) ideology distorts individual perception. Brown's novel captures the competing ideological forces at work in the minds of those living in early America and poses troubling questions about religion and the Enlightenment philosophies on which the young nation was founded. It is also important to note that the novel is narrated by Clara Wieland (Theodore's sister) and that, according with Brown's feminist attitudes, she is revealed to be an intelligent, strong and determined woman.

The Female Gothic novels that followed in the wake of Wollstonecraft's *Maria* (and Brown's *Wieland*) concentrated increasingly on female psychology and the complex inner lives of women. Although it was not published until 1818, Jane Austen's *Northanger Abbey* was written in 1798, when the Gothic novel was at the peak of its popularity, but was also beginning to be satirised by its critics. Austen's Gothic parody has often been accused of killing off the Gothic novel, but it is important to point out that she did not intend to dismiss it completely and that her satire is more affectionate than cruel. *Northanger Abbey* also reveals that Austen recognised the imaginative power of the Gothic, as well as its utility for psychological, political and cultural critique. Reminiscent of *Maria*, Austen domesticates the Gothic and questions patriarchy in the present. Catherine Morland – the heroine, or, rather, anti-heroine of the novel – has an obsession with Gothic novels, which leads her to fabricate thrilling fantasies about what she will find at Northanger Abbey when she is invited to stay there. However, the majority of her expectations are foiled. For example, she suspects that General Tilney, the owner of the abbey, murdered his wife, but it turns out that she died of natural causes. Austen offers a complex psychological examination of her protagonist and reveals how her reading of Gothic novels shapes her perceptions. Although *Northanger Abbey* demonstrates Catherine's need to distinguish fact from fiction, it also blurs the relationship between reality and fantasy. Several of the fears associated with the Female Gothic, such as the terrors surrounding patriarchal despotism, are shown to be well founded in Austen's novel. For example, General Tilney may not have murdered his wife, but he is shown to be quite an unpleasant and despotic man. This is most clearly revealed when he throws Catherine out of Northanger. Austen suggests that the Gothic exists in women's everyday worlds and, throughout her novel, she addresses a number of issues that are central to the Female Gothic, such as women's lack of education, the dangers of excessive emotion, male despotism, and the marginalisation of women in history.

As one might expect, Female Gothic works continued to be very diverse. In 1805, Charlotte Dacre published *Zofloya, or The Moor*. In this novel, subtitled 'A Romance of the Fifteenth-Century', Dacre focuses on her oversexed and ambitious protagonist, Victoria, who has often been seen as a female equivalent of Lewis's notorious Ambrosio. Where Ambrosio was encouraged to commit illicit acts by a demon, Victoria is compelled to commit terrible deeds by Lucifer himself, who is disguised as a seductive Moor. Under his guidance, frustrated passions give way to horrific acts of physical violence. In the course of the novel, Victoria murders her husband, drugs and rapes his brother when he rejects her, and tortures, mutilates and kills his fiancé, Lilla. Dacre's subversion of traditional gender roles and positioning of Victoria as the hero-villain challenges conventional gendered types of Gothic writings. Indeed, *Zofloya* radically destabilises the categories of male Gothic writing and the Female Gothic. As Carol Margaret Davison astutely observes, Dacre 'employs the Female Gothic in *Zofloya* as a vehicle through which to launch a serious attack on women's heavily and problematically circumscribed role in the cultural imaginary' (2009, 158). Dacre's novel is also notable for its psychological complexity and the force with which it represents the irrationality, obsession and torment that love can evoke. Although it may at first seem difficult to imagine that 'Austen and Dacre lived in the same universe' (Clery 2004, 100), there are important links between their works. For example, both writers reinvigorated the Female Gothic and offered increasingly detailed examinations of their protagonists' motivations and thoughts. Developing the psychological introspection of *Northanger Abbey* – as well as *Caleb Williams*, *Maria* and *Wieland* – Dacre's novel focuses on Victoria's internal struggle, and her difficulty to differentiate between external reality and internal experience.

The Gothic's increasing focus on interiority, psychology and alternative states of consciousness had a large impact on many Romantic writers.[31] This was especially the case with Percy Bysshe Shelley, who was heavily influenced by Brown and Godwin. He was a disciple of Godwin and was a great admirer of his philosophical anarchism. In 1810, Shelley published *Zastrozzi: A Romance*, which was his first attempt at writing a Gothic novel. This melodramatic and Gothic work draws on Godwin's *St Leon*, as well as Lewis's *The Monk* and Dacre's *Zofloya*. Shelley's novel focuses on the atheist and anti-institutional protagonist, Zastrozzi, and touches upon his earliest thoughts on irresponsible self-indulgence and violent revenge. Shelley followed up *Zastrozzi* with another Gothic novel, entitled *St. Irvyne; or the Rosicrucian* (1810).[32] This work is modelled on Godwin's *St Leon* and also develops the psychological aspects of *Caleb Williams*. Although the novel has been criticised for its confusing plot and abrupt ending, it has received acclaim for the way it associates the Gothic castle with the human psyche. As Frederick Frank argues, Shelley turns the 'Gothic castle into a recondite iconography of the mind itself under the unbearable stress from contradictory fears and drives'. Both of Shelley's Gothic novels reveal that, similarly to Godwin, Wollstonecraft and Brown, he 'understood how the deepest power of the Gothic lay in its capacity to call into question man's basic self-understanding and faith in systems of thought' (Frank 1977, xxi–xxii).

Mary Shelley – Wollstonecraft's and Godwin's daughter and Percy's wife – was also interested in the political and philosophical import of the Gothic. She was influenced by her parents' political and fictional works, as well as her husband's Gothic narratives. In 1818, Mary Shelley published *Frankenstein*, which relates the exploits of Victor Frankenstein, a Genevan student of natural philosophy, who builds a hideous humanlike creature out of corpses and brings it to life. The novel bears close relation to *Caleb Williams* and *Wieland* in terms of its confessional-style narration, criticism of unjust laws and focus on extreme psychological states. Rather than dwelling on the supernatural aspect of Frankenstein's creation, she chooses, instead, to concentrate on her monster's consciousness and psychological development. Her mother's concern with education in the *Rights of Woman* is in evidence here, as well her father's views on the social construction of consciousness in *Political Justice*. Furthermore, with its emphasis on dreams and the insight that they provide into consciousness, *Frankenstein* is reminiscent of *Zofloya*. Similarly to Dacre's novel, *Frankenstein* presents a challenge to gendered categorisations of Gothic writing. Although the novel is often discussed in relation to the Female Gothic, numerous critics have drawn attention to the blurring of traditional gender boundaries in Shelley's novel and suggested that the Creature allows for an exploration of a specifically female consciousness. *Frankenstein* sophisticates existing Gothic themes and pioneers new Gothic preoccupations: the novel asks difficult questions about the nature of evil, domestic despotism, nature and nurture, and the conflict between science and religion, civility and consciousness.

In its later manifestations, the Gothic novel would become even more concerned with consciousness and disturbed mental states. In 1820, Charles Maturin published *Melmoth the Wanderer*, which is something of a 'greatest hits' of Gothic themes and conventions.

Melmoth, who has sold his soul for the promise of prolonged life, offers relief from suffering to each of the characters, whose terrible stories succeed one another, if they will take over his bargain with the devil. Maturin greatly increases the structural complexity of *Frankenstein* and writes a Gothic novel that is both labyrinthine and bewildering. *Melmoth* has the same paranoiac atmosphere as *Caleb Williams* and, similarly to Godwin, Maturin employs first-person narration to portray the force of terror and despair, as well as the paradoxical nature of extreme emotional states. Maturin's psychological Gothic novel explores the irrational urges that are often concealed at the centre of human personality. *Melmoth* is also intensely anti-Catholic and portrays Roman Catholicism as a grotesque institution that, throughout history, has created a multitude of monsters.

Similarly to *Melmoth*, James Hogg's *The Private Memoirs and Confessions of a Justified Sinner* (1824) reveals religious anxieties and locates terrors in the human mind. Like *Melmoth*, Hogg's novel has a very complex narrative structure and the reader is presented with conflicting accounts of events. *Private Memoirs* features Robert Wringhim, a young man who believes himself 'saved' according to the Calvinist doctrine of predestination and, guided by the influence of a malign stranger named Gil-Martin, commits a series of horrifying crimes. Wringhim is increasingly haunted by Gil-Martin and, similarly to Caleb, eventually loses his own identity. Hogg makes the reader question whether Gil-Martin is a projection of Wringhim's troubled psyche or is the devil incarnate. There is also a suggestion that Wringhim becomes possessed by the devil. Hogg's narrative serves as a warning of the physical and psychological consequences of religious fanaticism and extreme Calvinism. The complex narrative structure of Hogg's novel also undermines the religious certainties on which Wringhim's beliefs are founded.

Inherited from its early contentious relationship with Enlightenment modes of historical representation, the Gothic continues to be preoccupied with the nature of the past; whether it is the complex authorship and epistolary nature of *Frankenstein*, the elaborate series of tales that comprise *Melmoth*, or the challenging structure and religious content of Hogg's *Private Memoirs*.[33] The Gothic is haunted by its own history. Even though some Gothic works were no longer *set* in specific historical periods, they still utilised Gothic *attitudes* towards the past. In all its various incarnations, the Gothic remains obsessed with macabre histories, repressed pasts, the survival of barbaric customs in the present, and the ideological legacy of the past. Indeed, humankind's 'Gothic' relationship with the past continues to be a source of fascination for such works. Throughout the Romantic period and beyond, sinister histories would continue to haunt the Gothic imagination.

Notes

1 As Anthony Mandal observes, after the publication of Horace Walpole's *The Castle of Otranto* in 1764, there was only a scattering of Gothic novels and the genre largely failed to gain traction. It was 'not until the appearance of Ann Radcliffe's novels from 1789 onward, as well as her many imitators in the 1790s, that a true "market" for Gothic fictions emerged' (Mandal 2014, 159). Mandal contends that one of the underlying reasons for this 'period of slow burn followed by a veritable explosion' was the Gothic's 'flexibility as a form, allowing it to permeate all sorts of literary genres and markets: the circulating-library novel, poetical works, popular drama, chapbooks and bluebooks' (159). Radcliffe was the 'totemic figure of this era' (165) and her writings gave rise to many imitations and adaptations. Many of these were 'hack works that made little attempt to disguise their derivative nature' (167), and, due to the formulaic nature of these productions, the Gothic became a target for satire and parody in works such as Jane Austen's *Northanger Abbey* (1798–99). For a good discussion of the Gothic's surge in popularity and the imitations that Radcliffe's works inspired, see Mandal, 'Gothic and the Publishing World, 1780–1820' (2014).
2 Lewis had lost interest in writing his novel, *The Monk*, until he read *The Mysteries of Udolpho* in May 1794. Radcliffe's work inspired him to complete it: 'I was induced to go on with it by reading "the Mysteries of Udolpho", which is in my opinion one of the most interesting Books that ever have been published' (Lewis 1794).
3 As Norton notes (2000, 106), '[n]ovels of sensibility (such as Goethe's *Werther*) flowed into the channel of terror earlier in Germany than in England, and developed into the well-defined sub-genres *Ritter-, Räuber- und Schauerroman* (novels about knights or robbers, and shudder novels)'. English translations of these stories, such as Johann Christian Friedrich von Schiller's *The Ghost-Seer, or Apparationist* (1795), proved popular in England during the 1790s and were very influential on English works. This strain of Gothic fiction became known as the School of Horror or 'the German school'. In contrast to Radcliffe's fictions, which tend to be set in Italy or France, the settings employed by the School of

Horror are often German, sometimes Spanish and sometimes English. Furthermore, rather than creating terror through suggestion and implied supernatural occurrences, the German school employed real demons and gory scenes.

4 Watt argues that, even though Reeve's *Memoirs of Sir Roger de Clarendon* 'cannot be regarded as a Gothic romance by any modern criteria', it 'nonetheless offers an instructive statement of purpose which serves to illuminate its choice of an English medieval setting' (1999, 59). This choice of setting is particularly significant in the context of the French Revolution; a subject Reeve was quite vocal about. She initially supported the French Revolution, but withdrew her support when it turned violent. After the September Massacres at Paris in 1792, she writes to Walker, 'What times do we live in? – My politics are all overthrown' (Reeve 1792). Reeve continued to comment on the French Revolution in the *Memoirs of Sir Roger de Clarendon*. In accordance with her classical republican political views, she deplores despotic government and levelling politics. Speaking of the situation in France, she argues that it was 'a faction of bold, ignorant, flagitious men, who associated together to oppose the constitution, the laws, and the king; and to overturn all kinds of government. They seduced the populace to espouse their party, by holding out the word *equality* as a bait to catch them, and then keep them under by the worst kind of despotism' (1793, 1: 225). 'Let Britain shudder at the scene before her, and grasp her blessings the closer', she implores (1: xx). For a broader discussion of Reeve's attitude towards the French Revolution, see Kelly's 'Clara Reeve, Provincial Bluestocking: From the Old Whigs to the Modern Liberal State' (2003, 115–25).

5 As Thomas Preston Peardon observes, Burke's *Reflections* triggered a new phase of English nationalism in historical writing. Burke's notion that English liberty was more secure than elsewhere in Europe because its roots stretched far back into the distant past was particularly influential. 'This teaching of Burke marked a new emphasis on national differences in government and history', notes Peardon (1933, 164). As the war with France intensified throughout the 1790s and into the nineteenth century, there was a greater emphasis on English exceptionalism, war sentiment and the need to defend time-honoured English freedoms. Peardon discusses a number of historical works that exhibit such views, such as Robert Macfarlane's *History of the Reign of George III* (1790–96), Herbert Marsh's *The History of the Politicks of Great Britain and France* (translated into English in 1800) and Robert Bisset's *The History of the Reign of George III to the termination of the late war* (1803).

6 Wollstonecraft was actively involved in the French Revolution. In 1792, she travelled to France to improve her French and to see the Revolution first hand. Her *Rights of Woman* had already been published in French and she was welcomed into an international group of literary and political writers. These included Helen Maria Williams (the English poet), Joel Barlow (an American political writer), Thomas Paine (the exiled author of the *Rights of Man*), and Brissot (the moderate French revolutionary leader who was guillotined during the Terror). Wollstonecraft felt part of the French community and dedicated the *Rights of Woman* to Talleyrand (a French diplomat) hoping, in vain, to influence legislation before the French Assembly on women's education. While she was in France, she saw Louis XVI being escorted through the streets to be tried for treason and a guillotine covered in blood. Wollstonecraft's experiences extinguished her earlier enthusiasm for the Revolution and, for a time, challenged her belief in human perfectability. See Tom Furniss, 'Mary Wollstonecraft's French Revolution' (2002), for a thorough account of Wollstonecraft's experiences in revolutionary France.

7 For a good discussion of Wollstonecraft's treatment by early reviewers, see Regina M. Janes, 'On the Reception of Mary Wollstonecraft's *A Vindication of the Rights of Woman*' (1978).

8 Godwin did not just commentate on and critique contemporary society; he was actively engaged in 1790s politics. In December 1792, he attended Thomas Paine's trial *in absentia* for writing the *Rights of Man* (1791–92). In February and March 1793, he published four letters in the *Morning Chronicle* attacking the government's use of spies and informers to intimidate reformers. While he was writing *Caleb Williams*, Godwin supported a number of middle-class radicals who were facing prosecutions for their political views. For example, he visited the Scottish radicals Thomas Muir and Thomas Palmer, who were found guilty and sentenced to transportation to Australia, while they were in the hulks at Woolwich. In 1794, Godwin often visited Joseph Gerrald as he prepared for his trial, following his arrest for sedition at the British Convention in 1793. Godwin also visited him while he was awaiting transportation in Newgate. Before the trials of his friends Thomas Holcroft, John Thelwall and John Horne Tooke, Godwin published an anonymous pamphlet entitled *Cursory Strictures on the Charge delivered by Judge Eyre to the Grand Jury* (1794). This work severely undermined the charge of treason against the three men and played a significant role in their acquittal. This work also secured Godwin legendary status among prominent radicals of the day.

9 See Pamela Clemit, 'Godwin, *Political Justice*' (2011, 96–9), for more details on the reception of Godwin's political treatise.

10 As Clemit notes (1993, 26), Godwin had read Radcliffe's *The Romance of the Forest* and *The Mysteries of Udolpho*. Ingrid Horrocks contends that Godwin 'was not only reading *Udolpho* as he moved towards' the completion of *Caleb Williams*, but that he 'may have met with Radcliffe and entered into discussion with her' (2007, 33). Horrocks cites one of Godwin's journal entries from April 1794, which refers to having 'tea at Radcliffe's, talk of morals and fortitude'. She draws attention to further journal entries that refer to Godwin 'call[ing] on Radcliffe' (quoted in Horrocks 2007, 33).

11 Godwin was very impressed with *The Canterbury Tales* (1796 onwards) and was keen to meet the Lee sisters, having desired to meet Sophia as early as 1786. It is likely that Godwin knew of *The Recess* – a popular novel with Gothic elements that, like *Caleb Williams*, was written in the first person – and possible that he had read it (or at least part of it). He finally met both sisters on a visit to Bath in March 1798. This meeting occurred only six months after the death of his wife. However, he 'was enchanted with Harriet from the first' and 'decided at once' that she would be 'a suitable successor to Mary Wollstonecraft' (St. Clair 1989, 201). Godwin proposed marriage to Harriet on 5 June 1798, but she refused him. She initially feared what people might say about her marrying an atheist who promoted radical ideas. After a series of letters from him, she was later put off by his condescension towards her in their discussions of religious faith. For more information, see St. Clair, *The Godwins and the Shelleys* (1989, 201–5).

12 See Mitzi Myers, 'Mary Wollstonecraft's literary reviews' (2002), for more details on the works that Wollstonecraft reviewed during her time at the *Analytical Review*.

13 This is particularly the case with *Caleb Williams*. As Monika Fludernik points out (2001, 857), it has not only been considered in relation to the 'Gothic novel', but has been read as an 'English Jacobin novel', canonised as a 'Romantic novel', viewed as the first 'spy novel', and has been remarked upon as 'one of the first fictional studies of abnormal psychology'.

14 Four revised editions of *Caleb Williams* appeared during Godwin's lifetime (1796, 1797, 1816, and 1831). Godwin made some substantial revisions and changes to later editions of the novel. Between the 1794 and 1796 editions, he changed some of his characters' names: 'Jones' (Falkland's agent and Caleb's pursuer) became 'Gines'; 'Gines' (Falkland's caretaker) became 'Warnes'; 'Doctor Arnold' became 'Doctor Wilson'; 'Wilson' became 'Larkins'; and 'Barton' was altered to 'Jeckols'. Throughout this chapter, I use the first edition of the novel, which was published on 26 May 1794. As Pamela Clemit suggests, this version 'brings us closer to Godwin's original intentions in 1794 and

presents his unique blend of politics and psychology in its purest form' (*CW* xxviii).

15 Ian Ousby notes that, even though the Treason Trials came after *Caleb Williams* had been completed, the legal proceedings that feature in the novel 'grew out of the political milieu of which the trials are the clearest expression' (1974, 49). For more detailed discussions of surveillance in *Caleb Williams*, see James Thompson, 'Surveillance in William Godwin's *Caleb Williams*' (1989) and David S. Hogsette, 'Textual Surveillance, Social Codes, and Sublime Voices: The Tyranny of Narrative in *Caleb Williams* and *Wieland*' (2005).

16 Godwin himself supervised the publication of *Political Justice* in 1793, 1796 and 1798. These editions differ considerably. See Isaac Krammick's 'Note on the Text' for details of these changes (Godwin 1985, 57–8). Throughout this chapter, I mainly use the 1798 edition, which was the third and final revision (Godwin 1985). However, I do, occasionally, also refer to the original 1793 edition (Godwin 2013).

17 Godwin's novel may focus mainly on Caleb's experiences, but it also records the tragic history of a young woman. Emily Melvile is the cousin and dependent of Barnabas Tyrrel, a tyrannical landowner who oppresses his tenants. Tyrrel has a 'brutal' disposition, but Emily becomes 'his favourite' and is adept at 'softening his rage' (*CW* 51). However, their relationship quickly deteriorates when Emily falls in love with Tyrrel's bitter enemy, Falkland. Tyrrel determines to 'wreak upon her a signal revenge'. He imprisons Emily in her room, tries to force her to marry a local labourer, has her arrested 'for a debt contracted for board and necessaries for the fourteen last years' (*CW* 78), and sends her to prison, where she dies of a fever. Emily is ultimately killed by the law. Tyrrel's response to being accused of Emily's murder is particularly telling in this respect: 'Murderer? – Did I employ knives or pistols? Did I give her poison? I did nothing but what the law allows. If she be dead, nobody can say that I am to blame!' (*CW* 88). In contemporary eighteenth-century society, it is the law – not a dagger, sword or poison – that becomes the Gothic tyrant's preferred 'weapon of tyranny' (*CW* 42). As Nancy E. Johnson observes, Godwin's tragic account of Emily influences *Maria*, where Wollstonecraft 'takes on this paradigmatic woman' and uses her 'as a model for the fate of women in a state where domestic tyranny is reciprocally supported by political despotism' (2011, 109).

18 See Eric Lindstrom, 'Imagining *Things as They Are*' (2010), for a comprehensive discussion of the nature, origin and development of the notion of 'things as they are' in the eighteenth century.

19 The representation of chivalry in *Caleb Williams* has received a lot of critical attention. It is widely recognised that the novel rejects

Burke's notion of chivalry as a positive force in the *Reflections*. See David McCracken, 'Godwin's Caleb Williams: A Fictional Rebuttal of Burke' (1969–71) and Pamela Clemit, *The Godwinian Novel* (1993), 43–63. For a more recent discussion of chivalry and national identity in Godwin's novel, see Charlie Bondhus, '"An Outlandish, Foreign-Made Englishman": Aristocratic Oppression and Ethnic Anomaly in *Caleb Williams*' (2010).

20 Godwin originally intended his novel to have a different ending. His diary suggests that he finished the first version of the novel on 30 April 1794. However, he was disappointed with it, and wrote the published version on the 4 and 8 May. In the original ending, Caleb fails to convince the magistrate that Falkland is guilty of murder. The two fragments that comprise the original ending of the novel are written by Caleb in prison, with Jones as his warden. Caleb's narration is erratic and disorganised, suggesting that he has gone mad. He has been informed that Falkland is dead, but he does not seem to remember his master. In his delirium, Caleb concludes that true happiness lies in being like a gravestone that reads, 'HERE LIES WHAT WAS ONCE A MAN!' (CW 311). The merits of these two different endings have been debated by critics. However, it is significant that, in the published ending, the action is relocated from Caleb's external environment to his mind. As Butler points out (1987, 68), the 'revised ending locates the action in Caleb's consciousness, which is as it should be'. I agree with Butler on this point. The emphasis on Caleb's mind and his inner voice – which ventriloquises his deceased master's anachronistic social views – is very much part of Godwin's plan to draw attention to the disturbing (and destructive) ideological legacy of the past.

21 Godwin would draw on the theme of ventriloquism again in his later work, *Fleetwood* (1805), which actually features a ventriloquist and a puppet (Godwin 1853, 34).

22 Wollstonecraft's relationship with sensibility is complex. She does warn about the dangers of romantic fantasies, but she also recognises that female sensibility and imagination are sources of freedom. As Barbara Taylor discusses (2003, 72–4), this tension between sensibility, romantic excess and female liberation is particularly evident in Wollstonecraft's *Letters Written during a Short Residence in Sweden, Norway, and Denmark* (1796). Wollstonecraft is not a detractor of sensibility or romantic love; what she fears is emotional excess and how it displaces reason.

23 In many respects, this an early example of the free indirect style found in Jane Austen's novels.

24 The extent to which Wollstonecraft is consciously critiquing the Maria and Darnford dynamic has been a subject of intense debate among

critics. As Claudia L. Johnson points out (2002, 203), some critics contend that 'the novel itself is unwittingly seduced by romance', while others maintain that it 'opens out a new space for critical distance'. For example, Poovey suggests that the 'narrator falls victim to the same sentimental idealism that cripples Maria' (1984, 105), while Kelly takes a more emancipatory view (1992, 206–23). I believe that Wollstonecraft has much more (conscious) control over her work than Poovey suggests. She (deliberately) employs free indirect speech not only to render her protagonist's thoughts, but to create an ironic distance between the narrator and Maria. As Johnson suggests (2002, 203), 'Wollstonecraft's irony seems clear' throughout *Maria*. For example, when the narrator questions, 'what chance had Maria of *escaping*' (*M* 32, emphasis added), the reader is 'being told that this love is yet another form of incarceration from which escape is as necessary as it is unlikely' (Johnson 2002, 203).

25 For more information on Caleb's and Falkland's attitudes towards Alexander, and how these relate to Godwin's ambiguous views on Alexander in *Political Justice*, see Andrew M. Stauffer, *Anger, Revolution, and Romanticism* (2005, 90–1).

26 Godwin takes particular aim at the historiography of David Hume and William Robertson, arguing that neither of these historians 'experience … emotions nor excite them' and that their historical writings are only 'of use as a whetstone upon which to sharpen our faculty of discrimination' (2000, 460–2).

27 In *Political Justice*, Godwin contends that the 'complete reformation that is wanted, is not instant but future reformation'. Social change is to be effected not by violent means, but by the distribution of knowledge. 'When the true crisis shall come', he argues, 'not a sword will need to be drawn, not a finger to be lifted up', as the 'adversaries will be too few and too feeble to dare to make a stand against the universal sense of mankind' (2013, 123).

28 Wollstonecraft had a keen interest in eighteenth-century historiography. In 1794, she published *An Historical and Moral View of the Origin and Progress of the French Revolution*. In this work, Wollstonecraft aims to examine the causes and effects of the French Revolution with a 'philosophical eye' (1794, 522). She focuses on larger patterns of social behaviour and argues that it is necessary 'to guard against the erroneous inferences of sensibility' (vi). For Wollstonecraft, historical writing should be governed by 'reason', as it is the 'only sure guide to direct us to a favourable or just conclusion' (vi). As Jane Rendall points out (2011, 80), Wollstonecraft signals the 'subversion of "philosophical history" as a masculine genre'. Very few women wrote history in the eighteenth century and almost none claimed to be a philosophical

historian in the same way as Hume, Robertson or Edward Gibbon. Rendall argues that the title of Wollstonecraft's historical work echoes Robertson's 'View of the Progress of Society in Europe' and notes that the *Analytical Review* called her 'our philosophical historian' (80).

29 The subject of women's education is central to many of Wollstonecraft's writings. For example, her first book, *Thoughts on the Education of Daughters* (1787), is a didactic work that encourages mothers to teach their daughters self-discipline, analytical thinking and honesty. In 1789, she published *The Female Reader*, which is an anthology of literary extracts 'principally intended for the improvement of females' (Wollstonecraft 1789, iv). The *Rights of Woman* begins with a call for the equal education of women and also includes a vision of a national school system. Wollstonecraft believed that women would only be able to become rational adults if they were educated properly as children, and so she also utilised the popular genre of children's literature to promote women's education. In 1788, she published *Original Stories from Real Life*, which begins with a teacher educating two young girls and expands into a series of didactic tales. As Alan Richardson points out, this didacticism is also present in both of her novels, *Mary* and *Maria*: they 'centrally address the self-education of their heroines while seeking to fill a pedagogical role in relation to their female readers' (2002, 24).

30 Intertwined with historical settings and subjects, it is widely acknowledged that the Gothic played a major role in the development of the historical novel in Britain. As Anne H. Stevens points out, with the Gothic becoming less dependent on historical settings, the historical novel began to inhabit some of the historical space that it vacated and became a more distinctive genre in its own right (2010, 49). With the divergence of these genres, they developed distinct generic identities and became associated with certain features and characteristics: readers of historical novels get 'increasingly detailed depictions of historical settings and personages' while readers of the Gothic came to expect macabre incidents and sensations of terror and horror (76).

31 Many of the Romantics were very well read in the Gothic and, despite their aversion to the flood of Gothic tales and imitations that inundated the literary marketplace towards the end of the eighteenth century, they utilised its conventions in their own writings. Samuel Taylor Coleridge was heavily influenced by the genre. For example, his poems *Christabel* (1798–1801) and *The Rime of the Ancient Mariner* (1798) focus on events in the past, employ brooding atmospheres and flirt with the paranormal. In *Manfred* (1816–17), Lord Byron utilises a number of Gothic conventions, such as a castle, supernatural occurrences and sublime landscapes. The protagonist,

Manfred, takes his name from Walpole's *Otranto* and Byron offers a portrait of a tormented and defiant Gothic hero-villain. John Keats was also attracted to the Gothic. For example, his *The Eve of St Agnes* (1819) features Gothic architecture, superstition and ancestral conflict. See Michael Gamer, *Romanticism and the Gothic* (2000), for more information on how Romantic writers viewed and responded to the Gothic.

32 Shelley did not outgrow his early love for the Gothic and his later works reveal his continued fascination with the macabre. For example, *The Revolt of Islam* (1817) features brother–sister incest (at least in the first version), violence, madness, cannibalism, and bloody counterrevolutionary violence. *The Cenci* (1819) has father–daughter incest, sexual betrayal, rape, patricide, torture, and religious corruption in a fusion of the Gothic with the Jacobean.

33 Another notable work influenced by the Gothic and its depiction of tortured psychological states is Thomas De Quincey's *The Confessions of an English Opium-Eater* (1821). This work reveals the nightmares, paranoia and despair experienced by the author as a result of his drug addiction.

References

Alliston, April. 1990. 'The Value of a Literary Legacy: Retracing the Transmission of Value through Female Lines'. *Yale Journal of Criticism* 4: 109–27.

———. 1996. *Virtue's Faults: Correspondences in Eighteenth-Century British and French Women's Fiction*. California: Stanford University Press.

———. 2000. Introduction to *The Recess*, by Sophia Lee, edited by April Alliston, ix–xliv. Lexington: University Press of Kentucky.

Ankersmit, F. R. 2001. *Historical Representation*. Stanford, CA: Stanford University Press.

———. 2005. *Sublime Historical Experience*. Stanford, CA: Stanford University Press.

Austen, Jane. 2003. *Northanger Abbey*, edited by Marilyn Butler. London: Penguin.

Barbauld, Anna Laetitia. 1810. *The British Novelists*. Vol. 22. London: F. C. and J. Rivington.

Barker-Benfield, C. J. 1992. *The Culture of Sensibility: Sex and Society in Eighteenth-Century Britain*. Chicago, IL: The University of Chicago Press.

Beard, Mary R. 1946. *Woman as Force in History*. New York: Macmillan.

Beebee, Thomas O. 1999. *Epistolary Fiction in Europe, 1500–1850*. Cambridge: Cambridge University Press.

Biro, John. 1993. 'Hume's New Science of the Mind'. In *The Cambridge Companion to Hume*, edited by David Fate Norton, 33–63. Cambridge: Cambridge University Press.

Blackstone, William. 1765–69. *Commentaries on the Laws of England*. 4 vols. Oxford: Clarendon Press.

Blake, William. 2005. 'London'. In *The Norton Anthology of Poetry*, edited by Margaret Ferguson, Mary Jo Salter and Jon Stallworthy, 744–5. New York: Norton.

Blakemore, Steven. 1997. *Intertextual War: Edmund Burke and the French Revolution in the Writings of Mary Wollstonecraft, Thomas Paine, and James Mackintosh*. London: Associated University Presses.

Bolingbroke, Henry St. John. 1752. *Letters on the Study and Use of History*. London: A. Millar.

Bondhus, Charlie. 2010. '"An Outlandish, Foreign-Made Englishman": Aristocratic Oppression and Ethnic Anomaly in *Caleb Williams*'. *Eighteenth-Century Fiction* 23: 163–94.

Bongie, Laurence L. 1965. *David Hume: Prophet of the Counter-Revolution*. Oxford: Clarendon Press.

Botting, Fred. 1996. *Gothic*. London: Routledge.

Braudy, Leo. 1970. *Narrative Form in History and Fiction*. Princeton, NJ: Princeton University Press.

Broadie, Alexander, ed. 1997. *The Scottish Enlightenment: An Anthology*. Edinburgh: Canongate Classics.

Bronner, Stephen Eric. 2004. *Reclaiming the Enlightenment: Toward A Politics of Radical Engagement*. New York: Columbia University Press.

Brown, Charles Brockden. 2013. *Collected Writings of Charles Brockden Brown: Letters and Early Epistolary Writings*. Vol. 1, edited by Philip Barnard, Elizabeth Hewitt and Mark L. Kamrath. Lewisburg, PA: Bucknell University Press.

Burke, Edmund. 1893. 'A Letter to a Member of the National Assembly'. In *The Works of the Right Honourable Edmund Burke*, Vol. 2, 519–58. London: Henry G. Bohn.

——. 1958–78. *The Correspondence of Edmund Burke*, edited by Alfred Cobban and Robert A. Smith, 10 vols. Cambridge: Cambridge University Press.

——. 1986. *Reflections on the Revolution in France*, edited by Conor Cruise O'Brien. London: Penguin.

——. 2004. *A Philosophical Enquiry into the Origin of Our Ideas of the Sublime and Beautiful*, edited by David Womersley. London: Penguin.

Butler, Marilyn. 1987. *Jane Austen and the War of Ideas*. Oxford: Clarendon Press.

Butterfield, Herbert. 1951. *The Whig Interpretation of History*. London: G. Bell and Sons.

Cannon, John, ed. 1988. *The Blackwell Dictionary of Historians*. Oxford: Basil Blackwell.

Carson, James. 1996. 'Enlightenment, popular culture, and Gothic fiction'. In *The Cambridge Companion to the Eighteenth-Century Novel*, edited by John Richetti, 255–76. Cambridge: Cambridge University Press.

Chaplin, Sue. 2007. *The Gothic and the Rule of Law, 1764–1820*. Basingstoke: Palgrave Macmillan.

Chard, Chloe. 1999. Introduction to *The Romance of the Forest*, by Ann Radcliffe, edited by Chloe Chard, vii–xxiv. Oxford: Oxford University Press.

Clemit, Pamela. 1993. *The Godwinian Novel: The Rational Fictions of Godwin, Brockden Brown, Mary Shelley*. Oxford: Clarendon Press.

——. 2011. 'Godwin, *Political Justice*'. In *The Cambridge Companion to British Literature of the French Revolution in the 1790s*, edited by Pamela Clemit, 86–100. Cambridge: Cambridge University Press.

Clery, E. J. 1995. *The Rise of Supernatural Fiction 1762–1800*. Cambridge: Cambridge University Press.

——. 2004. *Women's Gothic: From Clara Reeve to Mary Shelley*. 2nd edn. Tavistock: Northcote House.

Colley, Linda. 2005. *Britons: Forging the Nation 1707–1837*. London: Yale University Press.

Cooke, Jennifer. 2008. 'Katherine Mansfield's Ventriloquism and the Faux-Ecstasy of All Manner of Flora'. *Lit: Literature Interpretation Theory* 19: 79–94.

Cowart, David. 1989. *History and the Contemporary Novel*. Carbondale: Southern Illinois University Press.

Coykendall, Abby. 2005. 'Gothic Genealogies, the Family Romance, and Clara Reeve's *The Old English Baron*'. *Eighteenth-Century Fiction* 17: 443–80.

Davison, Carol Margaret. 2009. *Gothic Literature 1764–1824*. Cardiff: University of Wales Press.

Day, Robert Adams. 1966. *Told in Letters: Epistolary Fiction before Richardson*. Ann Arbor: The University of Michigan Press.

De Sade, Marquis. 1989. 'Reflections on the Novel'. In *The 120 Days of Sodom and Other Writings*, translated by Austryn Wainhouse and Richard Seaver, 91–116. London: Arrow Books.

Dickinson, H. T. 1977. *Liberty and Property: Political Ideology in Eighteenth-Century Britain*. London: Weidenfeld and Nicolson.

Duncombe, William. 1728. *Remarks on Mr Tindal's translation of Monsr. De Rapin Thoyras's History of England*. London: J. Roberts.

Ehlers, Leigh. 1978. 'A Striking Lesson to Posterity: Providence and Character in Clara Reeve's *The Old English Baron*'. *Enlightenment Essays* 9: 62–76.

Fielding, Henry. 1970. *An Apology for the Life of Mrs Shamela Andrews*. Folcroft, PA: The Folcroft Press.

——. 2005. *The History of Tom Jones*, edited by Thomas Keymer and Alice Wakely. London: Penguin.

Fludernik, Monika. 2001. 'William Godwin's *Caleb Williams*: The Tarnishing of the Sublime'. *ELH* 68: 857–96.

Forbes, Duncan. 1985. *Hume's Philosophical Politics*. Cambridge: Cambridge University Press.

Frank, Frederick S. 1977. Introduction to *Zastrozzi and St. Irvyne; or, The Rosicrucian*, by Percy Bysshe Shelley, edited by Frederick S. Frank, ix–xxv. New York: Arno Press.

Furniss, Tom. 2002. 'Mary Wollstonecraft's French Revolution'. In *The Cambridge Companion to Mary Wollstonecraft*, edited by Claudia L. Johnson, 59–81. Cambridge: Cambridge University Press.

Gamer, Michael. 2000. *Romanticism and the Gothic*. Cambridge: Cambridge University Press.

Godwin, William. 1795. 'Correspondence: To the Editor of the British Critic'. *The British Critic* 6: 94–5.

——. 1804. *Life of Geoffrey Chaucer*.Vol. 1. London: T. Davison.

——. 1853. *Fleetwood*. London: Richard Bentley.

——. 1985. *Enquiry Concerning Political Justice*, edited by Isaac Kramnick. Middlesex: Penguin.

——. 2000. 'Of History and Romance'. In *Caleb Williams*, edited by Gary Handwerk and A. A. Markley, 453–67. Peterborough, Ontario: Broadview Press.

——. 2013. *An Enquiry Concerning Political Justice*, edited by Mark Philp. Oxford: Oxford University Press.

Goldsmith, Oliver. 1771. *The History of England, From the Earliest Times to the Death of George II*. 4 vols. London: T. Davies.

Goode, Mike. 2009. *Sentimental Masculinity and the Rise of History, 1790–1890*. Cambridge: Cambridge University Press.

Gray, Thomas. 1825. *The Works of Thomas Gray*. Vol. 1 of *Poems and Correspondence*. London: Harding, Triphook and Lepard.

Grenby, Matthew O. 2014. 'Gothic and the Child Reader, 1764–1850'. In *The Gothic World*, edited by Glennis Byron and Dale Townshend, 243–53. Abingdon: Routledge.

Handwerk, Gary, and A. A. Markley. 2000. Introduction to *Caleb Williams*, by William Godwin, edited by Gary Handwerk and A. A. Markley, 9–46. Peterborough, Ontario: Broadview Press.

Hardman, John, ed. 1999. *The French Revolution Sourcebook*. London: Arnold.

Hazlitt, William. 1845. 'On the English Novelists'. In *Lectures on the English Comic Writers*, 124–56. New York: Wiley and Putnam.

Heiland, Donna. 2004. *Gothic and Gender: An Introduction*. Oxford: Blackwell.

Heller, Tamar. 1992. *Dead Secrets: Wilkie Collins and the Female Gothic*. New Haven, CT: Yale University Press.

Hicks, Philip. 1996. *Neoclassical History and English Culture*. Basingstoke: Macmillan Press.

Hogsette, David S. 2005. 'Textual Surveillance, Social Codes, and Sublime Voices: The Tyranny of Narrative in *Caleb Williams* and *Wieland*'.

Romanticism on the Net: 38–39. http://www.erudit.org/revue/ron/2005/v/ n38-39/011667ar.html (accessed 25 November 2015).

Holmes, Frederick M. 1997. *The Historical Imagination: Postmodernism and the Treatment of the Past in Contemporary British Fiction*. Victoria, New Zealand: University of Victoria Press.

Horrocks, Ingrid. 2007. 'More than a Gravestone: *Caleb Williams*, *Udolpho*, and the Politics of the Gothic'. *Studies in the Novel* 39: 31–47.

Howard, Jacqueline. 2001. *Reading Gothic Fiction: A Bakhtinian Approach*. Oxford: Oxford University Press.

Hume, David. 1825. *Essays Moral, Political and Literary*. Vol. 1 of *Essays and Treatises on Several Subjects*. Edinburgh: James Walker.

——. 1826. *An Enquiry Concerning Human Understanding*. Vol. 4 of *The Philosophical Works of David Hume*. London: Adam Black and William Tate.

——. 1854. 'Of the Study of History'. In *The Philosophical Works of David Hume*. Vol. 4, 508–13. Boston, MA: Little, Brown and Company.

——. 1911. *A Treatise of Human Nature*. 2 vols. London: J. M. Dent.

——. 1932. *The Letters of David Hume*, edited by J. Y. T. Greig. 2 vols. Oxford: Clarendon Press.

——. 1938. *An Abstract of A Treatise of Human Nature, 1740: A Pamphlet hitherto unknown*. Cambridge: Cambridge University Press.

——. 1954. *New Letters of David Hume*. Edited by Raymond Klibanksy and Ernest C. Mossner. Oxford: Clarendon Press.

——. 1976. *The Natural History of Religion*. In *The Natural History of Religion and Dialogues Concerning Natural Religion*, edited by A. Wayne Colver and John Vladimir Price, 23–98. Oxford: Clarendon Press.

Hume, Robert D. 1969. 'Gothic versus Romantic: a re-evaluation of the Gothic novel'. *PMLA* 84: 282–90.

Hurd, Richard. 1762. *Letters on Chivalry and Romance*. Dublin: Richard Watts.

Hutcheon, Linda. 1995. 'Historiographic Metafiction'. In *Metafiction*, edited by Mark Currie, 71–91. Harlow: Longman.

Janes, Regina M. 1978. 'On the Reception of Mary Wollstonecraft's *A Vindication of the Rights of Woman*'. *Journal of the History of Ideas* 39: 293–302.

Johnson, Claudia L. 2002. 'Mary Wollstonecraft's novels'. In *The Cambridge Companion to Mary Wollstonecraft*, edited by Claudia L. Johnson, 189–208. Cambridge: Cambridge University Press.

Johnson, Nancy E. 2011. 'Wollstonecraft and Godwin: dialogues'. In *The Cambridge Companion to British Literature of the French Revolution in the 1790s*, edited by Pamela Clemit, 101–16. Cambridge: Cambridge University Press.

Jones, Peter. 1993. 'Hume's literary and aesthetic theory'. In *The Cambridge Companion to Hume*, edited by David Fate Norton, 255–80. Cambridge: Cambridge University Press.

Keats, John. 1895. *The Letters of John Keats*. Edited by H. Buxton Forman. London: Reeves and Turner.

Keen, Maurice. 1984. *Chivalry*. New Haven, CT and London: Yale University Press.

Kelly, Gary. 1976. *The English Jacobin Novel 1780–1805*. Oxford: Clarendon Press.

——. 1992. *Revolutionary Feminism*. Basingstoke: Macmillan.

——. 1996. *English Fiction of the Romantic Period 1789–1830*. London: Longman.

——. 1999. *Bluestocking Feminism: Writings of the Bluestocking Circle, 1738–1785*. 6 vols. London: Pickering and Chatto.

——. 2002. *Varieties of Female Gothic*. 6 vols. London: Pickering and Chatto.

——. 2003. 'Clara Reeve, Provincial Bluestocking: From the Old Whigs to the Modern Liberal State'. In *Reconsidering the Bluestockings*, edited by Nicole Pohl and Betty A. Schellenberg, 105–26. San Marino: Huntington Library.

Kilgour, Maggie. 1995. *The Rise of the Gothic Novel*. London: Routledge.

Lerner, Gerda. 1981. *The Majority Finds its Past: Placing Women in History*. Oxford: Oxford University Press.

Levine, Joseph M. 1991. *The Battle of the Books: History and Literature in the Augustan Age*. Ithaca, NY and London: Cornell University Press.

Lewis, Jayne Elizabeth. 1995. '"Ev'ry Lost Relation:" Historical Fictions and Sentimental Incidents in Sophia Lee's *The Recess*'. *Eighteenth-Century Fiction* 7: 165–84.

——. 1998. *Mary Queen of Scots: Romance and Nation*. London: Routledge.

——. 1998. *The Monk*, edited by Christopher MacLachlan. London: Penguin.

Lewis, Matthew. 1794. Lewis to his mother, 18 May. Quoted in Norton 2000, 117.

Lindstrom, Eric. 2010. 'Imagining *Things as They Are*'. *Studies in Romanticism* 49: 477–506.

Looser, Devoney. 2000. *British Women Writers and the Writing of History, 1670–1820*. Baltimore, MD: The Johns Hopkins University Press.

Lukács, Georg. 1969. *The Historical Novel*. Translated by Hannah and Stanley Mitchell. London: Peregrine.

Macaulay, Thomas Babington, Lord. 1861. 'Horace Walpole'. In *Critical and Historical Essays Contributed to the Edinburgh Review*, 260–81. London: Longman, Green, Longman and Roberts.

Mack, Ruth. 2009. *Literary Historicity: Literature and Historical Experience in Eighteenth-Century Britain*. Stanford, CA: Stanford University Press.

Mandal, Anthony. 2014. 'Gothic and the Publishing World, 1780–1820'. In *The Gothic World*, edited by Glennis Byron and Dale Townshend, 159–71. Abingdon: Routledge.

Mayer, Robert. 1997. *History and the Early English Novel: Matters of Fact from Bacon to Defoe*. Cambridge: Cambridge University Press.

McCracken, David. 1969–71. 'Godwin's *Caleb Williams*: A Fictional Rebuttal of Burke'. *Studies in Burke and His Time* 11–12: 1442–52.

McEvoy, Emma. 2007. 'Gothic and the Romantics'. In *The Routledge Companion to the Gothic*, edited by Catherine Spooner and Emma McEvoy, 19–28. Abingdon: Routledge.

McIntosh-Varjabédian, Fiona. 2006. 'Probability and Persuasion in 18th-Century and 19th-Century Historical Writing'. In *Tropes for the Past: Hayden White and the History/Literature Debate*, edited by Kuisma Korhonen, 109–18. Amsterdam: Rodopi.

McIntyre, Clara Frances. 1970. *Ann Radcliffe in Relation to her Time*. Hamden, CT: Archon Books.

McManners, John. 1969. *The French Revolution and the Church*. Westport, CT: Greenwood Press.

Mellor, Anne K. 1994. Introduction to *The Wrongs of Woman, or Maria*, by Mary Wollstonecraft, edited by Anne K. Mellor, v–xviii. New York: Norton.

——. 2007. Introduction to *The Wrongs of Woman, or Maria*, by Mary Wollstonecraft. In *A Vindication of the Rights of Woman and The Wrongs of Woman, or Maria*, edited by Anne K. Mellor and Noelle Chao, 235–43. New York: Longman.

Mighall, Robert. 1999. *A Geography of Victorian Gothic Fiction*. Oxford: Oxford University Press.

Miles, Robert. 1995. *Ann Radcliffe: The Great Enchantress*. Manchester: Manchester University Press.

——. 2001. 'Nationalism and Abjection'. In *The Gothic: Essays and Studies 2001*, edited by Fred Botting, 47–86. Cambridge: Brewer.

——. 2002. 'Europhobia: the Catholic other in Horace Walpole and Charles Maturin'. In *European Gothic*, edited by Avril Horner, 84–103. Manchester: Manchester University Press.

——. 2003. 'The Gothic and Ideology'. In *Approaches to Teaching Gothic Fiction: The British and American Traditions*, edited by Diane Long Hoeveler and Tamar Heller, 58–65. New York: The Modern Language Association of America.

——. 2004. Introduction to *The Italian*, by Ann Radcliffe, edited by Robert Miles, vii–xxxviii. London: Penguin.

——. 2005. 'Radcliffe, Ann (1764–1823)'. *Oxford Dictionary of National Biography*. Oxford: Oxford University Press. http://www.oxforddnb.com/view/article/22974 (accessed 25 November 2015, subscription required).

——. 2014. 'Popular Romanticism and the problem of belief: *The Mysteries of Udolpho* (1794)'. In *Ann Radcliffe, Romanticism and the Gothic*, edited by Dale Townshend and Angela Wright, 117–34. Cambridge: Cambridge University Press.

Monthly Review. 1763. 'Review' of Catharine Macaulay's *The History of England*. *Monthly Review* 29: 372–82.

Mossiker, Frances. 1961. *The Queen's Necklace: Marie Antoinette and the Scandal that Shocked and Mystified France*. London: Phoenix.

Myers, Mitzi. 2002. 'Mary Wollstonecraft's literary reviews'. In *The Cambridge Companion to Mary Wollstonecraft*, edited by Claudia L. Johnson, 82–98. Cambridge: Cambridge University Press.

Nordius, Janina. 2002. 'A Tale of Other Places: Sophia Lee's *The Recess* and Colonial Gothic'. *Studies in the Novel* 34: 162–77.

Norton, David Fate. 1993. 'An Introduction to Hume's Thought'. In *The Cambridge Companion to Hume*, edited by David Fate Norton, 1–32. Cambridge: Cambridge University Press.

Norton, Rictor. 1999. *Mistress of Udolpho: The Life of Ann Radcliffe*. London: Leicester University Press.

——. 2000. *Gothic Readings: The First Wave 1764–1840*. London: Leicester University Press.

O'Brien, Karen. 2005. *Narratives of Enlightenment: Cosmopolitan History from Voltaire to Gibbon*. Cambridge: Cambridge University Press.

Okie, Laird. 1991. *Augustan Historical Writing: Histories of England in the English Enlightenment*. Lanham, MD: University Press of America.

Ousby, Ian. 1974. '"My Servant Caleb:" Godwin's *Caleb Williams* and the Political Trials of the 1790s'. *University of Toronto Quarterly* 44: 47–55.

Paine, Thomas. 1985. *Rights of Man*, edited by Eric Foner and Henry Collins. London: Penguin.

Parreaux, André. 1960. *The Publication of 'The Monk': A Literary Event 1796–1798*. Paris: Didier.

Paulson, Ronald. 1983. *Representations of Revolution (1789–1820)*. New Haven, CT: Yale University Press.

Peardon, Thomas Preston. 1933. *The Transition in English Historical Writing 1760–1830*. New York: Columbia University Press.

Penelhum, Terence. 1993. 'Hume's Moral Psychology'. In *The Cambridge Companion to Hume*, edited by David Fate Norton, 117–47. Cambridge: Cambridge University Press.

Perry, Ruth. 1980. *Women, Letters and the Novel*. New York: AMS Press.

Phillips, Mark Salber. 2000. *Society and Sentiment: Genres of Historical Writing in Britain, 1740–1820*. Princeton, NJ: Princeton University Press.

Piggott, Stuart. 1976. *Ruins in a Landscape: Essays in Antiquarianism*. Edinburgh: Edinburgh University Press.

Pittock, Murray G. H. 2007. 'Historiography'. In *The Cambridge Companion to the Scottish Enlightenment*, edited by Alexander Broadie, 258–79. Cambridge: Cambridge University Press.

Pointon, Marcia. 1997. *Strategies for Showing: Women, Possession, and Representation in English Visual Culture, 1665–1800*. Oxford: Oxford University Press.

Poovey, Mary. 1984. *The Proper Lady and the Woman Writer: Ideology as Style in the Works of Mary Wollstonecraft, Mary Shelley and Jane Austen*. Chicago, IL: The University of Chicago Press.

Porter, Roy. 2000. *Enlightenment: Britain and the Creation of the Modern World*. London: Penguin.

Price, Richard. 1790. *A Discourse on the Love of Our Country*. London: George Stafford.

Punter, David. 1996. *The Literature of Terror: A History of Gothic Fictions from 1765 to the Present Day*. 2 vols. London: Longman.

Radcliffe, Ann. 1795. *A Journey Made in the Summer of 1794*. London: G. G. and J. Robinson.

——. 1998. *A Sicilian Romance*, edited by Alison Milbank. London: Penguin.

——. 2000. 'On the Supernatural in Poetry'. In *Gothic Documents: A Sourcebook 1700–1820*, edited by E. J. Clery and Robert Miles, 163–72. Manchester: Manchester University Press.

——. 2001. *The Mysteries of Udolpho*, edited by Jacqueline Howard. London: Penguin.

——. 2004. *The Italian*, edited by Robert Miles. London: Penguin.

Rapin de Thoyras, Paul M. 1717. *Dissertation sur les Whigs & les Torys. Or, An Historical Dissertation upon Whig and Tory*. Translated by Mr. Ozell. London: E. Curll.

Reeve, Clara. 1785. *The Progress of Romance*. 2 vols. Dublin: Price, Exshaw, White, Cash, Colbert, Marchbank, and Porter.

——. 1788. *The Exiles, or Memoirs of the Count de Cronstadt*. 3 vols. London: T. Hookham.

——. 1791a. *The School for Widows: A Novel*. 3 vols. London: T. Hookham.

——. 1791b. Reeve to Joseph Cooper Walker, 12 April. Quoted in Kelly 2003, 117.

——. 1792. Reeve to Joseph Cooper Walker, 7 September. Quoted in Kelly 2003, 117.

——. 1793. *Memoirs of Sir Roger de Clarendon, the natural son of Edward Prince of Wales, commonly called the Black Prince*. 3 vols. London: Hookham and Carpenter.

——. 1829. Undated letter. Quoted in Scott 1829, 241.

Reeve, Clara, trans. 1772. *The Phoenix; or, The History of Polyarchus*, by John Barclay. 4 vols. London: John Bell and C. Etherington.

Rendall, Jane. 2011. 'Wollstonecraft, *Vindications* and *Historical and Moral View of the French Revolution*'. In *The Cambridge Companion to British Literature of the French Revolution in the 1790s*, edited by Pamela Clemit, 71–85.

Richardson, Alan. 2002. 'Mary Wollstonecraft on Education'. In *The Cambridge Companion to Mary Wollstonecraft*, edited by Claudia L. Johnson, 24–41. Cambridge: Cambridge University Press.

Richardson, Samuel. 1964. *Selected Letters of Samuel Richardson*, edited by John Carroll. Oxford: Clarendon Press.

——. 1985. *Pamela*, edited by Peter Sabor. London: Penguin.

Richter, David H. 1996. *The Progress of Romance: Literary Historiography and the Gothic Novel*. Columbus: Ohio State University Press.

Robbins, Caroline. 2004. *The Eighteenth-Century Commonwealthman – Studies in the Transmission, Development, and Circumstance of English Liberal Thought from the Restoration of Charles II until the War with the Thirteen Colonies*. Indianapolis, IN: Liberty Fund.

Robertson, Fiona. 1994. *Legitimate Histories: Scott, Gothic, and the Authorities of Fiction*. Oxford: Clarendon Press.

Robertson, William. 1761. *The History of Scotland during the reigns of Queen Mary and of King James VI till his accession to the crown of England*. 2 vols. London: A. Millar.

Runia, Eelco. 1999. *Waterloo, Verdun, Auschwitz*. Amsterdam: Meulenhoff. Translated and quoted in Ankersmit 2005, 144.

Scott, Walter. 1829. *Biographical and Critical Notices of Eminent Novelists*. Vol. 3 of *The Miscellaneous Prose Works of Sir Walter Scott*. Boston, MA: Wells and Lilly.

Shaw, Philip. 2006. *The Sublime*. Abingdon: Routledge.

Shklovsky, Viktor. 2004. 'Art as Technique'. In *Literary Theory: An Anthology*, edited by Julie Rivkin and Michael Ryan, 2nd edn, 15–21. Oxford: Blackwell.

Silver, Sean R. 2009. 'Visiting Strawberry Hill: Horace Walpole's Gothic Historiography'. *Eighteenth-Century Fiction* 21: 535–64.

Smith, Andrew. 2007. *Gothic Literature*. Edinburgh: Edinburgh University Press.

Smith, Bonnie G. 1998. *The Gender of History: Men, Women and Historical Practice*. London: Harvard University Press.

Smollett, Tobias. 1990. *The Adventures of Ferdinand Count Fathom*, edited by Paul-Gabriel Boucé. London: Penguin.

Southey, Robert. 1881. *The Correspondence of Robert Southey with Caroline Bowles*, edited by Edward Dowden. Dublin.

Sowerby, Robin. 2000. 'The Goths in History and Pre-Gothic Gothic'. In *A Companion to the Gothic*, edited by David Punter, 15–26. Oxford: Blackwell.

Spector, Robert Donald. 1984. *The English Gothic: A Bibliographic Guide to Writers from Horace Walpole to Mary Shelley*. Westport, CT: Greenwood Press.

Spencer, Jane. 1986. *The Rise of the Woman Novelist: from Aphra Behn to Jane Austen*. Oxford: Basil Blackwell.

Stauffer, Andrew M. 2005. *Anger, Revolution, and Romanticism*. Cambridge: Cambridge University Press.

Stevens, Anne H. 2003. 'Sophia Lee's Illegitimate History'. *The Eighteenth-Century Novel* 3: 263–91.

——. 2008. 'Forging Literary History: Historical Fiction and Literary Forgery in Eighteenth-Century Britain'. *Studies in Eighteenth-Century Culture* 37: 217–32.

——. 2010. *British Historical Fiction before Scott*. Basingstoke: Palgrave Macmillan.

Sweet, Rosemary. 2004. *Antiquaries: The Discovery of the Past in Eighteenth-Century Britain*. London: Hambledon and London.

Taylor, Barbara. 2003. *Mary Wollstonecraft and the Feminist Imagination*. Cambridge: Cambridge University Press.

Thomas, Sophie. 2005. 'The Fragment'. In *Romanticism: An Oxford Guide*, edited by Nicholas Roe, 502–20. Oxford: Oxford University Press.

Thompson, James. 1989. 'Surveillance in William Godwin's *Caleb Williams*'. In *Gothic Fictions: Prohibition/Transgression*, edited by Kenneth W. Graham, 173–98. New York: AMS Press, 1989.

Todd, Janet. 1986. *Sensibility: An Introduction*. London: Methuen.

——. 1989. *The Sign of Angellica: Women, Writing and Fiction, 1600–1800*. London: Virago.

Townshend, Dale, and Angela Wright. 2014. 'Gothic and Romantic engagements: The critical reception of Ann Radcliffe, 1789–1850'. In *Ann Radcliffe, Romanticism and the Gothic*, edited by Dale Townshend and Angela Wright, 3–32. Cambridge: Cambridge University Press.

Trott, Nicola. 2003. 'The Picturesque, the Beautiful and the Sublime'. In *A Companion to Romanticism*, edited by Duncan Wu, 72–90. Oxford: Blackwell.

——. 2005. 'Gothic'. In *Romanticism: An Oxford Guide*, edited by Nicholas Roe, 482–501. Oxford: Oxford University Press.

Ty, Eleanor. 1993. *Unsex'd Revolutionaries: Five Women Novelists of the 1790s*. Toronto: University of Toronto Press.

Wallace, Diana. 2013. *Female Gothic Histories: Gender, History and the Gothic*. Cardiff: University of Wales Press.

Wallace, Diana, and Andrew Smith. 2009. 'Introduction: Defining the Female Gothic'. In *The Female Gothic: New Directions*, edited by

Diana Wallace and Andrew Smith, 1–12. Basingstoke: Palgrave Macmillan.

Walpole, Horace. 1767. Walpole to Madame Du Deffand, 13 March. Quoted in Kilgour 1995, 17.

——. 1768. *Historic Doubts on the Life and Reign of King Richard the Third*. London: J. Dodsley.

——. 1791. *The Mysterious Mother*. London: J. Archer, W. Jones and R. White.

——. 1829. *Supplement to the Historic Doubts on the Life and Reign of King Richard III*. In Vol. 2 of *The Works of Horace Walpole*, 185–220. London: G. G. and J. Robinson and J. Edwards.

——. 1937–83. *The Yale Edition of Horace Walpole's Correspondence*. Edited by W. S. Lewis. 48 vols. London: Oxford University Press.

——. 1973. 'Maddalena'. In *Great British Tales of Terror*, edited by Peter Haining, 21–43. Harmondsworth: Penguin.

Warburton, William. 1970. Preface to Vol. 3 of *Clarissa Harlowe*. In *Novel and Romance 1700–1800: A Documentary Record*, edited by Ioan Williams, 122–4. London: Routledge and Kegan Paul.

Watt, James. 1999. *Contesting the Gothic: Fiction, Genre and Cultural Conflict, 1764–1832*. Cambridge: Cambridge University Press.

——. 2003. Introduction to *The Old English Baron*, by Clara Reeve, edited by James Trainer and James Watt, vii–xxiv. Oxford: Oxford University Press.

Wein, Toni. 2002. *British Identities, Heroic Nationalisms, and the Gothic Novel, 1764–1824*. Basingstoke: Palgrave Macmillan.

Whale, John. 2005. 'Non-fictional Prose'. In *Romanticism: An Oxford Guide*, edited by Nicholas Roe, 538–54. Oxford: Oxford University Press.

White, Hayden. 1985. *Tropics of Discourse: Essays in Cultural Criticism*. Baltimore, MD: The Johns Hopkins University Press.

——. 1987. *The Content of the Form: Narrative Discourse and Historical Representation*. London: The Johns Hopkins University Press.

Williams, Aubrey. 1971. 'Interpositions of Providence and the Design of Fielding's Novels'. *South Atlantic Quarterly* 70: 265–86.

Williams, David. 1999. Introduction to *The Enlightenment*, edited by David Williams, 1–70. Cambridge: Cambridge University Press.

Winkle, Sally. 1989. 'Innovation and Convention in Sophie La Roche's *The Story of Miss von Sternheim* and *Rosalia's Letters*'. In *Writing the Female Voice: Essays on Epistolary Literature*, edited by Elizabeth C. Goldsmith, 77–94. Boston, MA: Northeastern University Press.

Wollstonecraft, Mary. 1788. 'Review' of Charlotte Smith's *Emmeline* for the *Analytical Review*. Quoted in Anne K. Mellor, *Mothers of the Nation: Women's Political Writing in England, 1780–1830*. Bloomington: Indiana University Press, 2002, 89.

——. 1789. *The Female Reader*. London: J. Johnson.

——. 1794. *An Historical and Moral View of the Origin and Progress of the French Revolution*. Vol. 1. London: J. Johnson.

——. 1985. *A Vindication of the Rights of Woman*, edited by Miriam Brody. London: Penguin.

——. 2008. *A Vindication of the Rights of Men*. In *A Vindication of the Rights of Woman and A Vindication of the Rights of Men*, edited by Janet Todd, 1–62. Oxford: Oxford University Press.

Wootton, David. 1993. 'David Hume, "the historian"'. In *The Cambridge Companion to Hume*, edited by David Fate Norton, 281–312. Cambridge: Cambridge University Press.

Wright, Angela. 2007. *Gothic Fiction*. Basingstoke: Palgrave Macmillan.

Zaczek, Barbara Maria. 1997. *Censored Sentiments: Letters and Censorship in Epistolary Novels and Conduct Material*. London: Associated University Presses.

Zimmerman, Everett. 1996. *The Boundaries of Fiction: History and the Eighteenth-Century British Novel*. Ithaca, NY: Cornell University Press.

Index

Note: 'n.' after a page reference indicates the number of a note on that page.

Lightning Source UK Ltd.
Milton Keynes UK
UKHW021919250919
350436UK00005B/283/P